Worlding Brazil

This book looks at the development of thinking about security in Brazil between 1930 and 2010. In order to do so, it develops a new framework for thinking about intellectual history in Brazil and applies it to the development of knowledge on security in that country.

Building on the Gramscian literature on 'late modernization' and 'conservative revolution' and drawing on the idea of 'Theory of Emotional Action' proposed by Brazilian sociologist Jessé Souza, this book sets out to establish an innovative framework with which to analyse the development of 'thinking about security' in Brazil in three specific historic contexts. This theoretical framework is then used to argue that one specific discourse of Brazilian identity has been the main source of knowledge production in that country since the 1930s. In doing this, the book offers thought-provoking arguments about the role of intellectuals in Brazil and reassesses the exclusionary ideas embedded in the politics of identity and security.

This book not only introduces a novel framework to analyse intellectual production outside the core, it also sheds light on how security has been historically thought of outside the core and will be of interest to students and scholars of International Relations, Critical Security Studies and Latin American Studies.

Laura Lima holds a PhD from Aberystwyth University. She is the editor, with Shannon Brincat and João Nunes, of the volume *Critical Theory in International Relations and Security Studies: Interviews and Reflections*, published by Routledge.

Worlding Beyond the West

Series Editors

Arlene B. Tickner
Universidad de los Andes, Bogotá
and
Ole Wæver
University of Copenhagen

The *Worlding Beyond the West* series editorial board are:

Naeem Inayatullah (*Ithaca College, USA*), Himadeep Muppidi (*Vassar College, USA*), Pinar Bilgin (*Bilkent University, Turkey*), Mustapha Kamal Pasha (*University of Aberdeen, UK*), Sanjay Seth (*Goldsmiths, University of London, UK*), Quin Yaqing (*China Foreign Affairs University, China*), Navnita Chandra Behera (*Jamia Milia Islamia University, India*) and David Blaney (*Macalester College, USA*).

Historically, the field of International Relations has established its boundaries, issues, and theories based upon Western experience. This series aims to explore the role of geocultural factors in setting the concepts and epistemologies through which IR knowledge is produced. In particular, it seeks to identify alternatives for thinking about the "international" that are more in tune with local concerns and traditions outside the West.

Worlding Brazil

Intellectuals, identity and security

Laura Lima

Routledge
Taylor & Francis Group

LONDON AND NEW YORK

First published 2015
by Routledge

2 Park Square, Milton Park, Abingdon, Oxfordshire OX14 4RN
711 Third Avenue, New York, NY 10017

Routledge is an imprint of the Taylor & Francis Group, an informa business

First issued in paperback 2017

British Library Cataloguing in Publication Data
A catalogue record for this book is available from the British Library

Library of Congress Cataloging in Publication Data
Lima, Laura
Worlding Brazil: intellectuals, identity and security/Laura Lima.
    pages cm. – (Worlding beyond the West; 6)
    1. National security–Brazil. 2. Brazil–Foreign relations–Philosophy.
    3. International relations and culture–Brazil. 4. National characteristics,
    Brazilian. 5. Brazil–Intellectual life–20th century. I. Title.
    JZ1548.L55 2014
    355'.033081–dc23   2014018439

ISBN: 978-0-415-71689-5 (hbk)
ISBN: 978-0-8153-7785-6 (pbk)

Typeset in Times New Roman
by Sunrise Setting Ltd, Paignton, UK

To my parents, Josélia and Ademir; my brothers, Léo and Yuri; my grandmother, Beatriz

Contents

Illustrations

Tables

Figures

Abbreviations

ABRI	Associação Brasileira de Relações Internacionais (Brazilian Association of International Relations)
ADN	*A Defeza Nacional* (*National Defence*)
ADESG	Associação dos Diplomados da Escola Superior de Guerra (Alumni Association of Escola Superior de Guerra)
ANPOCS	Associação Nacional de Pós-Graduação e Pesquisa em Ciências Sociais (National Association of Postgraduate Studies and Research in Social Sciences)
CAPES	Comissão de Aperfeiçoamento de Pessoal de Nível Superior Commission for Improvement of Staff of Higher Education
CDN	Conselho de Defesa Nacional (Council of Nacional Defence)
CEBRAP	Centro Brasileiro de Análise e Planejamento (Brazilian Centre of Analysis and Planning)
CFE	Conselho Federal de Educação (Federal Council of Education)
CI	Contexto Internacional (International Context)
CNMC	Comissão Nacional de Moral e Cívica (National Commission of Moral and Civic Values)
CNPq	Comissão Nacional de Desenvolvimento Científico e Tecnologia (National Commission of Scientific Development and Technology)
CSN	Conselho de Segurança Nacional (Council of National Security)
CSS	Critical Security Studies
DOU	Diário Oficial da União (Federal Official Gazette of Brazil)
DSN	Doutrina de Segurança Nacional (Doctrine of National Security)
EMC	Educação Moral e Cívica (Moral and Civics Education)
EPB	Estudos Políticos Brasileiros (Brazilian Political Studies)
ESG	Escola Superior de Guerra (Higher War College)
FEB	Força Expedicionária Brasileira (Brazilian Expeditionary Force)
GEP	Geocultural Epistemologies Project
IBRI	Instituto Brasileiro de Relações Internacionais (Brazilian Institute of International Relations)
INEP	Instituto Nacional de Estudos e Pesquisas Educacionais Anísio Teixeira (Anísio Teixeira Institute of National Studies and Education Research)

iREL	Instituto de Relações Internacionais, Universidade de Brasília (Institute of International Relations)
IR	International Relations
IRI	Instituto de Relações Internacionais, Pontifícia Universidade Católica do Rio de Janeiro (Institute of International Relations)
ISEB	Instituto Superior de Estudos Brasileiros (Higher Institute of Brazilian Studies)
IUPERJ	Instituto Universitário de Pesquisas do Estado do Rio de Janeiro (University Institute of Research of the State of Rio de Janeiro)
LDN	Liga da Defeza Nacional (League of National Defence)
LSN	Lei de Segurança Nacional (National Security Law)
MB	Manual Básico (da Escolha Superior de Guerra) Basic Manual (of the Higher War College)
NPT	Non-Proliferation Treaty
OSPB	Organização Social e Política Brasileira (Brazilian Political and Social Education)
PF	Princípios Fundamentais (Fundamental Principles)
PNO	Objetivos Permanentes Nacionais (Permanent National Objectives)
PUC	Pontifícia Universidade Católica (Pontifical Catholic University)
RBPI	Revista Brasileira de Política Internacional (Brazilian Journal of International Politics)
TEA	Teoria da Ação Emocional (Theory of Emotional Action)
TSN	Tribunal de Segurança Nacional (Tribunal of National Security)
UB	Universidade do Brasil University of Brazil
UDF	Universidade do Distrito Federal (University of the Federal District)
UK	United Kingdom
UnB	Universidade de Brasília (University of Brasília)
UNCTAD	United Nations Conference on Trade and Development
UNDP	United Nations Development Programme
USA	United States of America

Acknowledgements

Graças à admirável colaboração encontrada, todos os meus problemas foram resolvidos no plano da serena continuidade. Posso resumir a minha recordação grata afirmando que jamais um único deveu a tantos.

(Thanks to the fine collaboration I found, all my problems were resolved at the level of serene continuity. I wish to summarize my gratitude by affirming that never was there one indebted to so many.)

Luís da Câmara Cascudo
Cidade do Natal, Julho de 1964
(*Made in Africa* 1999: 10)

I am writing these acknowledgements years after I first stepped out of London Euston and started asking people on the street if they could show me the way to Aberystwyth. In the time gone by since that sunny September morning, I have learned there is only one constant in the many different ways to experience 'Aber': the train journey. Risking a truism, I am still inclined to warning others that arriving or leaving Aber by train is a long, often delayed, uncertain and uncomfortable event for all. In many ways, the making of this book has been a long train ride. I do not mean that in any negative way. I was lucky enough to learn from friends and colleagues the beauty and opportunities inherent to being uncertain and uncomfortable with what I know and who I am. I could not possibly express my gratitude for everything I learned from and with all of you. Thus, I would like to thank:

The *Commissão de Aperfeiçoamento de Pessoal de Nível Superior* (CAPES), for the full scholarship that made this research possible. At Routledge, Nicola Parkin and Peter Harris were incredibly helpful and supported my work with zeal through its more difficult phases. Professors Arlene Tickner and Ole Wæver for taking interest in my work and inspiring me with the Geocultural Epistemologies project. I am very grateful to Lindsay Drewett, who was very kind in patiently proofreading this manuscript. Dr Alistair Shepherd and Fiona Macaulay offered valuable comments and contributed to making my PhD viva a memory I truly cherish.

Ken Booth and Lucy Taylor were far more than my supervisors. They offered me guidance, help and support, and stayed positive even when I could barely see any light. I am incredibly thankful for having been a part of the Department of International Politics at Aberystwyth University. Its members of staff lent me intellectual and emotional help at the most crucial times. I would thus like to thank Richard Wyn Jones, Andrew Linklater, Jenny Matthers, Roger Scully, Howard Williams and Michael Williams. I also thank the constellation of human stars I had the pleasure of meeting at Aberystwyth: Soumita Basu, Shannon Brincat, Eurwen and Thomas Booth, Linnea Gelot, Mat Hale, Charlotte Heath-Kelly, Jonny Jones, Olga Jurasz, Miguel Lourenço, João Nunes, Aylin Ozet, Jen Pedersen, Daniel Pineu, Tristan and Tessa Price, Herman Salton, Carlos Santos, Nida Shoughry and Andreja Zevnik.

During my fieldwork, friends and relatives in Brazil were kind enough to host me in their homes. For that, I thank Antônio Carlos, Aline and Jerônimo Vilela, Cida and Juanito, Carlos Lacerda, Alice Gismonti, Fernanda Pereira, Abinoam and Kênia Marques, Erica Resende and Carlos Freitas. A number of professors and supervisors were extremely important throughout my academic career in Brazil. For that, I would like to thank Mônica Lessa, Williams Gonçalves, Bernardo Kocher, Ademar Seabra and Paul Amar.

I have the honour and am quite proud of coming from a family whose members have a penchant for being larger than life and would fit in well in García Marquez's *100 Years of Solitude*. In the past 10 years, I have only returned to Natal four times, but not a day goes by that I do not think of them. Léo e Yuri, *vocês são meu ouro de mina, minha primeira saudade, meu último riso. Desculpem-me pelos anos de distância – a dor de não tê-los por perto nunca diminui.* Papai e Mamãe, *muito obrigada pelos princípios que me ensinaram.* Vovó Beatriz, *você é a rosa do meu cabelo, é o meu sorriso sempre em flor. É a sua voz que escuto quando penso em Natal.*

Rita Van Raemdonck and Karel Vandersteen accepted me into their family from the very first day. Words are not enough to express my gratitude. Pieter and his daughter, Carla Vandersteen, are my most beautiful and fulfilling chapter. I am a better human being for spending my days with them.

Introduction
Worlds of international relations

This book is an investigation and critique of ways of thinking that not only guided some of my personal political choices but also those of at least three generations of my family. Thus, it seems appropriate that I introduce my work by familiarizing the reader with the biographical context that led me to explore the historical basis and development of thinking about security in Brazil from 1930 to 2010.

I come from a family of four generations of political activists. My great uncle, João de Deus, took part in the 1930 coup that brought Getúlio Vargas to power and was later involved in the 1935 communist rebellion, the *Intentona Comunista*, which took place in Natal, Recife and Rio de Janeiro. His niece, my paternal grandmother, Beatriz, was active in the Liberation Theology movement and, at 85 years of age, is still involved in Catholic women's associations in her region of Brazil. Following this line of political praxis, my father and some of his sisters became local activists and community leaders in the humble neighbourhood of Natal where they grew up. Political gatherings, local protests of *Diretas Já* (the Brazilian movement that called for redemocratization in the early 1980s) and the grassroots community politicization campaigns in which my family was involved deeply marked my early childhood. I grew up listening to adults around me dreaming of, and aspiring to, development just as emphatically as they feared and hated the armed forces and their security politics.

On the one hand, I learned to associate development – taken as *the* general solution to the problems of Brazil – with resistance and left-wing politics. As far back as I can remember, development was at the centre of any political discussion among friends, classmates and colleagues. On the other hand, being born in the late 1970s into a politically engaged family, I also learned to equate security with right-wing politics, the armed forces and the violent state practices perpetrated by the dictatorship, which not only restricted liberties and punished difference, but also took the lives of so many dissidents. For my family, and for so many others in Latin America, 'security' invoked the spectre of authoritarianism haunting every corner of politics.

Throughout my school years (1985–96), I saw the Brazilian national currency change six times and witnessed the so-called lost decade (the 1980s) give way to a second lost decade (the 1990s) as successive civilian governments followed neo-liberal prescriptions. By the time I started university and joined the student movement, Brazil had been a democracy for 12 years. In the midst of successive economic crises, there were those who declared their longing for the military governments (Toledo 2009, 211), while others proclaimed Latin American developmentalism moribund (see Baran 1984; Ianni 1986; Bielschowski 1988).

In discussions with my family, colleagues and friends, there was a general feeling that neo-liberalism had won and the post-redemocratization left was incapable of recruiting popular support. Nevertheless, it was still generally believed by those in my circles that the intellectual left was the only true defender of the Brazilian state. Among my immediate associates, I felt at home. We discussed possible solutions to underdevelopment, criticized the neo-liberal path taken by the state post–1985, talked about Brazil as the great country of the future and the possibilities of integration across South America, its prospects for leadership and its role as a representative of the developing world. However, once I stepped out of these circles, I felt that we, the intellectual left, were deeply alone. The people, in whose name we spoke, were far from any form of political engagement, while right-wing intellectuals thrived on privatization, free-trade policies and the general rollback of the state from public life.

In this context, the 9/11 attacks in the USA forcefully awoke an uncomfortable subject in Brazilian academia, society and politics. As security became the prevailing lens through which intra-continental relations would be analysed, it highlighted the fact that there were very few experts on international security in the country. The reason for such lack of debate on security is deeply rooted on what 'speaking security' has meant in twentieth-century Brazil.

In the years that had gone by since José Sarney took office as the first civilian president after the military dictatorship, security could not be comfortably discussed in open political debates. Civilians as well as the military were not inclined to discuss security publically due to the political resentment it invoked on both sides (Chapter 5 develops this). At the centre of this contention lay the military-led path to redemocratization and the political power the military still held after formal power was returned to civilians. The path back to democracy, *abertura* (opening) as it is called in Portuguese, had little to no civilian input. As a result, the armed forces not only were able to dictate which policy areas they would release to civilian control, but also managed to maintain unscathed their power and influence in politics (see Skidmore 1988; Stepan 1988; Hunter 1997; Castro and D'Araújo 2001).

After the long process of Brazilian democratization, the political uneasiness that surrounded the subject of security meant that security was seldom mentioned in the Brazilian international relations (IR) lexicon. It was often understood that thinking and talking about security was the metier of the military or of those deemed 'friends of the regime', and, as such, security-speak denoted authoritarian politics. Furthermore, there was an underlying concern that discussing politics through security would only reify the advantageous political position of the armed forces, since they were the only experienced sector on the subject. It was this impasse that first brought security studies to my attention and ultimately became the main reason why I went to Aberystwyth.

Whereas many of my colleagues have told me over the years that what attracted them to Aberystwyth was its flourishing research on Critical Security Studies (CSS), my rationale was a bit different. I pursued a PhD in CSS because the only thing worse than seeing my country be lost to neo-liberalism was to watch it recast the armed forces as security experts due of the lack of qualified non-military professionals. If security was going to stay on the political agenda in Brazil for years to come, I believed it was my personal duty to seek non-militaristic ways of discussing it. In hindsight, I had a misplaced perception that anything that was not military was democratic, inclusive and emancipatory.

It was against this background that Professor Ken Booth's *Reflections of a Fallen Realist* spoke to my own assumptions about Brazil, its place in the world and my own family history. Although that text was not specifically focused on Brazil, Booth (1997: 91) asked a series of thought-provoking questions that made me ponder my political assumptions. Below I have intercalated his questions with my own answers at that time (in italics):

Who do we think we are?

An academic and political activist.

What is the relationship between our identity and our interests?

My family history and my own interests are intertwined; I want to work for the development of Brazil.

What do we think we are doing?

Working for the development of my country.

Who do we represent? *The people.*

What values are we promoting?

Development, civilian ways of thinking about security, equality, justice, wealth distribution.

And why?

Because there are people who do not have access to them.

What is or should be the relationship between study in a university and the political world?

They need to work together and in tandem in order to bring development to the country and to its people.

How powerful are cultural and social pressures in determining the construction of the social identity of the security specialist?

Very powerful, I would not be who I am today had I not had my experiences.

As my answers to Booth's questions reveal, even as I was seeking to learn other ways of thinking about security, I remained deeply attached to the political and academic debates of my country. To paraphrase Booth's use of Anais Nin's quotation in that same paper, I did not understand the text as it was, I understood it as *I* was. In making this point, I am exposing to the reader my understanding, central to the critical theorizing of the Frankfurt School (Booth 2008: 41–5) and to the central argument of this book, that the observer, the analyst, the commentator on politics does not stand on an objective viewpoint, but is socially and historically situated.

I spent most of my first year in Aberystwyth re reading the Brazilian IR literature on security put forward in the previous two decades. If anything, these writings only reassured my fundamental political positions. First, the development of Brazil was the general remedy for the many social, economic and political difficulties of the country. Second, Brazil was a country of unrealized potential. Third, it was axiomatic that Brazil should take a more assertive position in the international realm and stop acquiescing to the dominance of the USA in order to follow through with 'our' project of development. There was never anything as comfortable (and comforting) as repeatedly encountering my own political assumptions in what had been produced in Brazilian IR.

However, as the year progressed I began to realize how geographically placed and historically specific Brazilian IR was. That year there were two worlds of IR for me – and they were worlds apart. The first of these worlds concerned my own research object. It asked me to think about the Brazilian state, what security meant in my native country, its development and its foreign policy. The second world of IR surrounded me everywhere else. It asked me to look for the individual, to question masculinities, to search for women, to investigate agency and self-reflection, to celebrate diversity, to engage pluralism, ethics and cosmopolitanism.

To use the Gramscian lexicon, that was a personal time of organic crisis. While the work put forward in my home country pushed me to think about Brazilian development, 'Brazilian international identity' and its relationship with the USA, Europe and other Latin American countries; my research community in the UK thrived on questioning mainstream IR and pushing forward the critical agenda, investigating gender, emancipation and the very limits of the discipline. The debates which I was exposed to on a daily basis seemed to undermine everything I had learned to value in relation to both the Brazilian discipline and my political engagement.

My PhD project never really took off until I was intellectually prepared for the questions critical theory demanded I dare ask. Eventually I did dare. Thus coming to Aberystwyth represented the personal, political and academic value of asking uncomfortable questions (Booth and Vale 1995: 294), of assessing (and reflecting upon) the political assumptions about development, identity and security. In this sense, this book is the result of a critical engagement with myself and with my political place as an intellectual interested in CSS, but who is also deeply embedded in Brazilian politics and in the history of thinking about security in that country.

Geocultural epistemologies as critical engagement

Despite the many disagreements separating mainstream and alternative perspectives in IR, both disciplinary strands have long accepted the claim that IR is dominated by theories and approaches produced in the West (Hoffmann 1977; Alker and Biersteker 1984; Holsti 1985; Wæver 1998; Smith 2000; Crawford and Jarvis 2001; Friedrichs 2004). The acknowledgment that IR is practised and experienced differently in non-core settings has opened the opportunity for sociological enquiry into the 'many worlds' of IR and into the multi-layered web of complexities that connect the periphery and the core of the discipline.

In this aspect, the research initiative led by Arlene Tickner and Ole Wæver has been a fundamental influence on my attempt at understanding the specificities of thinking about security in Brazil. Their Geocultural Epistemologies project (GEP) has sought to reflect on the core–periphery divides of IR by emphasizing perspectives that politicize the making of the discipline outside the Anglo-Saxon condominium. In doing so, their work has not only paved the way for new avenues of enquiry, but also provided intellectual space for research that moves beyond the usual assertion that the discipline is defined and shaped by the core. More importantly, the GEP provided a platform for scholars around the world to explore the geographies of the discipline, to map patterns of disciplinary exclusion and to induce further sociological reflexivity in the field. For my own work, this has not only constituted an entry point to contesting the core–periphery divide in our discipline, it also has led me to explore how local forms and practices of IR are themselves infused with power relations constituted and reified by local actors and which are quite often independent of, although connected to, disciplinary boundaries produced in the core. The GEP informs this volume in two ways: the research questions it proposes and the idea of *worlding*. Each of them is explained below.

What is theory here? Why is this the case?

My initial exploration of Brazilian IR followed the two guiding questions Tickner and Wæver proposed in their co-edited volume, respectively: What is the state of IR here? and Why is this the case? Attempting to make sense of the first question naturally leads one to the second. However, it was the reply to that second question that made this volume possible. By this I mean that the study of the origins, agenda and the state of the art of Brazilian IR led me to enquire beyond Brazilian disciplinary boundaries and pursue a line of research that focused not on the shape and form of the discipline in Brazil but on how it has been locally shaped and reified.

Once I delved into the Brazilian IR literature, two patterns stood out. First, the set of underlying assumptions inherent to these writings. They mirrored the premises that had guided my political praxis, i.e. national development would be the answer to our problems, Brazil was a natural leader in South America, the country's natural wealth was already an indication of its great prospects, etc. These arguments were not only implicit in Brazilian IR texts, but also commonly found in other disciplines of the social sciences, in political debates, the arts, literature and daily news. Scientific and common-sense knowledge shared the same underlying principles and together seemed to form an ontology of Brazil: what it is, what it should be and how it ought to become. Thus, even though the research that led to the writing of this volume started from the questions introduced by Tickner and Wæver, it was this specific Brazilian ontology that first let me to explore the politics of knowledge production in IR outside the boundaries of the discipline. This meant that, instead of looking specifically at IR, I became interested in how this specific ontology was shared by and reified in different areas of knowledge.

Second, upon analysing the security literature in Brazilian IR, what came to the forefront was that the end of the military regime had virtually no impact on the discipline (Chapter 5 discusses this in detail). Moreover, arguments put forward by this literature had not changed in nearly four decades. To cite but one example, the concept of security found at the military think-tank *Escola Superior de Guerra* (Higher War College, ESG) at the height of the dictatorship was similar to the one shared by researchers in a scholarly series of conferences held nearly three decades later:

> On the concepts of security and defence, the panellists shared the idea that, even though these are complex concepts, there is a consensus around the fact that defence is basically an 'action' and security is a 'state'
>
> (Vidigal *et al.* 2004: 124)

> Security is a state and defence is an act or a set of acts. Defence has the aim of stopping a foreseen threat and security is established as an integral doctrine against any threat.
>
> (Távora 1959)

This finding came as a personal shock, since no other institution had its name as strongly connected to the regime as the ESG and its Doctrine of National Security. Throughout the past decades, academic researchers have looked at the ESG and the *Doutrina de Segurança Nacional* (Doctrine of National Security, DSN) as an access point into military and authoritarian thinking in Brazil. It became a cottage industry to attribute to the ESG all policies and practices pursued by the military regime (see Comblin 1978; Alves 1984). A great part of this enterprise aimed at drawing the links between military thought and authoritarian regimes in Brazil as an attempt to find common denominators that would in hindsight explain the regime. This entire literature works with the assumption that military thought constitutes a minimum core of ideas shared by the armed forces in general. There are several consequences to such essentialization of military thinking. First, it works with the assumption that military thought does not vary with class, rank, generation or international political divisions. Thus, it overlooks internal dissidence and political struggle within the ranks, giving the impression that all members of the military naturally identify himself/herself with the sort of thinking produced by the sector that is in power at a determined point. Second, and most importantly, it gives military thought an unconditional status of opposition to civilian thought. Third, it denies military thought any contextualization within specific political and economic processes, since it perceives it to have a single, immutable core throughout Brazilian history. Fourth, it not only supposes a predetermined orientation to either civilian or military thought based on profession, but also overlooks specific political alliances that did not conform to the rigidity of these labels.

Take, for instance, the concept of authoritarian utopia (D'Araújo 1994: 9; Fico 2004: 37–8) that seeks to explain military thinking in Brazil through a core set of common beliefs shared by the armed forces. The authoritarian utopia would be a minimum common ground on which different factions of that institution would agree upon independent of their political inclination. D'Araújo (1994: 10) summarizes it in four ideas: (a) military superiority over civilians, (b) the need to discipline the people, (c) the need to develop the state and to become a world power and (d) a clear differentiation between the elite (who should command the development effort) and the people (who should be educated and disciplined).

I am reluctant to accept these terms, not only because it is simplistic to assume that this kind of thinking was characteristic only of the military, but because it is important to engage with how these thoughts also populate non-military writing – an engagement that is lacking in this literature. All of these characteristics, including military superiority over civilians, were also espoused by non-military sectors (for works that make this argument, see McLain 1967; Marson 1979; Mercadante 1980; Diniz and Boschi 1989). In this sense, denying the existence of the authoritarian utopia in civilian life is a shortcoming that masks its scope and breadth in at least two ways. First, it gives a false idea that only the military in Brazilian society espoused the authoritarian utopia. Second, and stemming from the former, it bypasses discussions of how these views were/still are very much present in Brazilian society as a whole. This penetration of militarized ways of thinking into society is sometimes called 'militarism'. Militarism is defined as having three characteristics, namely, the adoption and exultation of the values, ideals and ideologies traditionally favoured by the military, the increase in or predominance of the role of the military in both domestic and foreign politics, and the adoption or encouragement of policies which emphasize the use of organized violence to solve either internal or external problems (see Skjelsbæk 1980; Cheeseman and Kettle 1990: 19–20). However, a standard work on the idea of militarism, noting its controversial usage, states that the concept of militarism has not been 'particularly useful to academic discussion' (Berghahnh 1981: 123). Consequently, I use the more general and less controversial term 'militarization' to refer to the various characteristics that are said to make up militarism.

Totalizing ideas concerning support for the regime based on gender, race and work affiliation also fall short of encompassing the multitude of behaviours at play. Examples of left-wing activism within the military realm also call into question the validity of the civilian/military dichotomy. Brazil has a history of left-wing military journals (*O Patriota*, *A Marinha Vermelha* and *Revista do Clube Militar*) and of partisans of the Brazilian Communist Party who hailed from the army (Reis 2000: 51; Fico 2004: 34). On the other end of the spectrum, there were conservative civilians who strongly supported the 1964 coup (Fico 2004: 40–3). Lest we forget, during the whole month of March 1964 – before the coup – thousands around the country were joining conservative demonstrations that openly favoured a military regime (Saes 1984; Codato and Oliveira 2004). On 2 April 1964 alone, the day after the coup, one million people marched the streets of São Paulo in celebration and support of the new regime (Simoes 1985; Costa 1989: 55–66). Conservative Catholics were met with Theology of Liberation dissidents (Simoes 1985; Cordeiro 2009); women's associations were as much a reality as those women who were persecuted by the regime (Ferreira 1996; Pedro and Wolff 2010). Likewise, repression within the military itself was also a norm (Cunha and Cabral 2006; Cunha 2008). More than 1000 military staff had either their careers stalled or were expelled from the corps (Gaspari 2002: 240). In the aftermath of the coup, no less than twenty (of the 102) active-duty generals were expelled from the armed forces (Carvalho 1982: 198).

That is, any sort of typology of the nature and project of the regime falls short of its purpose, since it is built on the assumption that the dictatorship was a regime forced on civilians by the armed forces and experienced uniformly throughout society. When one starts looking at the regime without the lens of civilian/military dichotomy, other richer and more contextualized narratives start to emerge, narratives that cannot and will not conform to mainstream, preconditioned views of the regime. That is, by looking at Brazilian thinking about security through the civilian/military dichotomy, the literature has not only essentialized its understandings of both, but has also failed to grasp the political meanings ascribed to security. In other words, the framing of intellectuals as either military or civilian has downplayed and overlooked affinities as well as differences within these two labels, forcing both sides to conform to static conceptualizations of left and right and/or civilian and military.

In order to explore this Brazilian epistemology and still be able to overcome the theoretical and methodological insufficiencies of the literature that seeks to understand the way security has been thought in Brazil, this book borrows from Brazilian sociologist Jessé Souza (Souza 2006d; and see De Souza 2011: 2) his 'Theory of Emotional Action'(TEA). In recent years, Souza has argued that there has only been one body of thought that is cohesive enough to be called 'theory' in Brazil. For Souza, the foundations of Brazilian social theorizing are traceable to the works of two academics. The first is the 1933 volume by Gilberto Freyre entitled *Casa Grande & Senzala*, whilst Sérgio Buarque de Holanda (1936) authored the second book, *Raízes do Brasil*. Souza argues that the strength of these books lie in the processes engendered by their release. They established a specific epistemology of social thought in Brazil by producing the first positive perceptions of Brazilian identity. This paradigm found both reason and popularity in the 1930s in Brazil due to its ontological claims about Brazilian identity. As a theory, the TEA describes an essentialized Brazilian identity as the most basic structuring concept around which processes take shape, actors interact and history unravels. As such, these assumptions about Brazilian identity have been the only basis to inform social theorizing in Brazil for the better part of the last eight decades. By analysing the core of these ideas on identity independently from political and professional affiliation, Souza was able to trace the roots of contemporary social theorizing and to understand it as a set of ideas that have permeated both left and right wings as well as civilian and military thought. In sum, by locating and contextualizing the birth of contemporary social thought in Brazil, Souza aptly demonstrates that the hegemonic form of theorizing in the country has masked the processes that have engendered contemporary forms of inequality and exclusion. By understanding Brazilian identity as the ontological claim of social theorizing in twentieth-century Brazil, one can apprehend all other intellectual claims put forward in that country, including those in the Brazilian IR literature, where speaking and writing security has enabled specific intellectual claims and practices derived from the ontological assertion of Brazilian identity. This volume, then, seeks to take the arguments raised by Jessé Souza and further them through analysing the development of thinking about security in Brazil. Furthermore, Souza's TEA helps me put forward a different take on the authoritarian utopia, namely one that is able to investigate social theorizing beyond the political lines that divide civilian from military thought. I perceive the authoritarian utopia to be a set of core values and ideas found in both academic and political debates in Brazil and which are espoused by different sectors of society independent of professional or political association. Souza's TEA also helps connect specific historic contexts with the hegemonic form of social theorizing by analysing the meanings and practices attributed to security in each one of them. I am specifically interested in those people who have negotiated the meanings of security in recent Brazilian history, why and through which means. If one is to accept the claims that IR has offered little 'international' theorizing and, as the literature has suggested, that its rationale is often nationally based, then critical engagement with geocultural epistemologies must necessarily include the assumption that 'local thinking' is for someone and for some purpose. By approaching my political assumptions and Brazilian IR thought as knowledge that is politically situated, I was able to trace my own intellectual tradition to axiomatic processes in Brazilian history that inform, but also go beyond, the disciplinary gates of IR.

Worlding

The second connection between the GEP and this volume is the idea of *worlding*. Tickner and Wæver define 'worlding' as the process through which reality is made intelligible and by which we determine who we are in relation to 'others' (Tickner and Wæver 2009a: 9). It refers to the multiplicity of ways knowledge is re-ordered and re-adapted in specific geocultural contexts so that, while it works with familiar forms of theorization, it also reifies other types of local exclusion.

Thus 'worlding Brazil' means the way in which theorizing/thinking has affected how Brazil is represented and thought of. That is, worlding Brazil is the epiphenomenon of political theorizing in the country (see discussion in Chapter 1). One of the tasks proposed, then, is not only to trace the epiphenomenom back to a specific theory, but also to analyse the content and implications of particular representations of Brazil. This task involves challenging how intellectuals have historically 'worlded' Brazil, how they have affected politics and its representations, as well as the contingencies of doing so. Before presenting the book's structure, I would like to highlight some of the key concepts used throughout the volume.

Key concepts

Thinking

When analysing debates on security in Brazil, I use thinking instead of theorizing. I use Waltz's differentiation between thought and theory (Waltz 1990). He initially used that distinction to draw a line between traditional realist thought and his structural neorealist theory. Waltz argued that the former was never able to transcend the development of concepts into the systematization of knowledge about objects, processes, movements, acts and interactions required by theory (Waltz 1990: 24). That is, realist thought focused on defining certain constants in foreign policy and in the interaction between states, but it could not offer an organization of regularities and repetitions in ways that enabled the fashioning of a theory. The argument here is that security discussions in Brazil fall into Waltz's category of *thought* (or thinking). For Waltz, thinking could include normative ideas and projects, but theory is social scientific. For social scientists in IR, adopting a Waltzian conception of 'theory', states are seen as 'like units' and are not concerned with the 'heterogeneity of states'. But this is exactly what Brazilian intellectuals have been concerned with – the peculiarities of Brazilian identity and its impact on state development, internally and externally. This is why, in relation to the concept of security in Brazil, I adopt 'thinking' instead of 'theorizing'.

In the context of the *Estado Novo*, analysed in Chapter 3, security concerned thinking about the militarization of society and the scrutiny of all aspects of societal interaction. In Chapter 4, security was related to thinking about a conservative method of modernization that did not preclude violent and authoritarian measures against political dissidence. In Chapter 5, security is discussed in its relation to the project of Brazilian *inserção internacional*. What comes to the forefront in all three cases are relational aspects regarding security and militarization, security and modernization, and security and foreign policy. These do more to reveal the political platforms of those who speak security than they do to systematize and organize knowledge about security. Before moving on to the next concept, *security,* I would like to make a distinction between my use of 'writing security' and that of David Campbell. Likewise, I would also like to specify the meaning of 'speaking security' to avoid giving the reader the impression that I am relying on the 'securitization' literature. In his 1992 *Writing Security*, Campbell sought to assess how the practice of writing security threats into US foreign policy constructed the identity of the USA (Smith 2005: 50). His argument is that identity is 'performative' and that there is no stable identity. Thus, for Campbell, writing security is a performance that seeks to constantly construct US identity. I am more concerned with the elites that get to define, write and speak security. That is, I am interested in how the political positions occupied by those who use the security lexicon impose their ideas about Brazilian identity, rationality and development. Where Campbell argues that identity is neither fixed nor final, my argument is that meanings attributed to identity are strategized by and dependent on the interest of those who write and speak security. The reason I am not delving into the literature that seeks to apply Speech Act Theory to security – the approach to security studies known as 'securitization' (see Wæver 1994, 1995) – is of a different nature. Even though I work with the political representations enabled by the security discourses in different contexts of Brazilian history, I do not share the securitization approach belief that states are (and ought to remain) the main referent of security (Wæver 1994). Furthermore, in the securitization school, speaking security requires an 'audience' that accepts the claim of the securitizing actor (for a critique of this point, see Booth 2008: 167). As Chapter 3, 4 and 5 convey, the audience to which authoritarian and conservative actors spoke security in those contexts were not given a choice to either accept or refuse the securitization of political processes in Brazil. Instead, security claims were often made despite and against its audience.

Security

This volume is informed by the approach of critical security studies, and it locates itself within the intellectual enterprise developed since the 1990s that has sought to politicize the concept of security, to investigate how and why specific accounts became dominant and their role in silencing alternative views on security, and to identify forms of engagement with security that may present alternatives to orthodoxy. This entails perceiving security – to do with threats and risks of danger to a referent – as derivative of 'different underlying understandings of the character and purpose of politics' (Booth 2008: 109). This point is elaborated in Chapter 1. Based on these understandings of security, this volume seeks to investigate the development, strategies and practices employed by Brazilian orthodoxy in the name of security. Due to this specific aim, I refrain from proposing different ways in which security could have been considered.

Intellectuals

The role of intellectuals in both knowledge production and political practices entailed by their thinking about security is a persistent theme of this volume. This comes from understanding politics as revolving around the interplay of interests and ideas (Wyn Jones 1999: 112), especially the politics of who gets to make claims about 'security' and for which purpose. Such an approach entails exploring how the TEA has been reified and reproduced in Brazil. I use the Gramscian concept of traditional intellectuals (Gramsci 1971a: chap. 1) to refer to the role occupied by those who have thought about security in Brazil since 1930. Thus, throughout the book, the term 'intellectuals' is used to mean traditional intellectuals – those I perceive to have played a role in maintaining – either through their theory or practice – those assumptions of security that reproduce the status quo (see Wyn Jones 1999: 120).

Coxian 'problem-solving' and the 'interests of knowledge'

'Problem-solving theory' and the 'interests of knowledge' are two ideas which structure the guiding principles behind this book. Both of them were introduced by Robert Cox in his seminal 1981 paper 'Gramsci, Hegemony and International Relations'. First, I will use the phrase 'problem-solving theory' a few times, sometimes preceded by the adjective 'Coxian' to indicate Cox's particular formulation of the concept. Cox introduced the idea of problem-solving theory (Cox 1983: 126) as the kind of theory that works with problems *within* the system. That is, it does not seek to transcend the status quo, since it works within the assumption of overall stability. Thus, I use the Coxian concept of 'problem-solving theory' when relating to knowledge production in Brazil in order to signal to the reader that the strand of theorizing analyzed in each context of thinking about security worked *within* the status quo. Second, another one of Cox's influential ideas in critical approaches to IR was summarized in his often-quoted 'theory is always *for* someone and *for* some purpose' (Cox 1981: 128). His idea was to place emphasis on the historical and political situatedness of knowledge-producers and on the interests engendered by the intellectuals' own position in a given context (Booth 2008: 48). In a recent interview, Cox stated that his phrase was 'a general encouragement to be critical, to refuse to accept a theory at face value, to look at it and see where it comes from, what it was designed to achieve and the context in which it was developed' (Brincat *et al.* 2011: 40). This idea of the interests of knowledge is the central inspiration to critique guiding this book. Understanding where ideas come from and what they were designed to achieve constitutes the initial and perhaps most fundamental step of critical thinking. In this sense, the book is guided by critical engagement with thinking about security in Brazil.

Book structure

The central question guiding this book is examined in six chapters which, after a theoretical discussion in Part I, follow a broadly chronological pattern in Part II, with conclusions and personal remarks in Part III. Part I sets out the theoretical approach and analytical framework of this book. It does so in two chapters. Chapter 1 works with Gramsci's concept of 'conservative modernization', which it uses to discuss the role of intellectuals in non-core settings and the relationship between the core and the periphery in terms of knowledge production in Brazil. Chapter 2 looks at the specific case of Brazilian knowledge production through Jessé Souza's idea of the 'TEA'. This chapter delves into the set of foundational ideas that have guided intellectual thinking in the country and develops the framework of analysis that structures the three different historic contexts explored in Part II.

Each of the chapters in Part II offers a novel contribution to the history of security thinking in Brazil through its sources and analysis. Furthermore, they test the validity of the claim that security thinking in Brazil has been seriously indebted to a very narrow and exclusionary set of assumptions about Brazilian identity – despite the political system or the political persuasion of different intellectual groups. This is achieved by looking at how security thinking was successively promoted by authoritarian actors under an authoritarian regime (Chapter 3), by authoritarian actors under a democratic regime (Chapter 4) and by democratic actors under a democratic regime (Chapter 5). Chapter 3 examines the traditional conceptions of the phrases 'national security' and 'national defence' in Brazilian political vocabulary. It further explores these terms as part of a project of militarization of the state and society which peaked during the *Estado Novo*. This chapter spans from 1930 to 1945 and refers to the meanings and practices of security pursued by authoritarian actors in an authoritarian regime. The arguments raised provide the initial context in which thinking about security was introduced in Brazil in the 1930s. As such, it highlights the early relationship established between 'Brazilianness' and development and argues that speaking security enabled authoritarian sectors to put forward their own project of development. The analysis of the legislation issued in Brazil between 1900 and 1945 was possible through the online public-access database Rede de Informação Legislativa e Jurídica. Its wide range of legislation enabled me to find the specific decrees, laws and decree-laws issued on security in that period.

Once the head of that authoritarian regime, Getúlio Vargas, was ousted from power in 1945, the political context in which security had previously been conceived changed. The redemocratization process required authoritarian and conservative sectors to rethink their modernization strategy and, thus, change the way security was conceptualized. This is the theme of Chapter 4, which deals with the developments in the conceptualization of security after the 1945 redemocratization until the end of the 1964 dictatorship. Thus, it covers the post-Second World War democratic regime (1945–64) and the military dictatorship (1964–85). The rationale behind this rather long timeframe is that the sort of thinking about security established during the democratic regime had been crystallized in the early 1950s and remained unchallenged until the end of the regime. This context, therefore, examines the conceptualization of security pursued by authoritarian actors in a democratic state. Chapter 4 sets out the grounds on which the development of thinking about security took place between 1945 and 1985. This chapter emphasizes the role of conservative actors, both civilian and military, in reproducing specific ideas of Brazilian identity and development through thinking about security. In doing so, it reveals how ideas of Brazilian identity were intimately connected to assumptions of rationality, whiteness and association with the West. It starts by arguing that the army-led democratization process brought about after the ousting of Vargas left unscathed the array of institutions and legal frameworks and, especially, the reputation of the military. As such, after the end of the *Estado Novo*, the armed forces reconvened with other conservative sectors at the ESG and produced the 'Doctrine of National Security' (DSN) – a modernization platform that had to compete with other political projects of its time. It then examines the DSN in the light of the framework presented in Part I of this volume. Through *being*, this chapter explores the meanings of the most basic concepts of the doctrine – society, nation, state and national power – and their relationship with thinking about security. *Becoming* examines the way development was put forward as inclusion in the realm of Western Christian democracies. The section entitled *the method* argues that, for the ESG, the DSN was a method of development that included very specific roles for the sector of the elite that shared ESG thinking about security while reinforcing ideas of rationality and Brazilianness. Lastly, this chapter examines 'worlding Brazil' in relation to the DNS. The research that provided the content of Chapter 4 was made possible through access to the library and documents available at the *Escola Superior de Guerra* in Rio de Janeiro and the material collected during fieldwork in Brazil in 2007 and 2010.

The end of the 1964 military regime brought about another change in the context of thinking about security in Brazil. The aim of Chapter 5 is, therefore, to look at how security has been conceptualized by scholars (democratic actors) in a democratic state. The framework presented in Part I enables this chapter to argue that thinking about security in Brazil has been characterized by continuity not only in terms of the basic claims about Brazilian identity and the teleological goal of development, but also in the way intellectuals strategize their own place in society and their own project of development. Chapter 5 starts by exploring the development of the education system in Brazil and its relation with ideas of national security. It then explores the history of security thinking in academic disciplines in Brazil. Finally it explores the idea of Brazilian identity in academia as a way of preparing the ground for the analysis of academic security thinking through being, becoming and the method. Through being, this chapter investigates how Brazilian academia has conceptualized security since the end of dictatorship. In becoming, the main concern is to explore how security writing has envisaged the path to development. The section entitled Method proposes that the method of development may be apprehended from exploring how the community of Brazilian scholars organized resistance when it perceived the state to be threatened by neo-liberal inclinations of the federal government. Finally, the last section of this chapter, Worlding Brazil, looks at how Brazil was worlded through security by Brazilian scholars. The analysis in Chapter 5 was greatly enriched by the open online availability of all issues of *Contexto Internacional* and *Revista Brasileira de Política Internacional* and by the interviews with Brazilian IR scholars. In order to protect the identities of those involved in this research and in the interest of frank disclosure, I have kept the identity of interviewees anonymous. Their words and views – translated and transmitted as accurately as possible and for the first time made public – are a significant contribution to knowledge about the development of thinking about security in Brazil. I was also lucky enough to be able to attend the very first meeting of *Associação Brasileira de Relações Internacionais* (ABRI, Brazilian Association of International Relations) in July 2007 in Brasília. My three stays in Brasília (July to August, October and November 2007) were of paramount importance to understanding and observing these issues. Apart from attending ABRI 2007, I was also able to observe five group discussions on security and was invited to take part in a symposium held in Rio de Janeiro every year, which is not open to the public. The aim of Part III of this volume is twofold. It not only draws conclusions on what security thinking has meant for Brazil, it also looks at how the attempt of bringing together those two worlds of IR reassessing political choices and reinventing my self. Chapter 6 looks at the personal history of those members of my family used in the introduction of this volume. It uses each individual and their condition as 'subject of security' to draw conclusions about knowledge production in Brazil. It examines the role of intellectuals in Brazil and their relationship with the reification of exclusionary structures of thinking in Brazilian society. Further to that, it looks at the framework developed in Part I and uses its three tenets (being, becoming and the method) to draw conclusions on how knowledge production in Brazil has been profoundly indebted to the place of intellectuals in its society.

Chapter 6 also offers an account of how the investigation of knowledge production in my native geocultural setting also meant addressing deep personal political assumptions – a long and often psychologically painful way to address my own scientific and cultural community. In this sense, 'worlding Brazil' meant re-worlding the self. Thus, in the final pages of this book, I look at how the global, the political and the personal were reshaped during its writing. As David Harvey (2010) has pointed out, 'one of the fundamental requirements for building a radically different world is to transform our 'mental conceptions of the world'.

Part I

The politics of worlding Brazil

1 International relations beyond the core

This chapter seeks to build on the research enterprise proposed by Tickner and Wæver. It looks at the contributions put forward in their co-edited 2009 volume as a way of assessing patterns in the development of IR in specific geocultural settings. It then suggests that, in order to keep to the original intent of the project, that is, analysing the core–periphery axis, there is an urgent need to map the patterns of institutionalization of IR in the non-core and relate it to waves of modernization in these countries. Critical scholarship needs to move beyond exploring how disciplinary mechanisms are produced in the core and reified in the periphery; it needs to investigate how power relations in the periphery are themselves hierarchical and infused with power. This means looking beyond the gates of the disciplinary history and investigating multiple and overlapping issues concerning knowledge production, such as waves of modernization, the interest behind the development of IR in different contexts, and how class and agency of local IR scholars influenced the making of the discipline. Rather than criticism towards the valuable contribution the GEP has provided, this should be perceived as an attempt to push the agenda forward. Here I identify three levels of analysis that may shed new light on the GEP, namely, 'the global', 'the local' and 'the personal'. In regard to 'the global', the chapter proposes to look at the development of IR in relation to the expansion of capitalism in countries of late modernization. That means moving beyond national/particular histories and understanding the development of IR outside the core within the structure of world history and international capitalism (see Gramsci 1985: 181). It argues that enquiries into the history of IR in the periphery must examine the relationship between international political processes and the proliferation of the discipline around the world. The second and third themes – 'the local' and 'the personal'– chiefly regard power relations in IR in the periphery and self-reflection outside the core. These questions are briefly introduced in this chapter and then further explored in consecutive parts of the book. Thus, Part II examines the politics of knowledge production in Brazil from a historical perspective. 'The local' aims at deepening the first level of analysis by proposing that the specific contours of modernization in Brazil need to be investigated and contextualized in order to understand how security has been thought of in the country. Lastly, the 'personal' level (explored in Part III) asks scholars to engage in self-reflection when relating to IR in their local contexts.

Deepening the geocultural epistemologies project

Since the 1980s, critical approaches to IR have been questioning much of the long-established conventional wisdom in the discipline, bringing to the field a diversity denied by prevailing forms of theorizing. IR scholars first turned to the history and sociology of the discipline to expose the construction of mainstream theoretical debates and established historiography of IR; the post-positivist turn opened room for multiple enquiries regarding the construction of IR narratives (Smith 1995; Schmidt 1998), its notably Western-centred agenda (Lapid 1989; Walker 1993; Wæver 1998; Holden 2001) and the general neglect of non-core theorizing in the discipline (Acharaya and Buzan 2007; Tickner and Wæver 2009b). In the aforementioned aspects, cross-fertilization with disciplinary and intellectual history (Levy 1997; Schmidt 1998; Armitage 2004; Teti 2007), and (to a lesser degree) philosophy and sociology of science has broadened and deepened the breadth and scope of our discipline (see Elman *et al.* 1993; Buger and Gadinger 2007). Hoffmann's seminal 1977 paper on the American blueprint of IR motivated research initiatives around the globe that sought to explore how the particular modes of thought of the discipline influenced its agenda and authoritative boundaries (for a more detailed account of this argument, see Tickner and Wæver 2009b: 2–6). Particularly interesting has been the work conducted on the state of IR in different national and regional academic settings (Behera 2007; Inoguchi 2007; Yaqing 2007; Chong and Hamilton-Hart 2009; Tickner 2009), which has turned the issue into a blossoming field of study (Bell 2009: 4). Within this particular set of literature, the GEP, led by Arlene Tickner and Ole Wæver, is the intellectual enterprise that motivates this book and that most closely influences it. The GEP aims at stimulating the production of critical knowledge about the core–periphery axis of our discipline (Tickner and Wæver 2009b: 3). It seeks to move beyond the commonly held views that there is no IR theorizing outside the West by exploring how the discipline has evolved in specific geocultural settings and its relationship with global IR. The support it has enjoyed and the book series it has produced are evidence of the potential it has to impact on the authoritative boundaries of the field. As mentioned in the Introduction, this volume is guided by the questions that structure Tickner and Wæver's co-edited 2009 volume *International Relations Scholarship Around the World*. They proposed two basic lines of enquiry, namely, 'What is the state of IR here?' and 'Why is this the case?' The response to those initial questions prompted scholars to appraise the discipline in different local contexts and to reflect upon the historic and sociological contingencies that have shaped IR in these various places. As a first step to a common effort of exploring IR outside the core, the GEP prospered in its focus on local histories of the discipline and their specificities. This ultimately brought to the forefront relevant aspects concerning the making and practice of IR outside the core (see Tickner and Wæver 2009c: chap. 18). Taken together, the different accounts of the development of IR in contrasting geocultural settings present a compelling argument that the contours of the discipline outside the Anglo-Saxon world are strongly dictated by national politics. The self-proclaimed main goal of the project, however, – that of examining the understudied core–periphery structure of the discipline – was left largely unexplored. Even though each paper examined how power structures established at the core dictated and affected the development of the discipline in specific contexts, the core–periphery – as a unit of analysis – remained consistently uninvestigated. As a result, readers were met with thought-provoking snapshots of IR outside the West that had little analytical engagement with the core–periphery structure as a whole. Nonetheless, the material produced has opened up space for systematic analysis of global patterns relating to the core–periphery axis of the discipline.

The global

Some of the main findings presented in *International Relations Scholarship Around the World* regarding IR in different geocultural contexts refer to the fact that the discipline, as it is practised outside the core, is often state-centric (Behera 2009: 134; Korany *et al.* 2009: 186; Ofuho 2009: 74–5; Schoeman 2009: 66), obsessed with an orthodox and parochial agenda (Drulak *et al.* 2009: 244; Tan 2009: 121) and not particularly interested in theorizing (Drulak *et al.* 2009: 245; Korany and Makdisi 2009: 177; Ofuho 2009: 76; Schoeman 2009: 55; Tickner 2009: 45). Unfortunately, what seems to be common to the whole spectrum of geocultural IR epistemologies in the periphery is its orthodoxy rather than its critical lenses. Such a verdict feels like the unexpected backlash of a project that at least implicitly contemplated finding critical knowledge in the margins of the discipline (see Tickner 2003: 745). Notwithstanding such a negative note, the first-hand accounts provided by that volume may offer important avenues of investigation of the core–periphery structure. In the case studies presented by the GEP, there seems to be two coinciding patterns relating to the institutionalization of IR in developing countries in the second half of the twentieth century. The first one concerns the time of institutionalization of the discipline in the periphery, whereas the second relates to the intended purpose of pursuing the establishment of IR in these countries. The contributions to the volume suggest that the institutionalization of IR in the periphery was much more connected to modernization projects and to post-Second World War politics than to disciplinary developments at the core. Tickner, for example, states that IR 'developed first in those countries that developed the earliest and became regional powers, namely, Chile, Mexico, Brazil, and Argentina' (2009: 36). About IR in the African continent, Ofuho linked the development of the discipline to the aftermath of African independence, when 'the newly emerging states faced the need to interact with the rest of the world' (Ofuho 2009: 72) Wang connects the beginning of IR studies in China to the post–1949 idea of seeking the 'recognition of the new China in the world' (Wang 2009: 104). Likewise, Indian IR seems to have also been driven by India's post-independence political agenda (Behera 2009: 134–5).

Accounts of the initial purpose for the establishment of IR departments in the periphery also diverged very little. The narratives in the 2009 volume point out to a perceived view in the periphery that IR could provide the necessary discursive tools for civil service staff to engage in diplomatic affairs and to represent their country to the world. They seem to indicate that IR is a specific language used not only to engage with the West but also to represent one's country through a modern lens. For instance, Wang (2009: 104) argues that there was a perception among Chinese IR scholars in the 1950s of 'a need to study the outside world and to prepare Chinese diplomats for the task of representing China in the world'. In the same vein, analysis of the institutionalization of IR in Turkey (Aydinli and Mathews 2009: 209), in the Arab countries (Korany and Makdisi 2009: 182) and in South (Behera 2009: 134) and Southeast Asia (Tan 2009: 120) all contain reference to the need of educating and preparing their elites to represent their country to the world. Both of these issues shed light on the fact that IR was understood and practised more as a code of access to dealing with and relating to the core and/or former colonial powers than as a scientific area of enquiry. In sum, the 'language of IR' seems to have been of fundamental importance to local elites at crucial points of each of these countries' histories and, perhaps even more poignantly, their national processes of state modernization (see also Tan 2009). For instance, the development of IR in South Africa during the Apartheid regime was deeply determined by the aim of maintaining the 'preservation of a white controlled state', whilst ensuring its legitimacy within the international community (Schoeman 2009: 3). In China, that process was connected to Mao Zedong's idea that his country should make its contribution to the world after 1949 (Wang 2009: 103–4). Even the example of Latin American IR offers insights into how its development in the periphery is intimately connected to representing one's country to the West. Tickner argues that IR was boosted in Latin America during the Cold War because the region's 'external affairs became mediated almost exclusively by its relationship with the United States' (Tickner 2009: 32). Much in the same vein, Sariolghalam (2009: 163–5) suggests that the political will of the revolutionary elites to distance themselves from Western modes of thinking determined not only the 'Islamicization' of mainstream knowledge production but also the exclusion of IR specialists from the policy-advising power they usually have in the periphery. That is, since representing Iran to the West as a modern/Westernized country was not a priority to the ortho-dox elite in power, IR specialists educated in Western modes of thinking were also kept at bay in politics. Given the aforementioned patterns of development of IR outside the core, the study of the history of IR in specific geocultural settings would perhaps provide richer accounts of the discipline if the connections between global politics and the local institutionalization of the discipline were systematically explored. If, as Gramsci rightly put it, 'the historical fact cannot have strictly defined national boundaries, history is always "world history" and particular histories only exist within the frame of world history' (Gramsci 1985: 181), then the local establishment of IR needs to be contextualized not only in relation to the discipline in the core but also within the wider framework of global history. The aforementioned patterns found in different continents may provide the background against which specificities experienced around the globe would not only speak about the margins but also give meaning to them by contextualizing the periphery of the discipline within the global system of capitalist exclusion. This poses an interesting question: 'How can one deal with the specific narratives of IR in different geocultural contexts in ways that would take into consideration power plays exercised at the international and local levels?' Gramsci's studies of the early stages of capitalism and its influence in the periphery of Europe offers important clues of how to assess the interplay between the international and the national in shaping local subjectivities (Morton 2007: 5). Particularly relevant is Morton's take on Gramsci's study of passive revolution as a method of historic analogy – to which we now turn. Gramsci first used the term 'passive revolution' when analysing the unification of the Italian state through *Ressorgimento*. Based on the principles set out by Marx in his preface to *The Critique of Political Economy*, Gramsci (1971b: 106) argued that a specific social formation would remain existent for as long as there was political space for manoeuvre and the necessary conditions for change had not been properly developed within that specific society. In the case of the Italian *Ressorgimento,* and unlike what had happened during the French Revolution, there were not Jacobins to establish a bourgeois state and eliminate the feudal classes. Rather, Italy's weak and reduced bourgeoisie allied itself with moderates and the big landowners, opting for the politics of *transformismo*, a centrist coalition of the government that isolated both the extreme right and extreme left (Morton 2007: 64). The bourgeoisie was therefore only able to assert its power by gearing the state towards bourgeois features, whilst ultimately reassuring the condition of subalternity of lower classes, especially the peasantry. This alliance between old hegemonic pre- and proto-capitalist classes with the Italian bourgeoisie represented what Marx described as the persistence of a social formation through political manoeuvre when the necessary conditions for change were yet to be developed.

Gramsci further developed his analysis of *Ressorgimento* by looking at what had happened in Europe in the Post-French Revolution period. It gave him a general framework for analysing the post-Napoleonic Wars period as a response of the traditional classes to the series of organic crisis that shook Europe throughout the nineteenth century and culminated with the processes of national unification (Thomas 1999: 145). The second half of the nineteenth century witnessed the 'efforts of the traditional classes to prevent the formation of a collective will and to maintain economic-corporate power in an international system of passive equilibrium' (Gramsci 1971b: 132). He further argued that the concept of passive revolution applied not only to the Italian case but, more generally, to countries that procured the modernization of the state through national wars or reforms that excluded radical revolution from its agenda (Gramsci 1996: 232). The insights provided by the case of Italian *Ressorgimento* allowed Gramsci to turn the concept of passive revolution into a principle of research and interpretation (Gramsci 1971b: 114). He applied those ideas to the case of Italian Fascism of his days

(Gramsci 1978) and Roosevelt's New Deal – in his notes collected under the title *Americanism and Fordism* (Simon 1982: 56) – and the passage from absolutist state into other stages of state formation in Eastern Europe.

Against the peril of being treated as a historic cause – which Gramsci was himself aware could happen to his interpretation of non-revolutionary revolution (Gramsci 1971a: 114, 116, 180) – Gramsci offers a method of (what Adam Morton calls) 'historical analogy' (Gramsci 1971a: 54; Morton 2007: 58, 68–9). For Gramsci, the passive revolution needs to be understood as a process that reveals breaks and continuities engendered by the order of capital within a path of general trajectories permeated by historical specificities (Morton 2007: 68). It is in this sense that Gramsci took time explaining, for example, the contingencies of uneven development between the South and North of Italy, the centralization of the absolutist state and the 'gelatinous' character of civil society in Russia, and the relationship between colonialism, imperialism and the political and economic activities of Fascist Italy. As Morton (2007: 70) puts it, 'this is an interpretative approach to historical sociology focusing on interrelated instances of state transition within world-historical processes, where the particulars of state formation are realised within the general features of capitalist modernity'. By linking the uneven development of capitalism in the periphery (general features) to relations within society (particulars of state formation), Morton (2007: 70) argues that Gramsci successfully binds together the history of Europe and of its colonies not through simple mimetic processes but through ways that assimilate the coexistence and interaction of interconnected and overlapping histories.

Through his reappraisal of Gramsci's account of *Rissorgimento* in ways that elucidate class struggle at the international and national level within the development of capitalism, Morton (2007: 74) points out that Gramsci prompts us to think of state formation beyond the arid history of state classes (which leaves the constitution and experience of subalternity unaccounted). Neo-Gramscians have de-historicized culture and taken it as a reductive idea of 'dominant ideology', argues Pasha (2013: 155). This risks taking hegemony as an elitist discourse that is unilaterally apprehended and followed in the periphery. Thus the concept of passive revolution is a tool to understand how historic specificities within general trajectories engender new social identities and subjectivities in terms of what the ruling classes have made of the other classes through whom they work and function.

More importantly, Gramsci reminds us that the concept of passive revolution applies to 'those countries that modernise the state through a series of reforms without undergoing a political revolution of a racial Jacobin type' (Gramsci 1996: 232). It then also refers to the path to modernity led by the dominant classes in different peripheral countries of uneven development or, as Morton rightly argues, 'the survival and reorganization of state identity through which social relations are reproduced in new forms consonant with capitalist property relations' (Morton 2007: 41).

My argument is that Gramsci's method of historical analogy may be applied not only to the expansion of capitalism, but also to the core–periphery axis of the discipline in ways that move beyond the Neo-Gramscian acceptance idea of the expansion of capitalism (Pasha 2013: 160–3). It is the role of intellectuals outside the core, the relevance of culture to the hegemonic process and its articulation as authoritative knowledge that then come to the forefront of analysis. Pasha asks us to see culture and its materialization (language) as the place of both consolidation and fragmentation of hegemonic power in which, and through which, multiple subjectivities and cultural projects struggle to forge specific collective identities. Hence the importance given by both Pasha and Morton to Gramsci's idea of passive revolution on the global scale.

For them, local passive revolutions (state-led modernization processes) are mutually conditioning moments within the single phenomenon of modernity. In leading the struggle for renewal, traditional intellectuals give materiality to the public spirit of the time through the production of ideas, world views and philosophies that 'give shape to the prevailing consciousness and help to naturalize it' (Pasha 2013: 161). These defining moments of consolidation of modernization in the Global South may offer important contributions as to how a confluence of past residues intermingles with core hegemonic discourse and the interests of the local historic bloc and gradually shapes the public spirit.

This is why Pasha (2013: 155–8) invites us to bring back culture as *the* central aspect of Gramsci's conceptualization of hegemony; because, through culture, materialized in the work of intellectuals, one can investigate the 'archaeology of consciousness'; that is, how the intricate working of a hegemonic bloc in a particular setting may be apprehended from the complex networks of individuals, institutions, government structures, etc.

This means recognizing that power relations are reproduced in the periphery with different, localized meanings that, albeit related to and using the language of the core, are embedded in local power struggles. In this context, intellectuals have a central role to play in the formation of the local public spirit, since material practices are reproduced in intellectual work (Pasha 2013: 16). This is where 'The Global' level of analysis in this volume meets 'the local'– where IR, as a language of the West, was absorbed and reshaped to fit the local context and meaning of modernity.

The local

There are still two other issues to be raised about what might have been missing from the accounts in Tickner and Wæver (2009a). The first one concerns the political place of intellectuals in the periphery. If, as suggested, IR is a specific language, initially learned and used by the elite of the foreign service in the periphery, that also means one needs to investigate how local disciplines of IR were shaped and defined by the worldviews and experiences of those who practise it. The search for critical voices in non-core scholarship has often romanticized the role of intellectual thinking in different contexts and has therefore failed to address how the social and political position occupied by intellectuals in the periphery affects their scholarship. There is an established view that non-core intellectuals are in an unfortunate position, especially if compared with their counterparts in the West. Intellectuals in the non-core may be in a situation of disadvantage in relation to academics in the core concerning language, available funding and the agenda-setting power widely enjoyed in the West, but conferring them the status of subaltern risks being complacent and naive about power relations in the periphery. In places where poverty, violence, lack of access to education and health are the rule rather than the exception, having a PhD and studying abroad – only some of the many privileges of being an academic in the periphery – gives them not only political advantage but also gate-keeping powers in their own settings. Lest we forget the Spivakean argument that however unfavourable their situation may be – the foreign elite, the indigenous elite, the upwardly mobile indigenes – anyone with access to the cultural sphere of the hegemonic order is not subaltern (De Kock 1992: 245). The stamp of subalternity to academics in the non-core may be a tempting one, but it does not quite give us the whole picture. Non-Western academics are, in their own societies, perhaps the best equipped people to understand Western thought. This gives them space to negotiate and articulate their claims of 'Westernness' (and hence modernity) to those within their cultural context and of subalternity to those in the West (for a similar argument, see Enloe and Rejai 1969:150). Such advantageous position – of being the middlemen between Western and non-Western scholarship – was not explored in the first volume of the GEP. Disregarding the fact that non-Western intellectuals also actively engage in power plays and also act as local gatekeepers of orthodoxy would give at best a biased view of how and why IR developed the way it did in specific contexts. Career intellectuals in the periphery (not only IR specialists) are often part of the upper classes and their knowledge about the world is also dependent on that condition. While criticism towards the IR establishment in the West being populated by white, elite, educated men has long made its way to the literature (see Ship 1994; Enloe 2000), the same cannot be said about a systematic approach to gender and class in non-Western academia. Even though many of the contributions presented in the 2009 volume touch upon the privileged background of the IR establishment, the consequences of its early institutionalization in diplomatic circles is presented as a given and not fully problematized (see, especially, Aydinli and Mathews 2009; Ofuho 2009; Schoeman 2009; Wang 2009). Understanding these multiple and overlapping layers of power that are constitutive of intellectual writing in the periphery means breaking away from one-dimensional analysis that perceives non-core theorizing as either the extension of what is done in the West or succumbs to the complacent, often romanticized, view that intellectuals in the periphery give voice to the silent majorities of their region. Or, as Mustapha Pasha (2013: 201) has called it, the Western gaze of critical scholarship to the Global South, the act of including the periphery only as a narrative of resistance without acknowledging power plays at work within the periphery itself. This is, of course, not a case of denying that – to some degree and in different circumstances – there has been uncritical acceptance of certain conceptualizations or, conversely, that intellectuals from the periphery have advanced critical enquiry into silences. It is rather a matter of emphasizing and giving due regard to the existence of multiple power practices involved in intellectual writing outside the core, including those internalized by each one of us in our own scholarship. The second point relates to the specific language of IR. It is worth quoting a remark by Tickner and Wæver:

> A strange absence in ancient, self-conscious, and large cultures like China, India, Japan, or the Arab world, and in countries like Israel and Iran with deeply ingrained religious traditions, is that IR seems to receive hardly any influence from strong cosmologies. In such cases one would expect to find, at least as a part of International Relations scholarship, approaches that differ in fundamental ways from Western ones. If the basic understandings of categories such as subject-object, individual-collective, earthly and transcendent, time and knowledge, among others, are different from standard Western thinking, it seems reasonable that they would be incorporated in IR too. Why then do we not find what we are looking for?
>
> (Tickner and Wæver 2009b: 337)

In searching for critical voices in the non-core of the discipline, Tickner and Wæver seem eager to understand why non-Western IR scholars are yet to profit from their own native philosophical traditions through the incorporation of different cosmologies of thought in their work. Concerning this specific goal, Bilgin had already alerted such line of questioning only reflected a 'misplaced Western mindset' (Bilgin 2008: 19–20; see also Tickner and Wæver 2009c: 338) characterized by the thought that one would necessarily find critical opportunities outside the core. That is, even though the literature is looking at the discipline in non-core settings, it does so in ways that reifies a postcolonial relationship between the core and the periphery of the discipline. It looks for alternative knowledge outside the West in order to expand the horizons of the discipline at the core. For example, at the end of her paper 'Latin American IR and the primacy of *lo práctico*', Tickner (2003: 745) states that 'a somewhat troubling discovery is that IR, as it is professed in non-core settings such as Latin America, offers relatively little of the kinds of alternative knowledge that critical scholarship so eagerly seeks'. In sum, the literature supposes that non-core IR scholars would be likely to tap into their native philosophical resources because of their birth culture. This relationship, between the scholar, his/her native culture and authoritative/Western forms of knowing needs to be more carefully analysed. Uncovering the politics of writing IR in different geocultural contexts involves not only understanding how/which concepts are reinterpreted and appropriated to fit local agendas, but also enquiring how the Western(ized) education of non-Western scholars both limits and dictates authoritative knowledge in the periphery. Jo Sharp has argued that to be taken seriously and have their perspective perceived as authoritative knowledge, non-Western experience 'must be translated into the languages of science, development or philosophy, dominated by Western concepts and languages' (Sharp 2008: 109–12). Even though Sharp was referring to knowledge produced by indigenous people, her point may be extended to countries with 'strong cosmologies'. If everything about becoming a scholar means learning and accepting Western forms of authoritative knowledge, how likely is it that one will capitalize on religious and philosophical traditions that are often perceived as myth and folklore? Admittedly, my knowledge about IR outside Latin America and the Anglo-Saxon world is perhaps too limited to allow me to propose any reply to the question above and, in any case, such a response would be outside the aim of this chapter. However, it may be worth briefly revisiting Sariolghalam and Behera's contributions to the 2009 volume on Iranian and Indian IR and highlight what scholars from countries with strong cosmologies and non-Western philosophical traditions have to say about it. Sariolghalam acknowledges the recognition given to the study of political theory and political philosophy in Iran, but states 'Iranian philosophers [were] carefully studied but more attention was paid to Kant, Rousseau, Montesquieu, and Weber' (Sariolghalam 2009: 159). Thus although local philosophers were not completely disregarded in Iranian academia, there seems to have been a clear preference for Western philosophy. While the lack of mention of the influence of local cosmologies should not be perceived as a definitive proof of scholarly disregard for them, it may perhaps be noted as a clue that religious and native cosmologies are understood as pertaining to a different realm from academia. Or, as Behera informs us about Indian IR, it

> stands divorced from the Indian cosmology and its conceptions of subject-object, knowledge, individualism, and secularism bear no weight in this discipline. Scholars theorizing IR rarely, if at all, draw upon the myriad ways of knowing, ideas, and practices of India's "pasts" because the two operate in completely separate epistemological domains. There is a huge implicit, albeit untested, assumption that it has nothing to offer in terms of enhancing knowledge about its key matter – the state.
>
> (Behera 2007, 2009: 150)

Behera argues still further that South Asia's disregard of its own philosophers and their contributions cannot be understood without thorough investigation of the discipline's relationship to the birth of India and Pakistan in the late 1940s. In this vein, in India and Pakistan, as in Iran and Brazil, if respect is paid to any specific cosmology it is that of the nation-state. In this regard, and as argued before, the existence (or lack) of native philosophies in each setting seemed less relevant to the development of the discipline outside of the West than the objective of modernization pursued by each of these countries' elite. As Tickner and Wæver have themselves concluded, the local modes and shapes that IR has acquired over the decades in different geocultural settings is that its episteme was rethought and adapted to the local national identity discourse (Tickner and Wæver 2009c: 334). As such, the adaptation of IR to other national settings share one same ontology but differ in their nationally based epistemologies. This way, IR in each national state is not only state-centric but nationally so. That means that, for example: in Brazil, IR is about the Brazilian state; in India, it is about the Indian state; in South Africa, it is about the South African state. While there is no denying the fact that IR is an American science and as such carries with it a specific mode of thinking that is deeply entrenched in Western thinking, due regard must be given to the fact that it has been developed in the periphery in tandem with the perceived national mission of each country. This may be perceived through the aforementioned three tenets reported in nearly every account of IR in different settings, namely: its relationship with the state's agenda and foreign policy, the role of policy-advising of academics in each country and the lack of preoccupation with theory and emphasis on 'pragmatic' knowledge. Since the 2009 volume provided a thorough picture of IR's parochialism, state-centrism and over-reliance on foreign policy in each of the geocultural settings explored, the next step in deepening the project should include the political and historical processes that gave rise to these local epistemologies. This means uncovering processes of state-led modernization and enquiring about its relationship with the promotion and development of not only IR but other human and social sciences as well. It requires breaking away from idealized views about intellectuals in the periphery and investigating how intellectual work in the periphery is infused by power relations that are much more related to local – rather than disciplinary – politics.

The personal

Lastly, for a project grounded on the reflexive turn of IR, it seems unusual that the contributions offered in the 2009 volume rarely spoke about the role of self-reflection in the making of local disciplines (exceptions include Behera 2009; Ofuho 2009; Wang 2009). The interest of critical Western scholarship on different geocultural settings has not constituted an openly pragmatic attempt to politicize and push the discipline in the non-core to further self-reflection. This way, scholars in the periphery seem to have a place as experts of what goes elsewhere without actively contributing to self-reflection and politicization of their role in their home settings. In keeping with the critical nature of the GEP, it would perhaps further its scholarly intent to ask contributors to ponder on their own place in their local disciplines and to investigate (and expose) class, gender and gatekeeping practices in their own circles. IR historiography as it is being currently written follows a 'who-did-what-and-where' approach to writing history. However necessary this first step may be, we should take on the critical task of investigating silences. That means asking who and what has been silenced and, especially, by whom. IR is often written about as something that is out there, developing despite its scholars (and their gender, class, race, political assumptions and professional interests). It seems we are much more inclined to talk about political and economic pressure coming from outside the field rather than examining how power is exercised among us. Again, this is not a question of downplaying the constraints and challenges of academic life in or outside the West. It is about exposing the many layers of disciplinary politics in IR and how they affect its writing. One way to do this in the scope of this project is to look at how power relations have constrained and limited local IR disciplines. However, is it possible to do that without asking ourselves how we have contributed to the reification of such a state of affairs? From my own limited experience, my perception is that the research proposal that led to the publication of this book did not start until I took a long, hard look at my own political praxis and realized I was not an observer outside my own discipline. It was then that I realized I had been willingly contributing to the reification of its parochial state-centric agenda. I had voluntarily denied and overlooked aspects of my life and of Brazilian society in order to conform to what the discipline I studied framed as authoritative knowledge (Chapter 5 develops this). Most importantly, it was only when I realized I had conformed and compromised my own political creativity in the name of Brazilian IR that I could finally see the masculinist white elitist establishment that I was working so hard to maintain and to be a part of. Thus, acknowledging 'the personal' as a level of analysis of the core–periphery axis of the discipline rescues the self-reflective intent of critical IR to the making of the discipline in the periphery.

2 Unravelling the Theory of Emotional Action

The task of the present chapter is to explore how the development of contemporary Brazilian epistemology is embedded in a specific moment of passive revolution, namely, the first Vargas government. The period 1930–45 is thus perceived as a foundational time for the forging of Brazilian intellectual discourse. To this end, this chapter explores the advantageous position of intellectuals as the main subjects of modernization policies promoted by the state in the nineteenth and twentieth century. By doing so, it uncovers how intellectual praxis in the early twentieth century was part of a political platform that sought to reclaim the place of pride they had enjoyed in empire politics. It builds on arguments presented in Chapter 1 by investigating the relationship between the place of intellectuals in Brazilian society and the sort of knowledge that has been produced in the country. As such, the theme running through the chapter is that knowledge production in Brazil has been historically infused with the perspectives of the class that has produced it. Intellectuals of the first quarter of the twentieth century exercised dissent against the liberal republican system (1889–1930) by defending the centralization of the state. Notwithstanding the conservative turn that took over the first Vargas government after 1934, intellectual adherence to the state project remained almost unaffected. By helping to shape and pragmatically taking part in the modernization effort of the 1930s and 1940s, this generation voluntarily helped forge the institutional arrangements where both knowledge and subjectivities of modernization would be negotiated in the decades to come. However, in order to understand how politically crucial the Vargas government was to Brazilian knowledge production, this chapter first explores the imbricate relationship between politics and intellectual production prior to the 1930s.

Waves of modernization

Between the arrival of the Portuguese court in Rio de Janeiro (1808) and the end of the Second World War, Brazil underwent two great processes of organic crisis, each of them followed by waves of state-led modernization. They both took place in connection with, and in response to, crisis initiated in Europe and their aftermath in the periphery of the system. The first one was related to the late stages of the Napoleonic wars and the colonial crisis in the Americas. Following

Napoleon's invasion of the Iberian Peninsula in 1807, the Portuguese royal family and core state bureaucracy fled to Rio de Janeiro and arrived in the capital of their American colony early the following year. In order to accommodate the Portuguese state in Rio de Janeiro, royal decrees created state institutions that had been historically prohibited in their colonies. These included the institutionalization of the first national bank; the establishment of an official publishing house, printing offices and newspapers; the creation of the Royal Military Academy; the building of gunpowder factories and steel industries; and the creation of the Royal Academy of Fine Arts, two schools of medicine, the Royal Library, the Botanic Gardens and the Royal Museum (Carvalho 1980: chap. 3; Mattos 1989; Viotti da Costa 1997: chap. 1). Furthermore, revoking the 1785 Colonial Act guaranteed non-taxed trade with other countries, as well as the end of the prohibition to set up industries.

This sudden breadth of modernization not only responded to the demands that were taking the local Hispanic elites in the Americas to engage in wars of independence against Spain but also ultimately kept the Portuguese colony from crumbling into smaller independent republics. Thus the local response to the systemic crises triggered in Europe after the French Revolution was furnished by the alliance between the Portuguese crown and the local elite. Throughout most of the nineteenth century, the Portuguese/Brazilian crown allied itself with slave and plantation owners and, in return, had the support of the colonial elite to remain in power (Carvalho 1980: chap. 3; Mattos 1989; Viotti da Costa 1997: chap. 1). This maintained local power in the hands of the plantation owners, while the emperor was able to exercise control at the federal level. This tacit agreement was one of the main reasons, for example, for the endurance of the slave system in Brazil – which was kept in place until 1888 and a federal system that was economically centralized in Rio but which let landowners have near-absolute political and repressive power in their local contexts. Such arrangements maintained politics highly localized and geographically tied to small communities in the countryside, where, after all, the great majority of the Brazilian population lived throughout that century. The landowner was free to pursue and maintain his own local interests and that, in turn, guaranteed his allegiance to the central government.

Throughout the nineteenth century, the top-down modernization waves promoted by the imperial house since its arrival in Brazil largely benefited those who could, by merit or family relations, work for the institutional establishments of the state. In turn, this created educated and professional sectors connected to state bureaucracy who made a strong link between the centralized state and modernity. In sum, the successive waves of modernization implemented by royalty in the nineteenth century gave rise to a class whose loyalty stood with the state and not with the imperial house.

The dominant paradigm of Brazilian intellectual practice after independence (in 1822) was built around two ideas. The first was the image of an exuberant and naturally wealthy country found in the imagery produced in and about the tropics (Nabuco 2003: 22–3; Ventura 1991: 25). In the first decades of that period, the Brazilian emperor Dom Pedro II and his court intellectuals devoted themselves to presenting Brazil and Brazilian identity as an extension of Europe (and thus European*ness*) in the tropics (Schwarcz 1993: chap. 1). There was continuous praise of Dom Pedro II and to his devotion to the 'world of science'. To promote the view of an European oasis in the tropics, the state stimulated foreign visitors to come to Brazil collect material for research, financed artistic and literary works that would depict the qualities of the country and, following the emperor's careful instruction, Brazilian representations around the world promoted the image of Brazil as modern, industrious and civilized (Schwarcz 1993: 32; 2002, chaps. 7 and 15). Opposing those positive images associated with nature, a second, concomitant view, heavily influenced by racial theories, was also developed from the second half of the nineteenth century onwards. The adoption of these theories in Brazil in the mid-to-late nineteenth century marked the demise of the attempt by court intellectuals of portraying Brazil as the hub of science and civilization in the tropics. There was an increasing perception that the lack of progress in the country was a result of racial degeneration promoted through interracial breeding (Schwarcz 1993: chap. 3). Early in the second half of the nineteenth century, the curator of the Brazilian Royal Museum announced, 'If anyone doubts illnesses provoked by racial interbreeding, come to Brazil' (Romero 1868: 71). His words echoed what French diplomat Count Gobineau had stated about the country over a decade earlier in his 1855 *Essai Sur L'Ine-galité des Races Humaines*: 'It is a completely *mulato* population, corrupted in blood and spirit and frighteningly ugly'. Nineteenth-century intellectuals faced the task of providing solutions for the country's backwardness in an intellectual environment that precluded the possibility for development in a racially mixed cultural setting (Schwarcz 1993: 92). In the following decades, race and the perceived negative influence of miscegenation dominated readings of Brazilian culture. Furthermore, they predefined the preference for whites in immigra-tion policies (Azevedo 1987), justified Brazilian underdevelopment, explained criminal behaviour of socially disadvantaged classes and even guided racialized practices of medicine (see, for example, Romero 1868, 1882; Rodrigues 1899, 1915; Haeckel 1908; Lacerda 1911; Kehl 1913, 1923). Racial theories not only imposed a certain perception of the past and present of the country, they also announced the improbability of any development in Brazil. Race determined the departing point of Brazilian*ness* and the negative political and economic outcome of any modernization. It was around this same time that the concept of 'Brazilian people' and its negative role in any prospect of progress of the Brazilian state started appearing in intellectual work. It is in this sense that one can understand the defence of whitening policies of European immigration both before and after slavery abolition. In his defence of slavery abolition, intellec-tual and politician Joaquim Nabuco wrote: 'European migration will bring to the tropics a Caucasian blood stream that is vivacious, energetic and healthy so that we may absorb it here' (Nabuco 2003: 22–3). A paper presented at the first International Conference of Races is an example that this kind of thought was still very much alive in the twentieth century: 'the *mestiço* Brazil of today has in a century of whitening its perspective, its point of departure, and its solution' (Lacerda 1911: 1). Writings at the end of the nineteenth century and the beginning of the twentieth century were populated with this subjacent pessimistic view of the impracticability of the country. On this issue, historian Lilia Schwarcz (2002: 240) has pondered on the uncomfortable situation of this generation of intellectuals 'who oscillated between the adoption of determinism and the reflection of its implications; between the praise of "national modernity" and the confirmation that the country, as such, was not viable'.

Brazilian intellectuals in the late nineteenth and early twentieth century sought to overcome the problem of race through hygiene and sanitation policies (Luz 1982; Hochman 1998; Lima and Hochman 2000; Mota 2003) and education (Rocha 2003; Queiroga 2011). By then, the subjacent determinism of Brazilian inferiority turned to medical solutions as a remedy for backwardness and to the pessimist interpretation of unfeasible progress. Hygiene and education were perceived to be measures of palliative care as much as the intake of white immigrants had been in the wake of the emancipation of slaves. The need for dealing with the problem of race through hygiene and sanitation led renowned doctor Miguel Pereira's warning that 'Brazil is still an immense hospital' (Pereira 1922: 2), whereas another equally renowned federal judge stated 'education is the law that can modify race' (Pimenta 1919: 60).

Thus, until the 1930s, Brazilian identity and social theorizing were thought of in terms of the engendered incapacity of overcoming problems rendered by centuries of miscegenation. Caught between the unsustainable authenticity of the strand of national identity connected to European *Brazilianness* and the blatant pessimism engendered by racial theories, intellectuals of the early twentieth-century anchored its nationalist project not on the existence of a form of Brazilian identity but on the need for socially engineering one (Pécaut 1989: 21). This will to engineer a national identity and to take part in the national project of modernization led by Getúlio Vargas in the 1930s and 1940s can only be understood within the wider crisis of the liberal republican system in Brazil. It is this claim that makes this historical overview important to the development of the central argument of this chapter.

The hour of the state

Between the end of the nineteenth century and the first decades of the twentieth century, another moment of crisis took shape. This time, it was spurred by the antinomy between the slave-based agro-exporting economy and the industry sectors based on free labour. The wealth generated by the latter grew outside of the umbrella of government power and had little interest to collude with either slavery or the centralization of power in Rio de Janeiro.

A military coup established the Brazilian republic by ousting Emperor Pedro II from power in 1889. This move engendered a political reconfiguration in which there was a relay in the presidential office between the two most powerful states of the federation until 1930. Direct rule by export-based agrarian elites and an emerging industrialist sector located in the southeast region of the country characterized those decades. Thus, the liberal republican system was the attempt of the agro-exporting elite to decentralize the state – a move towards a liberal federation of states that guaranteed both local and national rule of the agrarian sector.

In the first years of the republic, and in tandem with the liberal corollary of state withdrawal, the central government systematically took out of the federal power the supervision of sectors that the empire had guided. State properties and revenues were constantly decentralized. Public lands were granted to private colonization companies or taken over by local leaders after the government ceded most of them to the provinces (Katzman 1974; Holloway 1980), the state monopoly over subsoil was terminated, and public enterprises such as the *Central do Brasil* railway and iron foundries were unsuccessfully put up for sale.

The decentralization of the state greatly upset sectors that had historically been the recipient of modernization policies during the empire: the civilian bureaucracy, the armed forces and liberal professionals. When the agro-exporting oligarchies attempted to weaken state structures and its bureaucracy, that class came to the rescue of the state. The relationship between the liberal oligarchies in power and the sectors that defended a strong state remained highly contentious throughout the first decades of the twentieth century (Topik 1980; Triner 1999).

The military, which had allied itself with the agrarian sector in order to bring the republic about, saw the relationship run its course after five years of military rule that followed the establishment of the republic. The agrarian sector, in fact, spent the next three decades attempting to keep the military away from politics. One example is the preferential treatment given to the navy in order to foster internal divisions in the armed forces (Sodré 1968: 186–9) or the 1910 presidential campaign of Rui Barbosa, which was structured around the slogan 'civilismo' – the idea of permanently pushing the military away from politics (Figueiredo 1971; Gonçalves 2000: 38). The central government still refused for many years to dissolve the locally run militias and to have a modernization project for the armed forces (Faria 1979: 170; Smallman 2002: chap. 1) – which rendered the relationship with the military even more tense.

As for intellectuals (writers, artists, journalists), the fall of the monarchy meant that they lost part of the state patronage on which they relied. Many intellectuals had indeed joined the campaign to abolish slavery and the republican cause, but once these campaigns came about in the 1888–9 period, intellectuals had to accept the reality of private demands of the publishing market and the need for isolation from their previous political space (Pécaut 1989: 23; Sevcenko 1983: 228). The resentment of intellectual sectors was then directed towards a republic that had not only taken away their privileged status, but also failed to bring about meaningful changes to the nation and, especially, to the state. Intellectual writing of the early decades of the twentieth century displayed the animosity between intellectuals and the agrarian system that no longer fostered their activities.

The dissatisfaction of these sectors with the liberal project peaked in the 1920s. Opponents questioned the legitimacy of the liberal republic that had depended on them for functioning but denied them political participation through the rigidity of the political party system. Economically, attempts to use federal funds to save the agro-exporting economy from cyclical crisis further deteriorated their political position in the country. During the 1920s, art, literature and political debates challenged the liberal system. Dissent came from all sectors that benefited from a strong centralized state: the armed forces, the civilian bureaucracy, political leaders outside the party then in power, the church and the recently founded Communist Party (Pécaut 1989: 22).

A crisis in the presidential election of 1930 quickly escalated and received wide support from various anti-government political sectors, including the armed forces. Led by Getúlio Vargas – who had been the runner-up in the fraudulent polls of that year – the Revolution of 1930 overthrew the liberal government that had been in power since the early decades of that century and enthroned Vargas as the head of the provisional government. He remained in power until 1945 when he was ousted by a military coup. Up to this day, the first Vargas office (1930–45) still stands as the largest and most comprehensive modernization and state-building effort in Brazilian history. By 1945, the armed forces had become central political actors and the contemporary Brazilian institutional framework had been delineated and defined (for the institutional set up of the *Estado Novo*, see Schwartzman 1983; Lamounier 1989; Hentschke 2006).

Political dissent against the liberal republican system came from various sectors of society which were united in one idea: it was necessary to rescue the state from the liberal system. These sectors, which the agro-exporting elite had struggled to keep at bay from the political process, became the spokespersons of the nation, charging themselves with 'the task of shaping the nation and preparing themselves to take a position of power' (Sevcenko 1983: 232). Elaborating his perspectives of intellectuals in the 1920s, Brazilian writer Sérgio Milliet stated 'we threw ourselves into political activism, we were convinced that only through power we could impose a new order' (Andreucci 2006: 49). By throwing themselves into politics, these intellectuals of the centralized state announced their vocation to becoming the ruling elite, to aid and reinvigorate the centralized state that had earlier promoted their modernity and to manufacture the nation in their image.

The supporters of Vargas became the intellectuals of the centralized state. In this sense, the idea of the centralized state took precedence over any concern with the well-being of the people. This is not to say that it did not include concern with marginalized classes, but these, when they occurred, were secondary to the notion of reclaiming their place as agents and recipients of modernity in connection to state institutions. The 'people' were outside the boundaries of modernity and, at this point, still very much thought of in terms of the multitude of ill-nourished uneducated 'mass' (Carvalho 1987: chap. 3). However, the great intellectual turn of this generation was not its claim to politics, nor its inherent elitism. The novelty of this generation was the successful conjugation of academic and state discourse, and the forging of Brazilian identity into one set of ideas that are still, both implicitly and explicitly, key to Brazilian politics and academic research (Souza 2006a: 10).

By taking part in the state building effort, this generation of intellectuals reclaimed the place in politics they once had (under the monarchic system). This shifted and re-cast the social sciences in terms of policy relevance. Claims of the unbiased nature of medical solutions for poverty and backwardness of the people now turned to the assertion that the social sciences were of prime importance to the political process. To cite an example, jurist and Minister of Education Francisco Campos (1940: 6) stated 'transformations are not put in practice by the primitive mentality of the people nor of its leaders but through the influence of sciences and arts, research philosophers, scientists, engineers, artists'. Even intellectuals of different political persuasions shared this outlook. The modernist Brazilian poet Mário de Andrade (Andrade 1972: 41–2) stated in 1939 that he believed 'if some Indian philosopher would wish to know what sociology is through what, under that name, is done among us he would have more or less this definition: "Sociology is the art of quickly saving Brazil"'.

Both Campos and Andrade displayed the claim to power of intellectuals of their generation – a call to lead a 'rational' form of governance in politics. On this aspect, Pécaut (1989: 31–2) has proposed that intellectuals of the 1925–40 generation were advocating their own cause and did not claim to represent a determined social class. In fact, they were claiming their own place and 'natural vocation' to be among the ruling elite. It is important to highlight the idea that the centralized state took precedence over any concern with the well-being of the people. This is not to say that it did not include concern with marginalized classes, but these, when they occurred, were secondary to the notion of reclaiming their place as agents and recipients of modernity in connection with state institutions. The 'people' were outside the boundaries of modernity and, at this point, still very much thought of in terms of the ill-nourished uneducated 'mass' (Carvalho 1987: chap. 3; Ferreira: 2006).

As much of a feat the alliance between the Vargas government and intellectuals might have been for the *Estado Novo*, the intellectual innovation of this generation was not its claim to politics, nor its inherent elitism. The novelty was the successful conjugation of academic and state discourse, and the forging of Brazilian identity into one set of ideas that are still key to Brazilian politics and academic research (Souza 2006a: 10).

It was within this very specific context of the post-1930 coup in Brazil that a particular form of theorizing took hold and became the hegemonic way of thinking about Brazil during the 80 years preceding 2014. The next section proposes the framework used by Brazilian sociologist Jessé Souza (Souza 2006b, 2006c, 2006d) to analyse knowledge production in the social sciences in Brazil in the twentieth century. Souza defends the argument that the development of the social sciences in Brazil is deeply embedded in the historical moment of the institutionalization and incorporation of contemporary Brazilian identity. As such, the views that inform both are embedded in a historically traceable social imaginary. Souza's argument is that the successful conjugation of identity politics, state modernization and the institutionalization of academia in Brazil led to the predominance of a particular form of reading and understanding reality, the Theory of Emotional Action (TEA).

The Theory of Emotional Action

In his investigations on the source of Brazilian inequality, sociologist Jessé Souza briefly examined how social sciences in Brazil have historically theorized its society and inequality. In doing so, Souza proposed that there has been only one paradigm that is both coherent and articulated enough to be deemed a 'theory' of Brazilian thought (Souza 2006b: 13). Jessé Souza's TEA has been one of the most important critical contributions to Brazilian social thought in recent decades. Souza not only offered an insightful critique of his own discipline, but also provided an analytical basis with which one may reassess other areas of knowledge production in Brazil. Souza's argument is that the self-defeating principles of turn-of-the-century racial theories underwent a complete reversal in the 1930s after the publication of Gilberto Freyre's *Casa Grande & Senzala* (1933) and three years later, the first edition of *Raízes do Brazil* (1936) by Sérgio Buarque de Holanda. It is the novel analysis of Brazilian culture introduced by these two authors that inaugurated and, most importantly, established the norm for thinking about Brazilian identity since then.

The conjugation of Freyre's and Buarque de Holanda's ideas led to what Jessé Souza calls the TEA – an academic and popular common sense in Brazilian culture that seeks to explain the culture of privilege, corruption, prejudice and the so-called Brazilian racial democracy as by-products of a culture of *homem cordial* (Souza 2006d: 107). This paradigm is composed of the idea that Brazilian society is governed by pre-modern rules of coexistence in which emotions, and not rationality, are the basic form of societal interaction. Although the arguments laid out by the TEA may seem simplistic and incomprehensibly narrow to be able to inform nearly a century of social theorizing, it is important to take into account that there are three processes involved in this form of theorization. They are the discourse itself, its significance and particular political meanings, and the intellectual practices that support its constant reification in time. On the one hand, these ideas provided a solution to the racial conundrum that had pervaded social theorizing in the previous decades; on the other, they essentialized Brazilian identity and further compared it with (the essentialized) rational 'other', the USA (explored later). Most importantly, Souza argues that readings of Freyre and Buarque de Holanda provided both intellectuals and the state with the 'theoretical' framework and fundamental discourse of national identity with which to legitimize modernization. This way, the reaction against the liberal republic – the system that had deprived intellectuals of the social status enjoyed under the monarchy – came through the denial of liberalism's individualism and the certainty of an innate national unity (that precluded class struggle). However challenging the arguments presented by Souza may be, they do not go as far as establishing connections between intellectual writing and political agency in twentieth-century Brazil. By not contextualizing the place of intellectuals in Brazilian history and society, Souza fell short of investigating how intellectual praxis in Brazil has been embedded in perspectives that both reflect and reify their place in society while masking inequality under the guise of national identity. As a result, the reader is left with the idea that the eight decades prior to 2014 have been pervaded by thoughtless mimicry of the founding ideas put forward by Freyre and Buarque de Holanda. I readdress Souza's arguments by proposing a narrative that includes intellectual agency in the making of the TEA. This way, not only the political status of Freyre, Buarque de Holanda and their generation comes to light, but also that of the following intellectual generations. Let us now explore the individual contributions of Freyre and Buarque de Holanda to the Brazilian ontology. *Gilberto Freyre and the positivization of racial miscegenation* In the 1933 introduction of *Casa Grande & Senzala*, Freyre briefly addresses how the ideas of his generation were intertwined with the political prospects of Brazil: 'it was as if everything depended on me and on my generation; [it depended on] our way of resolving century-old issues' (Freyre 1933: xxiii). As was the case with other intellectuals of the centralized state, a national project for Brazil was at stake for most of that generation. Freyre addressed those issues through the construction of a narrative on Brazilian miscegenation. Freyre's thesis argues that Brazil's racially mixed composition is the result of a Portuguese past that fulfilled in its colony all potentialities of that culture, including a benevolent form of slavery that introduced the non-white population to the extended colonial family through sexual and affective relations. Ultimately, Freyre (and Buarque de Holanda, who I shall deal with below) rescues if not the Portuguese empire in Brazil, at least its cultural heritage. So much of the liberal republican system had been about pushing away from the centralized state that the empire had left, shying away from Portuguese culture and replacing it with that of other European colonial powers (France and England, for example). It is with the same intent that, in the first chapter of his book, Buarque de Holanda reminds his readers:

> as unattractive as it may seem to some of our compatriots, in the Brazilian case, it is still our association with the Iberian Peninsula, specially Portugal, that maintains a long tradition that is established enough to nourish a common soul between us, despite everything that separates us.
>
> (Buarque de Holanda 1936: 11)

One has to keep in mind that a great number of this generation of intellectuals had ties with the imperial system in their immediate family history. In 1922, the 20-year-old Buarque de Holanda published a short story entitled *Antinous* in which he criticized the decree that maintained the ban against the Portuguese royal family in Brazil. In it, in a clear reference to the work of Dom Pedro II as the emperor of Brazil, he stated 'Look at everything around you. Everything, everything is the work of one man only. Of one brain only' (cited in Matos 2005: 159). Both Freyre and Buarque de Holanda looked at the consequences of Portuguese rule in Brazil through the lens of a generation that had watched the liberal republican system attempt to decentralize the state. For Freyre, this rescue of Portuguese culture took shape through what he terms the 'plasticity' of the Portuguese colo-nizers. According to him (Freyre 1933: chap. 3), due to their national history, the Portuguese were not only predisposed to face slavery in more amicable terms but would also include slaves in their family circles – either through sex, love or both – and through such relationships shape Brazilian culture itself. Effectively, the cru-cial point Freyre raised was that the mixed ethnic background of the Brazilian people should be a matter of pride of a people who were capable of developing a unique society of true diversity within the realm of Portuguese culture (Souza 2006d: 103). In a 1937 lecture in Lisbon during his European tour, which fol-lowed the success of his *Casa Grande & Senzala*, Freyre stated:

> In face of this problem of ever growing importance for modern peoples – [the problem of] miscegenation – there is a distinct Portuguese attitude, or better yet, Luso-Brazilian, Luso-Asian, Luso-African [attitude] that makes us a psy-chological unity over one of the human solutions to problems of biological and social order: the democratization of human societies through the mixture of races. the essentially human social democracy. The love of these men for native women and later for African ones, love beyond prejudice and conven-tion, powerfully affected the formation of Brazil, softening what the slavery system would make cruel and inhumane. There was never a greater victory of the human, all too human, over the economic [sphere].
>
> (Freyre 1938: 14)

Although in his 1933 volume Freyre does explore in detail the sadistic patriarchical behaviour involved not only in slave/owner relations but also with the immediate (white) family of slave-owners, it is the 'positive' outcome of these relationships in Brazilian culture that interests him. In this sense, what Freyre does is to free the intellectuals of his time from both the dim prospects of development and the cultural weight of slavery. By reconstructing the slave system as something pos-itive (Schwarcz 1993: 188), he tried to liberate his generation from any need for a critical engagement with the (then) recent Brazilian past. It rescued the Portu-guese empire, for whose time of centralized state these intellectuals yearned. Fur-thermore, it gave this generation a blank canvas of national identity on which to discuss a project of modernization. In this sense, what Freyre presented the intel-lectual community of his time with was a way to be proud and accept Brazilian miscegenation. It was also a way for the Brazilian elite – who loathed the second-ary status of its colonial power in Europe and disdained its mixed population – to accept themselves as the result of colonial history. The idea of a homogeneous, peaceful Brazilian people that were able to overcome racism through an inher-ently sensual and emotional relationship between races was the idealized image of *Brazilianness* necessary for the effort of modernization of the magnitude pro-posed by Vargas.

The acceptance that miscegenation was positive for Brazilian culture also influ-enced the way intellectuals discussed the country's prospect of development. Since miscegenation was the wealth – rather than the curse – of Brazil, the prospects of development were not only plausible, but also attainable. This was no small feat at a time when the intellectuals of the centralized state engaged in a Gramscian war of position against the liberal republican system. The political demands for the return of a strong centralized state were then strengthened by the idea that a national project was possible, since tropical and *mestiço* Brazil was not condemned to failure.

The impact of Freyre's thesis is aptly described by Antônio Cândido, a renowned Brazilian professor of literature, who is also considered one of the greatest scholars of the twentieth century in Brazil. In a 2001 interview, which deserves to be quoted at length, Cândido said:

> Today it is hard for you to evaluate the impact of that publication [Gilberto Freyre's *Casa Grande & Senzala*]. It was a true earthquake, with favourable reaction from the great majority of readers, especially the most enlightened ones. To answer you, it might be worth telling how I came to know the book in 1934. I had two friends, the brothers Antonio Carlos and José Bonifácio de Andrada e Silva, who were leftists, one was my age and the other was one year older. As you may see by their family names, they were of an important family of politicians. They read *Casa Grande & Senzala* and told me what the book was about. The first reaction I remember is of Antonio Carlos looking at himself in the mirror, pulling his lips out as to make them look thicker and saying "I think I am a mulato!" I tell you this to indicate how *us*, not as an external fact, but as something that we were certainly part of, us who were of old families, forged in a time when sexual relationships between slave-owners and slaves were intense. We began to feel that somewhere in our ascendance there might have been a black forerunner. [Gilberto Freyre's] book showed us that the formation of the country could not be negatively interpreted through race. For us that was like a revelation, the explanation he gave through culture. . . that had an ever more important role in the way we understood things. Thanks to him [Freyre], a more dynamic vision of society started imposing itself. And that helped Brazilians to vent, to become freer from the compulsion of imitating European standards at all costs, including that compulsion for whiteness, that here [in Brazil] touches the ridiculous
>
> (Pontes 2001: 8–9)

The intention of the long transcription is not only to suggest the impact of Freyre's ideas on that generation, but also to advance their readily available reach in Brazilian society. Freyre's argument did not need theorizing of any sort; it was there – on the mirror that reflected Antônio Cândido's friend – available for anyone to look at and understand the power of miscegenation. Moreover, because it was there for everyone to see, it did not need to be discussed further. This engendered a Janus-faced process: the recipients and agents of modernity would profit from these novel approaches to identity; whereas those outside its sphere of positive influence were left with the feeble moral compensation that race relations in Brazil were fairer than elsewhere in the world. On the one hand, racial democracy became the theoretical shield that legitimized ideas that informed and celebrated Brazilian identity, while national economic development was the objective that brought together intellectuals and state bureaucracy in one modernization project. On the other, the judiciary system established by Getúlio Vargas heavily penalized blacks and *mestiços* (Flauzina 2006). Likewise, the public educational system sought to 'whiten' these populations and replace their history of exclusion with one of peaceful coexistence with whites (D'Ávila 2003), while sanitation policies displaced them from the urban perimeter and away from view (Santos 1985). In other words, while race still stigmatized socially and economically disadvantaged classes, it aided the elite's self-served modernization platform through its claim of a benign idea of race. It also blanketed issues of race and exclusion through the defence of an apolitical society that has resolved its issues through sexual relations (Davidoff 1982: 34). Commenting on the Brazilian myth of racial democracy, Martin Harris (1964: 64) advised: 'those who consider Brazil a racial heaven, should keep in mind that this heaven is populated by fictional creatures'. That is not true. That heaven is inhabited by real-life people whose abuse, exclusion and violence have been erased in the name of national identity. In his 1928 *Retrato do Brasil*, Paulo Prado – one of the most influential Maecenates of Brazilian modernism – summarized Brazil as a 'tropical and mestiço country, condemned to failure' (Prado 1928: 170). It is quite surprising that less than a decade later, the Brazilian *mestiços* were thought of as making up the strength and emotional wealth of the nation. That is, in about a decade, Brazil witnessed the rise and spread of a deeply rooted identity discourse that informed ideas on the cordiality of its people (Avelino Filho 1990; Schwarcz 1993), its racial democracy (T. Azevedo 1975) and its prospects as a country on the path of development (Chauí 2000). The short period that elapsed between the negative connotations and the positivization of Brazilian identity is still less crucial than the penetration this discourse attained in society. More importantly, although negative connotations of race would persistently frame, dictate and inform social policies and criminal justice (Bellintani 2009: chap. 3; Flauzina 2006: chaps. 2 and 3); intellectual, political and common sense discourse profited in the positivization of race and its intricate relationship with identity.

Sérgio Buarque de Holanda and personalismo/patrimonialismo

Following the publication of *Casa Grande & Senzala*, Sérgio Buarque de Holanda's *Raízes do Brazil* (1936) not only strengthened Freyre's thesis, but also reworked it in denser academic style. Profoundly influenced by Freyre, the contributions of Buarque de Holanda stemmed from his perception of Portuguese cultural heritage, which he expressed through the concepts of *personalismo* and *patrimonialismo*. Both concepts may be defined as the imposition of the personal sphere over societal relations as practiced by the Brazilian people (*personalismo*) and the Brazilian state (*patrimonialismo*). While Freyre's *Casa Grande & Senzala* was based on the result of his PhD study at Columbia University in the 1920s, Buarque de Holanda wrote *Raízes do Brasil* in the first years after the 1930 coup. As such, Buarque de Holanda engages much more with the ongoing political developments of his time. One of the very premises of the book was to establish a correlation between pre-modern and modern subjectivities in face of the contemporary Brazilian society. At play in *Raízes do Brasil* is a sense of unrealized modernity (Silva 2003). Buarque perceives an irreconcilable tension between the development of Portuguese heritage in the tropics and the ability to modernize, since it requires Brazilian culture to adapt to 'impersonal' forms of societal relations. That is, for him, modernity (and its institutions) is a product that is consumed and experienced by those societies which have made the leap from pre-modernity to modernity. In this sense, what seems to be at the heart of his concerns, and which emerges in the last chapter of his volume – entitled *Nossa Revolução* (Our Revolution) – is not only the relationship between a pre-modern culture and modernity, but also the way that modernity is being pursued by the post-1930 'revolutionary' movement. Attentive to the developments at play after Vargas rose to power, Buarque de Holanda (1936: 181) pondered on the relevance of what he calls a horizontal revolution. For him, this was a revolution 'that only benefits a few hundred, maybe thousands of people' and 'what we need is a good and honest vertical revolution' that would do away with 'the old colonial, aristocratic, patriarchical, *personalista* order' (1936: 180). It is a shame that the Buarque de Holanda of *Nossa Revolução* has received little attention in contemporary social sciences. Taken together, the differentiation he proposes between horizontal and vertical revolution and the criticism he offered on how the conservative sectors of the 1930 movement had hijacked the agenda seem one step away from the concept of a Gramscian passive revolution – nearly two decades before the first publication of Gramsci's *Prison Notebooks*. That passage of the book never received much attention from Brazilian intellectuals. The most celebrated part of his work has been *personalismo*, *patrimonialismo* and *homem cordial* – even though he declared he wished he could unsay (*desdizer*) those concepts (Buarque de Holanda 2004: 69). In fact, in his own opinion, Buarque de Holanda stated that the most important concept in that book was in *Nossa Revolução*; the idea of a vertical revolution. He comments 'it was a very hard argument to make then' (Buarque de Holanda 2004: 69). By 'hard', Buarque de Holanda meant 'politically dangerous', since at that time the National Security Law (1935) had just been passed and the left wing of the 1930 movement was the first to be persecuted by the 'revolutionary' government.

Out of the three concepts that make up the core of the arguments developed by Buarque de Holanda, 'personalismo' seems to be the most basic one. *Personalismo* is how Buarque de Holanda defines the culture of the pre-modern man, one that is not mediated through 'rational' civil relations between people:

> Sincerity, hospitality, generosity . . . virtues appreciated by foreigners who visit us, represent a definitive feature of the Brazilian character in which the influence of ancestral patterns of human coexistence is still active and are thus informed by rural and patriarchical environments. It would be a mistake to suppose these virtues to mean politeness and civility. Before anything, they are legitimate expressions of a deeply rich emotional depth.
>
> (Buarque de Holanda 1936: 141)

The deep emotional depth to which he refers is not only positive but also deeply negative. On the one hand, Brazilians are sincere, hospitable and generous, yet, on the other hand, their emotive behaviour can also drive them to favour friends, to purposefully harm others, to lie and to practice vengeance (Buarque de Holanda 1936: chap. 5). In other words, an individual that is ruled through emotion will not conform to expected norms of civil coexistence because she/he positions personal relations before societal ones. This culture of *personalimo* bequeathed Brazil with *homem cordial*, an individual shaped by family and personal relations and who is averse to discipline, to non-personal relations and to rationality.

Accordingly, these cultural traits of the Brazilian people led to the governance of politics through personal rather than public interest, a characteristic of Brazilian political culture which Buarque de Holanda (1936: 146) called *patrimonialismo*. Buarque de Holanda's reading of Brazil is embedded in the notion that contemporary political processes in the country are informed by pre-modern practices that rely on the lack of rationality in personal as well as public relations. From there, Buarque de Holanda extended these traits to the state, making it the realm of personal politics in Brazilian society. It is revealing that throughout his text, although emphasizing those characteristics in Brazilian culture, Buarque de Holanda makes several references to the fact that such behaviour is also present in other American countries (Buarque de Holanda 1936: 56, 61, 78). Once again, that seems to have been dropped from intellectual analysis of his work, making the *homem cordial* strictly Brazilian in his pre-modernity and incredibly amorous in his *personalismo*. That is, Buarque de Holanda's writings on Brazilian identity seem to consist of a patchwork of what could be adapted for the task of writing about identity by the intellectuals of the strong state. Here, the success of the TEA lies not only in the capacity of each individual to immediately relate to it, but also in its ability to silence violence, racism, inequality, poverty and exclusion, with the moral compensation of being a peaceful, fun-loving sensual people. However weak or poor the ideas that compose the TEA, it is their conjugation as state and academic discourse of national identity that contributes to the poverty of and academic debates in Brazil. As academic common sense, the TEA advances a sort of moral compensation to its bearers: if Brazilian identity produces the opposite of the idealized (developed and rich) Anglo-Saxon world, then it also works as a welcome emotional counter-point to the perceived rationality of these cultural contexts. In other words, these emotionally aware individuals in Brazil are warmer, more human, hospitable, generous, understanding and ever more sensual than those in societies who have presumably been primed for rationality in the public sphere. These are the most basic informing ideas from which social theorizing in Brazil has developed since the 1930s (Souza 2006b: 28). The aim of the next three sections of this chapter is to explore the key ideas of Souza's argument that are used in this thesis. At the centre of all these ideas is the word 'emotional': it therefore needs some explanation. First, emotional is the opposite of rational. Second, emotional is understood as the type of pre-modern behaviour of the *homem cordial*. Third, emotional is the reaction to criticism of this world view. Each of these three points is relevant to the way this book proposes to develop the analysis of security thinking in Brazil. The emotional/rational dichotomization is taken in the following chapters as the first and defining step of identity – *being* – which encompasses how tenets of identity are naturally found in Brazil: its natural resources, its vastness, its wealth, as well as the emotional aspects of its people. The second step explores the immanent character of Brazilian identity, *becoming*: the idea that Brazilian identity has a teleological aim to reach, namely, development. Finally, in relation to the reaction to criticism, this thesis develops two ideas. Initially, it is concerned with how the relation between being and becoming necessarily entail different appraisals of *method*. (That is, strategies through which being and becoming can realize development).

Being

Souza argues that Brazilian thinking works with the existence of a sort of antithesis to the *homem cordial* and to the Brazilian state. The USA represents that counterpoint. By the first decades of the twentieth century, the comparison between the USA and Brazil was an issue of disquiet among Brazilian intellectuals (Souza 2006d: 100). These were countries of continental proportions with a colonial past and a history of slavery. So, given this common history, the question that has pervaded the minds of Brazilian intellectuals for nearly a century is: How was it possible that the USA became a developed country and Brazil simply did not? Buarque de Holanda's answer to that question came through the conceptualization of the *homem cordial* who represents the opposite of the protestant ethics of individualism, emotional control, discipline and, most importantly, rationality.

Therefore, it is the underlying comparison between the USA and Brazil (both the states and its nationals) that pervades the work of Buarque de Holanda. The background to this latent scholarly comparison between the two countries has the marked influence of a specific aspect of neo-Weberian sociology (Souza 1998, 2006a: 25). It is the essentialist idea that non-Western societies had to go through stages that corresponded to those produced by the ethics and logic of Protestantism in the development of capitalism. As a result, failing to follow those steps would destine one to a pre-modern stage of development. Thus, locked in this logic of developmental stages, this type of academic work perceives the premodern*ism* of certain societies as the main cultural trait that hindered development (see, Bresser-Pereira 1999: 303–6; Faoro 2000: 200–23). This means disregarding two steps of enquiry. First, it leaves unquestioned the differentiation between the emergence of Western rationalism in Europe and in the USA. Second, it fails to problematize the exportation of its fundamental institutions: the capitalist market and the state. In this sense, both state and market – as consequent institutions of a specific form of rationalization – and its spread around the globe are not problematized but taken as fact and exempted of any form of justification. That is, pre-modern societies have their pre-modern condition based on the assumption that conformity to state and market in the model set by Europe and the USA is what essentially defines rationality. By having an aprioristic definition of what rationality is and means, and by never challenging how and why the consumption of its cultural artefacts are considered necessary, a great majority of Brazilian academia sought to explain their society as an emotional one. Therefore, rationality, in the sense understood in Brazilian sociology, is materialized in the existence of the USA, and it is against the backdrop of the essentialization of rationality as individualism, emotional control and the discipline needed to become a developed 'people' and 'state' that Brazilian identity is scholarly constructed. By attributing rationality to a foreign other (in this case, the USA), Brazilian social sciences have ascribed Brazil a pre-modern condition that is doomed to both covertly and overtly search for the contingencies and impossibility of Brazilian rationality. This sort of thinking supposes that those who cannot successfully adapt to modernity are incapable of doing so because of their cultural traits and not because of their systematic exclusion from any form of citizenship. Brazilian intellectuals seem to have preferred to understand their society's inability to enter modernity as an innate cultural trait. They could instead have enquired about the consequences of the way the state and the capitalist market created new subjectivities that were inherently exclusionary, or the way these institutions only benefited certain classes. Understanding the individuals who make up society as inherently emotional and, therefore, incapable of adapting not only disregards the need for processes of inclusion, but also renders inequality invisible. By inviting others to think – and to accept – that these problems are cultural and not historic or political, theorizing is shamefully diverted to glorifying culture, to praising an emotional identity that only serves those who *are* adapted to modernity. Contrary to what works within the paradigm of the TEA, Souza argues that inequality is not the result of a pre-modern condition. Rather, it is the result of the character of the great waves of modernization that started taking place in the nineteenth century and had its apex in the first Vargas government (Souza 2006a: 23). Souza develops his argument by advancing the thesis that inequality and its naturalization in society is modern and connected to the mode of appropriation of capitalist values and institutions in peripheral societies. Here, I would like to focus on what he calls 'processes of invisibility', that is, the understanding of the world through the essentializing lens of national identity. Processes of invisibility relate to the exclusionary nature of the form of theorizing that is based on a dialogical relationship with identity. On the one hand, such forms of theorizing are blind to political experiences that do not conform to a set of pre-established norms of identity. On the other hand, the set of prescriptions that arise from such myopic forms of theorization only reify the status quo. This engendered the sort of Coxian problem-solving theorizing (Booth 2008: 47–8) that can only offer prescriptions within this status quo, since it requires the uncritical acceptance of pre-established identity-related norms. This characteristic of the TEA comprises the first point of my analysis when exploring the meanings and conceptualizations of security since 1930: that a people or a country is naturally something and that there is value – and academic relevance – in assigning an emotional characteristic that has no other basis for existence but birth. As such, I call this tenet of the TEA 'being'. The following sections explore being by examining the assumptions which intellectuals have held to be natural, to be inherent to the conceptualizations connected to security.

Becoming

By subscribing to the view that there are innate characteristics of the Brazilian people, the last few generations of intellectuals have made Buarque de Holanda the great articulator of contemporary social sciences in Brazil (Souza 2006d: 105–7). Truth be told, he is deserving of the many tributes paid to him, but mainly because his work extended far beyond what was in fact an essay he wrote at the very beginning of his career. By constructing the *homem cordial* as the complete opposite of Protestant pilgrimage to the USA, Buarque de Holanda aims at explaining the traits of Brazilian culture in relation to rationality. *Personalismo* is what he perceives to be the general characteristic of Brazilian individuals. It profoundly determines how forms of societal living are driven by and based on emotion. That is, personal relationships (hence the name *personalismo*), in Buarque de Holanda's view, is what regulates the society of cordial men – in contrast to practices of discipline and reason (Souza 2006d: 106). Buarque de Holanda's *homem cordial* is guided by his heart, and therefore cannot and will not conform to principles of instrumental rationality.

The extrapolation of these perceived societal characteristics to the state follows the same reasoning; the emotional man bears the same sort of private relationship with public matters that he does with personal relations. That is, personal attachment dominates both public goods and political processes in Buarque de Holanda's conceptualization of *patrimonialismo*. This is how he describes the *patrimonialista* bureaucrat:

> For the patrimonial bureaucrat, public governance itself is a matter of his personal interest; work and the benefits extracted from it are related to the personal rights of the worker and not to objective interests, as it happens in the true bureaucratic State in which specialization and efforts to ensure juridical guarantees to the citizen prevails. It lacks the impersonal coordination that characterizes the bureaucratic state. It is possible to follow, throughout our history, the predominance of personal wills that are not accessible to an impersonal order. The Brazilian contribution to civilization will be cordiality – we will give the world the *homem cordial*.
>
> (Buarque de Holanda 1936: 146)

This argument has several consequences for Brazilian knowledge production since 1930. First, the essentialization of Brazilian culture as an integrated emotional whole, devoid of class struggles or any other relevant social and political processes, have taken academic works to focus on economic development as a solution to inequality, marginalization and citizenship. Second, and stemming from the former, political and economic contours are perceived to be determined by what the elite thinks and how it behaves – which not only disregards bottom-up agency, but also silences perspectives that are not of the elite. Third, the TEA has developed a specific grammar with which to think about the 'social' and the 'political' that is not only theoretically frail but also emotionally appealing to both common sense and academic work. This way, Brazilian social sciences in general are pervaded by a one-dimensional approach that is so deeply embedded in national identity that any attempt of criticism is met with great emotional resistance. Here the ideas of both Freyre and Buarque de Holanda were of fundamental importance in delineating that discourse by providing an intellectual appraisal of Brazilian identity that corroborated and justified the modernization project at hand (Souza 2006d: 100). Although Souza places the encounter between the state-building project of Getúlio Vargas (1930–45) and the ideas of Freyre and Buarque de Holanda as a turning point for the crystallization of the TEA, he does not provide any detail on how this process took place. Souza outlines the idea in one paragraph:

> The new ideas of Freyre became popular when they met the interest of the intervener state of Getúlio Vargas as a positive ideology of national integration. Large-scale industrialization in Brazil, which starts in 1930, needed a set of ideas that would call Brazilian people to join large scale efforts of national renovation. The thesis Freyre defends is precisely the substantial unity of Brazilians. We are all in the same boat and we should be proud of what we have already built; a society that harmoniously unites the opposites and, furthermore, we can be proud of what we are going to build. This thesis must have certainly sounded like music to the ears of the elite committed to the great national leap that inspired this era. After all, this idea starts being taught in schoolbooks (with very little change up to this day), in political propaganda, in samba songs, in newspapers, and in universities.
>
> (Souza 2006d: 104)

The excerpt above is self-evident to students of Brazilian history and politics that are well aware of the role of state discourse during Vargas' government and how it guided all efforts of modernization of the *Estado Novo*. However, outside these circles the analytical step taken by Souza is a lot less apparent. Souza does not seem interested in exploring how the aforementioned process took place; rather, he seems to find it sufficient to propose that the *Estado Novo* took up the ideas that informed the TEA. Again, my argument is that however correct Souza may be in advancing this idea, his analysis falls short of explaining why these ideas became so ingrained in the social sciences in Brazil. The TEA could profit from the inclusion of the role of intellectuals in politics. Since Souza does not explore the role of intellectuals, his analysis does not examine the conditions in which it was possible for the TEA to become the main source of common sense, intellectual work and state discourse. Souza (Souza 2006d: 97–9) argues that the strength of Freyre's and Buarque de Holanda's ideas was connected to the possibility of turning around that racial conundrum and perceiving Brazilian miscegenation not as an obstacle to development but as the very source of its future success as a nation. In this sense, only the appraisal of the political place of the intellectual and its connection with the birth of social sciences in the country can generate a narrative that can comprehensively uncover the ideas subjacent to Brazilian contemporary social sciences. The narrative proposed here corroborates Souza's arguments, but it goes further by arguing that intellectuals intently pursued the strengthening of state structures in both intellectual discussion and the modernization project. By doing this, they were ascertaining their political place as agents of modernization and part of the ruling elite. Both points above have been important for the development of security thinking in Brazil, as will be suggested in the following chapters of the thesis. One of the central arguments of each of the chapters is that thinking about security in Brazil cannot be analysed comprehensively without taking into consideration that speaking security allowed intellectuals to ascertain their place in society whilst also putting forward their own specific development project. The writings of Freyre and Buarque de Holanda provided a solution to the racial conundrum of the previous decades. The readings provided by these two authors transformed that pessimism in the pride of reason. Their totalizing views on Brazilian culture and history – which not only precluded political and identity differences but also eliminated class struggle – allowed for the continuation of the state as the main referent of the social sciences. This was met positively by the anti-establishment forces that had stood up against the liberal republic and which held strong claims of both centralization and strengthening of the state. A second issue also arises from understanding this tenet of the TEA as the intertwined works of identity, intellectual discourse and the project of modernization. While the first tenet works on the perceived innate characteristic of the Brazilian people, this second tenet relates to the immanent aspect of Brazilian identity, mentioned in the second section of this chapter. These ideas about Brazilian identity presuppose unity for the modernization project, and for the attempt of rationalization of society. That is, national identity *is* and *ought to become*. There is an idea of unrealized potential that pervades these writings.

In his conclusion to *Raízes do Brasil*, Buarque de Holanda wrote:

> The primacy of particular conveniences over collective interests is clearly revealed through the predominance of the emotive element over the rational. There is here a form of unilaterality that is in open opposition with the juridical and neutral point of view on which liberalism is based. Simple cordiality cannot generate good principles. It is necessary some normative solid element, innate in the soul of people, or even implanted through tyranny, in order to have social crystallization. The thesis that tyranny cannot accomplish anything in the long term is but one of the many illusions of the liberal mythology. It is true that the existence of such illusion is not an argument against liberalism and that there are other remedies beyond tyranny for the consolidation and stabilization of a national and social whole.
>
> (Buarque de Holanda 1936: 184–5)

Here, he offered two underlying interrelated aspects that became an inherent part of the TEA. The first is the paradoxical existence of the *homem cordial*. On the one hand, it provides a more optimistic view of Brazilian society, on the other, such essentialization also stands in the way of 'rationality' or, as he puts it, 'simple cordiality cannot generate good principles'. This is where the more pragmatic aspect emerges as the 'other remedies for the consolidation and stabilization of a national and social whole'. The very recognition of the existence of the *homem cordial* implies a task in hand; the engineering of what this people ought to be in order to generate the good principles of a rational society and also to constitute a national whole that is able to function as a great country. This view spoke not only to the project espoused by the state post-1930, but also for the role that intellectuals sought to legitimize for themselves when denouncing the liberal republic. A dialogic relationship existed between the essentialized view of society and what it ought to become, and this became central not only to Vargas' efforts of modernization but also to the social sciences in general. National identity in this discussion has two political meanings. The first is the pre-conditional acceptance of the *homem cordial*, a pre-modern being that is not adapted to a rational form of living. The second is the need for transforming the *homem cordial*, the *personalista* society and the *patrimonialista* state into their rational versions. Through a top-down process engendered by the state, the rationalization of society is then to be promoted by the state. Intellectuals, having evoked a 'natural' social order, created the means of attributing the state an unlimited margin of action for the political re-engineering of society (Pécaut 1989: 51). By reclaiming the centrality of the state to the modernization processes, Brazilian intellectuals put these aforementioned ideas at the centre of the views that have informed theorizations in the country. In his criticism of both Brazilian liberalism and the way that the 1930 movement was becoming progressively authoritarian, Buarque de Holanda states in *Nossa Revolução*:

> If on the political and social realm amongst us, liberalism became more of a destroyer of pre-existing forms than a creator of new ones, if it was above all a useless and costly affectation, it will not be through ingenious elaborations that we will meet our reality one day.
>
> (Buarque de Holanda 1936: 161)

The very last words of his statement give away the immanent project of identity – meeting one's own reality and realizing the potential of that identity. Much in the same way, the 2003 (forty-eighth) edition of Freyre's *Casa Grande & Senzala* had a series of poems written about the book and signed by renowned Brazilian authors. The opening poem is by Freyre and its first four lines are:

Eu ouço as vozes	I hear the voices
Eu vejo as cores	I see the colours
Eu sinto os passos	I feel the steps
De outro Brasil que vem por aí	Of another Brazil that is coming
	(Freyre 2003 [1933]: 9)

The Brazil that is *becoming* is a different one. It is another. It is, as Buarque de Holanda mentions, not there yet. In both cases, there is an idea of Brazil as something in the future and, most importantly, one that is different from the one they have at the time of writing. This 'another' Brazil, as our reality shall be one day, is the immanent tenet of Brazilian identity which I will examine under the label 'becoming' in the following chapters. 'Becoming' then refers to the ideas taken to represent what intellectuals have understood as the unrealized potential of Brazil. In other words, what they perceive Brazil to be becoming.

The method

The successful conjugation of intellectual, political and common sense discourse through informing views of national identity in Brazil achieved recognition to such an extent that criticism and critique face deep cognitive and emotional obstacles within Brazilian academia (2006d: 112). Reflecting on a panel discussion at the *Associação Nacional de Pós-graduação e Pesquisa em Ciências Sociais* (ANPOCS, National Association of Postgraduate Studies and Research in Social Sciences) in 2004, Souza comments on the reply of a colleague to his argument that Brazilian academia was in dire need of theoretical critique in order to transcend not only its theoretical poverty but the frailty of political outputs it suggested. His colleague, Luís Eduardo Soares (perhaps the most renowned intellectual on 'public safety' in Brazil and known for the quality of his theoretical arguments), replied that the problem was not the lack of theory, since everybody knew what the theory and the issues were and what was needed to resolve them (Souza 2006c: 118). The certainties expressed by Soares related to three different aspects: theory, subject and political output. None of these three issues was under discussion. Soares' opinion is not only his own in Brazilian academia. In relation to Brazilian IR, for example, after having been a student in the area for a decade and, furthermore, after having analysed a great share of knowledge production published since the 1950s, there have been no theoretical debates or disputes in the discipline. The only disagreements, when they do happen, are in terms of the *method* of development they propose. Examples of this are the neo-liberal/ developmentalist debates of the 1990s and early 2000s (explored in Chapter 5). If one looks at other times of disagreement in the conduct of state affairs, the historic dichotomization between civilian and military thought may be included as disciplinary debates. However, they were not debates. All of the above issues were in terms of 'on which side do you stand?'. They were loyalty tests. That is, the questions these disagreements put forward were in relation to the best method for bringing about development: Through authoritarianism or not? Through direct association with the West or not? Through a strong centralized state or not? Doing what Souza did at ANPOCS – or what he has done through his critique of Brazilian social theorizing – is taken as a personal insult in Brazilian academia. Critique and criticism are not tolerated well, because they challenge the place of theorizing as well as the place of theorists in the country. Since the 1930s, Brazilian intellectuals have placed themselves as agents of modernization, as the thinking class that defend the development of Brazil. Questioning the theoretical basis on which they stand is questioning the eight-decade-long place of social theorizing in Brazil.

As argued, Brazilian identity has informed social theorizing in Brazil in three ways. First, it implies innate characteristics of the people and of the state. Second, it supposes both of them have unrealized potential that need to be achieved. Third, it proposes a method of achieving that unrealized potential. These points go back to my use of the term 'authoritarian utopia' in the Introduction. By 'authoritarian', I do not mean the violent state practices pursued by either military or civilian governments. I do not even mean to make a distinction between civilian and military. Here, 'authoritarian' corresponds to the way the TEA imposes such cognitive and emotional impositions against criticism and critique. This way, the idea of authoritarian utopia moves beyond the dichotomies produced by these disagreements as it seeks to apprehend what is common to both sides. 'Authoritarian utopia' then refers to the way intellectuals, irrespective of their political and/or professional associations, have established themselves and their forms of theorizing as agents of modernization. It is in this sense that one can understand how the authoritarian utopia hailed from and galvanized different sectors of society and how it could not be predetermined based on professional association (civilian/military) as it has been presented in the literature. The existence of a common authoritarian utopia does not preclude the idea that there were (are) different persuasions of it. However, there is a minimum core of ideas common to the general political spectrum. Within this spectrum there were persuasions that tended to totalitarian ideas, while other sectors had more progressive views on the inclusion of marginalized sectors in the political process. What is important to stress is that none of these persuasions transcended the limits of either the state or identity as their main informing views. In doing so, they reproduced and reified a particular discourse, which was summarized in the TEA. The authoritarian utopia has imposed itself through the establishment of certainties of theories, subjects and political outputs that do not need to be discussed and cannot be challenged. This authoritarian utopia is crystallized in practices spread throughout society that serve not only to conceal prejudice, but also to exclude political differences, to normalize violence and to mask class struggle under the panoply of the state. In this sense, the contribution of this book is to analyse how the authoritarian utopia lives on in contemporary IR theorizing about security in Brazil and how understanding its conceptualizations are highly indebted to the insights of the TEA. The following chapters investigate the TEA by exploring how security thinking in Brazil has promoted different methods of realizing the potential of Brazilian identity and state. The role of intellectuals in Brazil since the 1930s cannot be understood outside the establishment of the political place of intellectuals in the country as agents of modernization. It is therefore the aim of the next chapters to explore how intellectual praxis, security theorizing and political discussion were anchored on and reproduced the informing ideas of Brazilian identity. Part II builds on the arguments made here, by looking at three defining moments of security thinking in Brazil. Each of these chapters will offer a further contribution to the idea of authoritarian utopia in the way they test the validity of the claim that security thinking (as well as social theorizing) in Brazil does not conform to the abstract division between civilian and military thought.

Moreover, Chapter 3 provides examples of discourses in the 1910s and 1920s which were already making ontological claims about Brazilian identity. It also looks at how this discourse was also used to justify a set of authoritarian legal measures and institutions put in place during the first office of Getúlio Vargas. Chapter 4 looks at the *Escola Superior de Guerra* (ESG) as a site of knowledge production about security and links the main political discourse of that institution – the Doctrine of National Security – to the assumptions of the TEA; and Chapter 5 looks at knowledge production in Brazilian IR. By investigating how intellectuals of different political persuasions (left/right) and professional associations (civil/military) have historically contributed to the perpetuation of the TEA, Part II not only furthers the initial findings proposed by Souza, it also provides a richer narrative of the politics of knowledge production in Brazil.

Part II

Worlding Brazil through security

3 Security as scrutiny

The aim of this chapter is to uncover the political meanings ascribed to security in Brazil between 1930 and 1945. It explores security thinking put forward by authoritarian actors under Vargas' first term in office. It starts by locating the history and nature of the engagement of armed forces in Brazilian politics before the 1930 coup that brought Vargas to power. It then examines how the armed forces introduced the phrases 'national defence' and 'national security' into the political and legal vocabulary of the country as a way of asserting their political power over civilians in Brazil. The aim of the chapter is therefore to expose how, upon being introduced into the political and legal vocabulary of the country, 'national security' and 'national defence' became inherently connected to the political place of the armed forces. This, in turn, put limits on the scope of the meanings of those phrases and on who got to talk about them. Overall, the chapter argues that the unique Brazilian discourse on security that emerged in this era: (1) charged the concept of 'security' with a particular political meaning and, stemming from this, (2) the discourse set up a boundary – with national security 'experts' as gate-keepers – that effectively removed the subject from the public or 'civilian realm' for most of the twentieth century.

Armed forces and the state in Brazil

In broad terms, the history of the armed forces in the first half of the twentieth century is marked by two processes. The first one is the struggle on the part of the Crown and, later, the republican government, to curb military influence in politics. After the First World War, however, it was the rise to power of its most authoritarian wing that characterized military politics. Between the arrival of the Portuguese royal family in Brazil in 1808 and the first decade of the twentieth century, the relationship between the regime in power and the armed forces was very tense and convoluted. After the declaration of independence of Brazil, the crown was particularly apprehensive of the republican ideas espoused by the army – a feature that was common to the armed forces of other countries in South and Latin America (Rouquié 1984: chap. 2). In order to counter the anti-monarchic armed forces and to suppress rebellious movements against the Portuguese crown, Emperor Pedro I authorized the creation of the Guarda Nacional

(National Guard) in 1831. In practice, the establishment of the National Guard promoted a class division between it and the armed forces, where the former would only take in men of substantial wealth and education, leaving poor, uneducated men the option of only volunteering to the latter (Carvalho 1982; McCann 1984). By the late 1800s, the armed forces had become the most outspoken critics of the monarchy (Smallman 2002: 15–18). In 1888, the crown broke its political and economic agreement with coffee oligarchies and abolished slavery in Brazil. The political response on the part of the oligarchies was fast and effective; they joined forces with the army and conducted a coup that ousted the emperor from power in the following year (1889). With the National Guard headed by the landowners of each state and the armed forces against the emperor, Pedro II had no option but to step down from power. However, once the new form of government was established, the armed forces and the oligarchies returned to their opposing differences regarding the type of regime that would be best suited for the country. The armed forces favoured a strong centralized state whilst the oligarchies implemented a liberal republican system that allowed greater autonomy of the states from the central government. Throughout the rest of the pre-1930 period, there was a constant political struggle on the part of the state, now ruled by the coffee-exporting oligarchies, to keep the armed forces (as far as possible) outside of politics. On the one side, military resentment against the republican system orbited around the lack of federal commitment to the modernization of the army and, on the other, civilian governments perceived any effort to modernize the army as opening an opportunity for the military to attempt taking power. Even though the armed forces were part of the coalition that established the republican system, their political allies not only kept the military at bay from politics, they also did not attend to any of the long-held demands of the armed forces such as training, education and provision of equipment.

Despite having taken part in the coup d'état that ousted Emperor Pedro II from power in 1889 and having established a military dictatorship (1889–94), the armed forces were successful neither in accommodating the demands of the agrarian oligarchies nor in putting forward their project of a strongly centralized state. In 1895, Prudente de Morais became the first civilian president of the Brazilian republic as the candidate of the coffee-exporting elite. He quickly moved on to give further privileges to local power to the detriment of central government. The exclusion of the armed forces from the political processes quickly returned to the political agenda of the day as much as it had been under the monarchy (Sodré 1968: 186–9; Hilton 1982: 639). The secondary status of the armed forces had in national politics only changed after the First World War broke out in Europe. From a weak, internally divided institution throughout most of its history in Brazil, the army was able to circumvent the central government in less than two decades and dictate the shape of institutions and legal charters – most of which are still in place today. Brazilian dependence on foreign supply was made obvious when contracts of armament supplies were not met by the German, British and US governments. Furthermore, the dependence of the Brazilian economy on the foreign market increased the need for industrialization, the modernization of the armed forces and the diversification of the economy in order to establish autonomy in those sectors (Hilton 1982: 639; Alexander 1956).

Not long after the war, the government hired a French mission to train the army in modern warfare (Hilton 1982: 635–8). Overall, the material and political conditions of the army seemed to improve: the state sponsored a push towards industrialization and the manufacturing of supplies (Hilton 1982; Bellintani 2009); it carried out military reforms in 1918 and 1919; the National Guard was made extinct in 1922 (Carvalho 2005: 23); and compulsory military service was implemented in 1923 (Carvalho 2005: 24–30). In essence, the experience of the First World War changed the status of the armed forces in Brazil and for the first time in years brought the army closer to the central government. Aided by the changes implemented in the 1910s and early 1920s, military activism in politics became more organized and various sectors of the armed forces joined the anti-establishment wave of those decades. In the 1910s, the army emerged in Brazilian politics side by side with other modernizing actors of that era. The same generation of Brazilian army officers was also responsible for political movements such as Tenentismo, the 18 do Forte and the Coluna Prestes. Exponents of this generation, such as Pedro Aurélio de Góes Monteiro and Luiz Carlos Prestes, would influence and define the contours of left- and right-wing Brazilian politics over the next few decades. Most importantly, the military wing of the conservative sector in power between 1934 and 1945 emerged from this generation. Its rise in Brazilian politics went hand in hand with the introduction (and practices) of national defence and national security. The way that such engagement was still proposed in the 1910s is central to early developments of thinking about security in later decades – when these young officers became the ruling elite of not only the armed forces but also Brazilian politics. By following their activism in Brazilian politics and legislation, this chapter uncovers the political meanings attributed to these two concepts in the first half of the twentieth century.

The militarization project in Brazil

The literature has been quick to categorize the militarization of society or the totalitarian tenets of post-1930 presidential terms as a project of the Brazilian armed forces. It is against this backdrop of civilian and military support for the militarization of society that the concept of authoritarian utopia needs to be analysed. One needs to systematically explore anti-establishment voices of the 1910s and 1920s outside the 'civilian versus military' framework for three reasons. First, it sheds light on pre-1930 conservative wings of political dissent. Second, it shows how anti-liberal dissent found supporters both inside and outside the military establishment. Lastly, it provides a background context to explore the specific meanings given to 'national defence' and 'national security' after 1930 (explored in the next section).

In the 1910s and 1920s, different dissenting factions of society were united through their common resentment for the liberal republican system. In this context, the two decades preceding the 1930 coup were vital for the formation of a consensus amongst the most conservative wing of the anti-establishment movement regarding the militarization of society. Both in and outside the barracks, the 1910s witnessed the growth in belief that the armed forces were the most equipped, physically and morally, to lead the development effort. Moreover, supporters of this view preached that the armed forces should be given not only the political mission of modernization, but also that of organizing society into a military structure. Perhaps the best example of both military and civilian activism in favour of the militarization of society is the military journal *A Defeza Nacional* (*ADN*, National Defence) and its civilian arm the *Liga de Defeza Nacional* (LDN, League of National Defence). The independently published journal *A Defeza Nacional* (1913) was edited by returnees of the military training mission in Germany (McCann 1983; 1984; Nunn 1983). Although most of the articles in the journal were of a technical nature (Carvalho 2005: 27), its (unsigned) editorials were responsible for most of its publicity (Coelho 2000: 81). The editorials gave the board of the journal more room to express their political opinions freely, especially since the journal faced strong opposition from senior officers in the armed forces (Carvalho 2005: 24). Being an unofficial publication of the armed forces, it provided a space for officers to discuss 'military innovations, current army affairs, and their dreams for Brazil's future' (McCann 1984: 748). Three years after the establishment of the ADN, the League of National Defence was set up as the civilian arm of the journal. It was headed by prominent intellectuals in the country such as Olavo Bilac, Pedro Lessa, Miguel Calmo and Rui Barbosa. The league promoted the ideas of *soldado-cidadão* (soldier-citizen) and *cidadão-soldado* (citizen-soldier) and sought to defend the leadership of the armed forces on state reform. It quickly rose to become one of the largest nationalist associations of its time, being responsible for the lobbying and approval of obligatory conscription (Nunn 1983; Beattie 2001: 218; McCann 2004: 216). *Soldado-cidadão* claims were limited to the right of military men to vote – which was prohibited at the time – while *cidadão-soldado* implied that each citizen was supposed to act like a soldier in the defence of his/her *pátria* (Bilac 1917: 34). The poet Olavo Bilac was the champion of the second cause amongst civilians. For him, the *cidadão-soldado* should be brought about by military training in public education and by the return of obligatory conscription to the armed forces to ensure 'the triumph of democracy, the leveraging of classes, the school of order, of discipline, of cohesion; the laboratory of dignity and patriotism' (Bilac 1917: 7).

The *ADN* also provides poignant material with regard to the ideas held by the sector of the armed forces that would be in power after 1930. In its first editorial, the *ADN* established the tone of the debates:

> The army, *the only truly organized force* amidst the *tumultuous mass* goes, sometimes, beyond its professional duties and becomes a determining factor of *political transformation* and social stabilization through *national defence*.
> (1913: 1, my emphasis)

As may be perceived from the quotation above, the political claims of that group were structured around three points: (1) the armed forces stood apart and above other sectors of society; (2) they were the only sector that could lead the country to development; and, most importantly, (3) their project was for the defence of the nation (and not of their own place in politics). The armed forces were presented as hierarchically above the *tumultuous masses*. Such apriorism not only revealed the armed forces as the *only truly organized force in society* but also its place in society in relation to the people. Likewise, *political transformation* was presented as the 'development of the nation' (*ADN* 1913: 2), the realization of the immanent potential of the state under the 'guiding hand of the armed forces' (*ADN* 1913: 2). Lastly, *national defence* hints at the authoritarian project of development envisioned by this faction of the armed forces. Although there are no references to national identity, the monthly editorials of *ADN* displayed the same political assumptions that would come to inform the TEA in later decades. The three argumentative steps of the TEA are inscribed into that editorial. What are the *tumultuous masses* if not the position of departure of the people (TEA's 'being')? What is the *development of the nation* if not the teleological aim of politics (TEA's 'becoming')? The method is proposed as: 'the military organization of the nation, so it can defend itself' (*ADN* 1913: 4). Lest we forget, the method of modernization (the militarization of society) is also a strategy to include the armed forces in political processes, since they are the only sector capable of leading development. As a critique of knowledge production in Brazil, the TEA enables one to see more clearly that writing about the present and future of Brazil reflects the will to inscribe the role of intellectuals in politics. Let us now consider the quotation from the first *ADN* editorial as a way of introducing the general ideas that would pervade thinking about security in the 1930s and the 1940s.

The truly organized force and the tumultuous mass

Establishing what and who is rational constitutes a central claim of theorizing in Brazil. This claim specifies those who are able to lead the modernization project and differentiates them from the rest of the population. Such moves entail the essentialization of society between those who can command and those who simply cannot. In addition, such dichotomy hinders considerations regarding class, race and gender, rendering invisible the political claims of multiple sectors of society.

As the following chapters will uncover, this normalization of social hierarchy and its resorting to the language of the 'masses', the 'people', the 'excluded' has been one of the convenient rules of social theorizing in Brazil: the will to initiate political changes in the name of the masses, but without their participation. The claims of this discourse were but rhetorical devices, an exhortative ploy to gain legitimacy for their elitist actions. The idea of moral superiority over civilians would guide the activism of the armed forces in politics over the following decades (Hilton 1982: 638; Nunn 1983: 135). They remained suspicious of the ability of civilians to conduct politics in any way that would be satisfactory to the requirements of the modernization effort on a scale needed by Brazil. Civilians were portrayed as unprepared for leadership and hierarchy, affected by emotions rather than reason, unpatriotic and extremely venal (Fico 2004: 39). In the case of the *ADN* editorials, a central concern involved establishing boundaries between military rationality and civilian irrationality. Following this line of assumption, a 1916 editorial stated 'Brazil is not a country, nation, or pátria, it is exploitation' (*ADN* 1915: 241). The exploiters were deemed to be 'politicians, judges, congressmen, civil servants, and graduates' whereas the exploited were:

> The farm labourers, the industrial workers, the commercial employees, the people who struggle, who work, who toil, who pay taxes with their sweat and blood. Only they have the right to give their lives for the patria; the others reserve themselves the right to sponge off it. In this sense, there is no doubt, Brazil is exploitation.
>
> (*ADN* 1915: 242–4)

One should not think that the officers procured any associative role with the 'tumultuous masses' of the 'exploited' of Brazil. They spoke in the name of the exploited but did not seek direct connection with them. The inherent hierarchical aspect in which political struggle was deemed to take place relegated the exploited to a non-place in debates. Rather, as suggested by Pécaut, it is their honour, their sweat and blood, and their struggle that is called upon as a as a moralizing discourse to lend legitimacy to their agenda, but which had no real intention of including as equals the exploited who they claimed to represent (Pécaut 1989: 30–2; Souza 2006d: 35).

Political transformation

As previously argued, speaking security has allowed different sectors of Brazilian society to put forward their own project for modernization. In the 1910s and 1920s, the intertwining of criticism towards the liberal system, the nascent nationalism (Pécaut 1989: 22) and the inherent elitism meant that political transformation – the becoming of the Brazilian state – was conceived in terms of the centralization of the state. To that formula, the conservative sectors added the modernization of the armed forces and national industrialization under the direct guidance of the military. As the 1913 *ADN* editorial shows, officers were *categorically investing themselves and the armed forces with a role of tutelage over civilians – one which they would pursue for many a decade to come. The conservative perspective was such that on the one hand the population could not be entrusted with the task of promoting development and, on the other, politicians had never given clear signs of acting on anything other than their 'individualistic interests' (Coutinho 1956: 287). Thus, it was up to the armed forces to do so. With their preconceived self-regard as a true national institution and 'one of the only forces with character enough to concentrate and act on national interests' (Goés Monteiro 1934: 156), this sector of the armed forces entrusted themselves with the tasks of breaking with the liberal system and modernizing the country. For them, the role of the armed forces was to keep civilian irrationality in check, making sure that non-military sectors could follow military principles of organization and thus contribute to the modernization of the country. They also equated the modernization of the armed forces with the modernization of the country itself. For them, development meant 'opening roads, having solid national industries, well fed, well trained, and educated troops that can lead the country' (*ADN* 1915: 2). In line with this thinking, a 1915 editorial stated that the armed forces needed to 'be prepared for its conservative and stabilizing function over the social elements and prepared to correct the internal disturbances so common in the tumultuous life of societies in formation' (*ADN* 1915: 3). 'To be prepared' meant that the armed forces needed to be organized and modern enough to fulfil its role of tutelage. The armed forces appear as 'the prime factor of political social transformation' (AND 1915: 2), because it was through the armed forces that 'narrow individual interests shall be abandoned in the name of the great collective interests' (*ADN* 1913: 2). Thus, they were to be not only 'an instrument of external defence' (*ADN* 1913: 1), but also the sector to lead the modernization effort. This is the purported truth that legitimizes their argument: '[it is] a historical fact that nascent societies needed the military to assist in their formation and development, and that only by obtaining a high degree of civilization could they free themselves from the tutelage of the military' (*ADN* 1913: 2). Therefore, what started as a moralizing call to politics reveals itself as a way of legitimizing claims to power. The *ADN* editorials highlight the claims of this specific project: the militarization of society and the scrutiny of civilian life by the armed forces – and these assumptions were exactly what security came to legitimize between 1937 and 1945. Before that argument can be analysed, however, it is necessary to examine the concept of 'national defence', since there is a direct connection between this concept and that of security during the *Estado Novo*.

National defence

By re-elaborating their political contentions with the liberal republic system in terms of a national need, this sector of the armed forces introduced 'national defence' into the political vocabulary of the country with a discursive meaning that the phrase did not have before. Through their formulation of national defence, officers framed their professional and political participation in the modernizing efforts that they claimed were needed both in the country and in their institution. The concept then became politically infused with the need for asserting the role of the armed forces in internal politics and their project of militarization. It was thus charged with their specific modernization programme and its inherent assumptions about the role of the armed forces, of the civilian elite, and of the people in society.

In this sense, 'National Defence' – in Portuguese, *A Defesa Nacional*, the very title of the journal – was a direct reference to its political programme. It is a play on words. In Portuguese, the term means both 'national defence' and 'defence of the nation'. The nation was out to defend itself from the liberal project of the oligarchies, from the exploitation of those who sponged off the sweat of others, from the narrow individualistic interests that 'stubbornly persisted in Brazilian society' (*ADN* 1913: 2), and from 'the racially "weak" uneducated masses' (*ADN* 1913: 3). The defence of the nation was also the defence of a *particular* nation, one in which the idea of rationality filtered out the racially mixed masses. It carried with it not just the political significance of modernization but also the general message of the anti-establishment forces: the need for a centralized, modern and strong state. The introduction of the adjective 'national' came to signify not only anti-liberal claims of the armed forces, but also, and more specifically, the nationalist authoritarian principles sponsored by the conservative sectors of both the military and civilian realms. It is in this respect that the push for the implementation of the concept of national defence came from the armed forces, but it was also of great importance for those sectors of civilians that defended the militarization of the state as a project of development (Carvalho 2005: 61). National defence also built the bridge between civilian and military demands, since it was within its scope that both sides demanded national industrialization, the strengthening of the state and the modernization of the bureaucratic apparatus of the country. For the military, the targets were heavy industries, roads and ports so they could push for autonomy and prepare for war (Nunn 1972: 40–6). For civilians, these demands were also a call for a national project of modernization – one that would also establish a militarized order so 'every citizen is a soldier of his pátria' (Bilac 1917: 8). The next section argues that the introduction of 'national defence' and later, 'national security' in the political and legal vocabulary in Brazil served the specific purpose of legitimizing the militarization of the state. In this sense, the emergence and spread of those two concepts in Brazil are traceable to specific moments in the rapid rise to power of the most conservative wing of the armed forces in the 1930s. Along with the rise of the most conservative military sector to power, one can trace specific conceptualizations that accompanied the discursive legitimization of the militarization of society. By exploring these processes, the next section uncovers the connection between national legislation and the wider project of militarized modernization.

Legislating 'national defence' and 'national security'

Once the success of the 1930 coup had been assured and Getúlio Vargas was the head of the provisory government, it was the lack of a common project among the many anti-liberal sectors that came to the forefront of politics (Carone 1965: 84; Fausto 1988: 47–50; Dreifuss 2008: 30). The first 4 years of Vargas' first term in power were of successive challenges to his leadership and constant political instability. It soon became obvious that navigating through the many political subdivisions of the supporters of the 1930 movement would prove nearly impossible and, most importantly, put the permanence of the revolutionary movement in doubt. It is in this context that the armed forces became instrumental to Vargas as the main source of support for his government. Here, the main obstacles to earning the loyalty of the army were its internal divisions and political strife within the forces. In order to rely on their support, Vargas needed to make sure that those institutions were not only internally cohesive, but also highly prepared to take up arms in case of the spread of rebellious movements against the central government. This required focus on the modernization and unification of the armed forces not only to attend the demands of the military, but also to guarantee repressive power in the event of political dissidence (Stepan 1971; Carvalho 1982; McCann 1983). To make sure he had the allegiance of the leading military ranks, Vargas promoted a witch-hunt inside the armed forces. It started by excluding opponents of his leadership at the very top of the military hierarchy while also promoting lieutenants to higher ranks so they could qualify for posts in government (Carvalho 1982: 208). An example of the latter was General Pedro Aurélio de Góis Monteiro – former editor of *ADN*, Vargas' right-hand man and perhaps the most influential figure in armed forces politics until 1964. Góes Monteiro received three promotions in 1 year in order to qualify for appointment as the Minister of War and Army Chief of Staff (which he served as both) by the end of 1932 (Carvalho 1982: 210). By the end of 1935, Vargas had successfully expelled military dissidents from the armed forces and had declared a State of Emergency. Moreover, he passed the National Security Law (1935), and less than a year later, set up the Tribunal of National Security, which attributed political crimes to military jurisdiction. With the help and support of the (now homogenized) armed forces, the provisional government was quickly becoming a de facto military dictatorship. In an interview with Aspásia Camargo (Camargo and Goés 1981: 136) about the process that led to the establishment of the *Estado Novo*, General Amaral Peixoto stated 'the coup would happen with Getúlio [Vargas], without Getúlio or against Getúlio!' Peixoto makes it clear that the decision to rule under a 'state of exception' came from the armed forces, leaving Vargas the choice of either joining the military and remaining head of government or standing against it and eventually stepping down from power. To sum up, Vargas' reliance on the armed forces made it so politically strong that ultimately it was the highest ranks of the military that demanded the establishment of the *Estado Novo* dictatorship. Vargas remained in office as the head of a military dictatorship until 1945 – when the armed forces ousted him through yet another palacian coup. From an internally divided institution that had been kept at bay from political power since the nineteenth century, the armed forces went on to establish de facto military dictatorship that lasted from 1937 to 1945. It was the same armed forces which forced Vargas out of power in 1945 and elected a general to succeed him as president. What is important to take from the increasingly authoritarian characteristic of the 1930 movement after Vargas took power is his over-reliance on the army and the most conservative wings of the anti-liberal forces. In practice, this meant that the conservative wing of the armed forces was the victorious faction of the 1930s' movement. Once the various methods of expulsion and dissent within the armed forces had pragmatically reduced political activism in the lower and middle ranks (preventing the existence of politics in the army), Góes Monteiro (1934: 163) famously stated that it was time to let go of politics in the army and do the politics of the army. 'Politics of the army' was how he framed the militarized modernization of the state in which he would personally be involved throughout Vargas' government. Being one of the former editors of *ADN*, Góis Monteiro revised the discussions that took place in the journal as national security and was himself responsible for the introduction of this concept in the political and legal vocabulary of Brazil. As the armed forces acquired more political power post-1930, the conceptual distinction between national defence and national security served to further the control of the armed forces over civilian life and to safeguard areas of military interest outside civilian control. The analysis of the legal use of 'national defence' and 'national security' may give interesting clues in relation to the conceptual use and differences between the former and the latter. Since neither one of these terms were properly defined in political writings until the 1950s, official legislation provided a way of assessing how these phrases were used and what they meant. I have examined laws, decree-laws and decrees issued by the Brazilian government at the federal level between 1900 and 1945. The analysis of federal legislation issued in Brazil sheds light on how the framing of political discussions as matters of national security was deeply tied to the status of the armed forces as a political actor. Table 3.1 shows federal legislation issued between 1900 and 1945 concerning defence, national defence, security and national security.

Some points need to be raised with regard to Table 3.1. First, 'national defence' appears in the legal vocabulary in the 1920s, whereas 'national security' only enters legislation the following decade. This raises the question of the conceptual difference between security and national security, as well as defence and national defence. Second, it begs the question of why such conceptual differences were introduced at those particular times. The short period of time in which 'national defence' and 'national security' were adopted in the country's political and legal vocabulary reflect not only the rapid growth in power and status of the military but also shed light on how authoritarian sectors strategized their role in politics and their own project of modernization under the guise of security. In sum, the introduction of 'national defence' and 'national security' in Brazil not only provided a form of discursive and rhetorical legitimacy for the military's authority over civilians on issues deemed of strict military interest, but it also meant the corruption of traditional views of civil–military relations. The next two subsections argue

Table 3.1 Use of the concepts of defence, national defence, security and national security in Brazilian legislation, 1900–45

	Defence	*National defence*	*Security*	*National security*
1900s	7	0	08	0
1910s	25	0	10	0
1920s	55	3	18	0
1930s	73	7	21	25
1940–45	22	49	35	38
Total	182	59	92	63

that the conceptual change in 'national defence' and the introduction of 'national security' in the legal and political vocabulary of the country had the overarching objectives of (a) safe-keeping specific areas of policy under military control while also (b) submitting civilian input in politics to military scrutiny.

The concepts of defence and national defence

Until the early 1920s, the phrase 'national defence' was not a part of the institutional and/or legal lexicon of Brazil. 'Defence' (without the adjective 'national') was used in two ways. Its first meaning concerned the protection of policy areas directly relevant to the state and the economy, while the second referred to military capabilities. Within the first meaning one can cite the defence of hygiene standards in the federal capital (Brazil-DOU 1902: 30,06); the defence of the rights of workers in the agricultural and rural industry (Brazil-DOU 1903: 138) and the economic defence of rubber (Brazil-DOU 1912: 5,127, 20,266). The same principle for defence of agriculture and cattle was used as a justification for setting up the Instituto de Defesa do Café (Institute for the Defence of Coffee) (Brazil-DOU 1922b: 20,266) and the Serviço de Defesa do Algodão (Secretariat for the Defence of Cotton) (Brazil-DOU 1921a: 17,869; Brazil-DOU 1922a: 7,863). Its second meaning (military capabilities) was also invoked by a 1915 decree that dealt with the distribution of troops and regiments in national territory (Brazil-DOU 1915: 2279). A 1916 decree authorized the preparation of defence of the main ports in Brazil (Brazil-DOU 1916: 14,161). It is important to highlight that in both cases, when there was military input, it was still limited by civilian deference to the subject at hand. The main body of these decrees clearly established that the armed forces had been consulted over whether such measures (and only the ones relating to military power) would have any positive effect on the defence of the country. However, after 1930, legislation on (national) defence and (national) security does not refer to the advisory status of the military. Rather, post-1930 legislation usually refers to 'the Chief of Military Staff orders' (Brazil-DOU 1931b: 12,402; 1932a: 19,730). Although 'national defence' debuts in Brazilian legal vocabulary in the early 1920s, it was still used as a synonym for 'defence'. In 1921 and 1923, 'national defence' first appears in federal decrees (Brazil-DOU 1921b: 19,761; 1923: 336), but the phrase is limited to military exercises and the defence of the territory. The 1921 decree refers to renovation works in a naval port, while the 1923 decree authorizes the number of troops that would engage in military exercises that year. However, by the late 1920s 'national defence' has a completely different meaning. In 1927, a federal decree established the Conselho de Defesa Nacional (CDN, Council of National Defence) as a consultation organ of the president which aimed at studying and coordinating 'all information on all financial, economic, war, and moral issues that concern the defence of the *pátria*'. This decree also introduced working cells in each ministry with the objective of collecting information to be discussed in CDN meetings (Brazil-DOU 1927: 25,512). This institutional arrangement remained in place throughout the *Estado Novo* and was taken up by the 1964 military dictatorship. That same year, President Washington Luís justified the set up of CDN in the following way:

> For the organization of the national defence, we need to count on everyone, those in the fields, those at the beaches, in the factories, behind the counters, in laboratories, in the public means of transportation, and those working with supply. The issue of national defence is [an issue] of the nation itself. Its enduring study must be done by experts with the collaboration of the representatives of those who produce since they all constitute the living force of the nation. National sovereignty resides in all of us and we must defend it. The Council of National Defence composed by the chiefs of the general staff of the army and the navy and other representatives of the [armed] forces must be created as an institution of coordination of indispensable measures of general character for the defence of the fatherland [*pátria*] and must be commissioned to ensure the continuity of such measures.
>
> (Brazil 1927: 61)

Both the decree that established the CDN and the presidential address that justified its creation conceptualized 'national defence' as the *defence of the nation*. Here, 'national defence' has the meaning introduced by *A Defeza Nacional* in the previous decade – corresponding to the 'defence of the nation'. As such, it not only required a completely different set of discursive legitimization, but was also deeply influenced by nationalist ideas that had taken over intellectual writing in the mid-1910s (Pécaut 1989: 24). In this sense, national defence was intertwined with the protection of the *pátria* (fatherland) and infused with ideas of a laborious, industrious and *not* racially 'weak' people. The *pátria* worth defending was composed of *men* who were apt to contribute to the modernization effort. Although the defence of the *pátria* included the physical defence of territory by the armed forces, it was not perceived as the ultimate form of defence. Rather, national defence expanded to mean the national effort of modernization – one that included the moral exhortation of the lower classes but devised no place for their agency. President Washington Luís called upon the lower classes to participate in the national effort, but set them apart from experts and representatives who held the credentials to study national defence. Such rapid conceptual change was not only a sign of the rise of the armed forces as a major political actor, but was also revealing of two other connected processes, namely, the crisis of the republican system and the necessity for the federal power to acquiesce to military demands during this crisis. In the 1920s, the institutional arrangement of the CDN still reflected civilian superiority over the military. For instance, less than half of the members (four out of ten) of the CDN were representatives of the armed forces (Figueiredo 2005: 30). Moreover, neither had they veto power nor could they represent the president when he was away. In later reformulations of that institution, those civilian prerogatives were dismissed (as will be explored later). During Vargas' first term in office, national defence underwent another change in conceptualization. After 1930, and most notably in the 1934 constitution, the meaning of national defence as protection of the *pátria* and the national effort of modernization was transferred to the term 'national security'. Only a year after the 1930 coup, national defence was invoked in relation to the development of a national industrial complex (meaning heavy industry in general). Decree 20246 (Brazil-DOU 1931a: 12,402) declared it mandatory that, when solicited, all industries should provide information to the Ministry of War and other military ministers on their development and capabilities as these were deemed 'of interest to the national defence'. Likewise, the nationalization of the railway system and its placement under the responsibility of the Chief of the Army's General Staff was made official by decree 21985 (Brazil-DOU 1932b: 19,730) as it was considered of utmost importance in preparation of national defence. The preamble of decree 1058 declared that the federal government was promoting the creation of basic industries and roads to fulfil the needs of the military with 'the necessary elements to the order and defence of the country' (Brazil-DOU 1939a: 1,825). In all of these cases, the industrialization effort was rapidly submitted to the control and surveillance of the armed forces. What started in 1931 with the duty to inform the armed forces of the development in certain industries ended the decade completely under military jurisdiction. Two processes were underway. First, in terms of development of national industries, the priorities were within those areas of direct interest to the armed forces. Second, by prioritizing these areas as primary military interest, the government completely relinquished policy-making of the issues to the armed forces. In the 1930s, therefore, the military acquired stakeholder and decision-making powers over not only military budget, training and armament, but also industrial development. No other civilian, apart from Vargas himself, had any input in these policies. By the time the armed forces were powerful enough to declare the *Estado Novo*, they had already assured that military issues were not under civilian scrutiny of any kind.

Security and national security

Once policy-making and policy-advising in areas deemed of great military interest were no longer under civilian scrutiny, it was time to launch the institutional apparatus that submitted the civilian realm to military scrutiny. It was the introduction of national security in the legal apparatus that enabled this second process. But first let us examine the thoughts of General Pedro Aurélio de Góes Monteiro. Such contextualization is necessary because he was the first writer to use the term 'national security' in political writings in Brazil. By the 1930s, Góes Monteiro had been defending the same ideas he had espoused since his time as editor of the *ADN* in the 1910s: (a) the superiority of the armed forces over other sectors of society, (b) the need to use the armed forces as an agent of modernization and (c) the centralization and strengthening of the state. In his 1934 volume, Góes Monteiro used the phrase 'national security' as a replacement for 'national defence'. This first reference stated that: 'the moment now requires reflection about the main problems of national security, particularly those connected to the armed forces and for which we need to find rational solutions' (Góes Monteiro 1934: 125).

Since nowhere in his writings does he define the concept of national security, this section uncovers its political meaning by examining the way General Góes Monteiro conceived societal relations.

General Góes Monteiro and the concept of national security

The introduction of 'national security' in the legal and institutional apparatus of Brazil was the intellectual work of one man, General Góes Monteiro (Coelho 2000: 105; Coutinho 1956: chap. 6). Together with jurist Francisco Campos, General Góes Monteiro was widely known in the country for being one of the ideologues of authoritarianism, for the militarization of the state and for holding a certain appreciation for the Nazi and Fascist regimes in Europe. The authoritarian experiences of Portugal, Italy and Germany strengthened his ideas on corporatism and the role of the armed forces in politics (Schwartzman 1988: chap. 6; Fausto 1995: 10). General Góes Monteiro invoked a moralizing discourse about the need to give the people better living conditions, while disregarding their place in the political processes. In his writings, the people appear as one incapacitated mass that cannot contribute to any meaningful political change. He stated: 'the masses, in their permanent struggle for life, seldom hold the vigorous character of a uniform mentality, of a racial fortress, of communion of interests, of a clear understanding of the necessity of organizing general labour' (Goés Monteiro 1934: 123). By describing the 'masses', Goés Monteiro also offers clues on the issues he perceived as indispensable for modernization. For him, the effort of modernization needed to be brought about by the uniformization of society and its labour. He supported the idea of a corporatist militarized state where politics could not endanger the process of modernization. In this aspect, civilians were perceived as less apt, since they often submitted 'themselves to dubious practices which have infected the national organism and made a true devastation of our national life' (Goés Monteiro 1934: 129–35). These ideas on the lack of probity and the capacity of civilians to make the 'national organism' function are key to the concept of national security in Brazil from the mid-1930s onwards. On the one hand, the government could entrust neither the incapacitated masses nor the dubious civilian elite to help modernization, while, on the other, it needed their labour for the modernization effort. The concept of national security provided the response to this authoritarian conundrum. Its corresponding legislation was introduced to institutionalize and provide legal legitimization for the scrutiny of civilian life by the armed forces. It institutionalized surveillance, policing and a general system for keeping the population in check while Vargas was leading the state-building efforts. Furthermore, it was within the context of the scrutiny of public life that General Góes Monteiro found space for the role of the armed forces in politics. He conceived the role of the armed forces as 'the duty to guarantee the internal order found not only in the material existence of institutions, but also in the political and moral integrity of the *pátria*' (Goés Monteiro 1934: 120). Under these conditions, 'the national armed forces must be forces of construction that support strong governments and which are capable of transforming and giving new structure to national existence' (Goés Monteiro 1934: 156–7). For the armed forces, Góes Monteiro reserved the joint task of keeping society in check through whatever means necessary and of rationalizing the modernization effort through the depoliticization of politics. This was an attempt to exclude democratic participation and discussion from politics and to reduce the conduct of state affairs to matters of management and order. This is in tandem with his statement on the nature of the regime he helped institutionalize in the 1930s:

> The regime we are going to set up should resolve the financial–economic crisis and the moral crisis. The most rational way to do this is establishing national security on solid basis with the aim of disciplining the people and obtaining maximum use of all branches of public activities. In sum, it means to adopt the principles of military organization.
>
> (Goés Monteiro 1934: 201)

Without ever defining the concept of national security, General Góes Monteiro was able to ascribe it a political meaning embedded in the militarization of society. Since its introduction in the political and legal vocabulary of Brazil, national security invoked authoritarian and often violent practices of the state in the name of modernization. An example of this is the issue of law 38 of 4 April 1935 (Brazil-DOU 1935: 6,857). Its preamble states that it 'defines crimes against political and social order'. The document has no mention of either security or national security. Still, within a day of its publication, the law received two unofficial names from the opposition: '*a lei monstro*' (the monster law) and 'the law of national security'(Kossoy and Carneiro 2004: 68). Even though 'national security' had only been in public use since 1934, within a year there were no doubts about its political meaning: authoritarianism, censorship, surveillance and the submission of civilians to military principles of organization and order.

The political meanings of national security (1934–45)

In Portuguese, 'safety' and 'security' are the same word – *segurança*. In the first three decades of the twentieth century, the use of the word 'security' related primarily to safety (as in 'health and safety') and public safety. Even when related to public safety, Brazilian legislation between 1900 and 1930 had no direct association with policing or surveillance. It was rather about maintaining streetlights and roads, and keeping streets safe (Brazil-DOU 1904: 1,174, 1905: 98, 1906: 6,536). Notwithstanding these early meanings, the phrase 'national security' entered federal legislation at the top of institutional arrangements and national legislation in the 1930s. Its first use in the legal vocabulary in Brazil was in the 1934 constitution. That constitution had eight 'titles' – chapter divisions of the chart – and one of them dedicated entirely to national security. It ruled the constitutional rights and duties of the armed forces (Brazil 1934: articles 160–5), the creation and jurisdiction of the CSN (Brazil 1934: article 159), the access to public lands (Brazil 1934: article 166) and the official relation of national industries and the armed forces (Brazil 1934: article 167). That charter also institutionalized the supra-ministerial *Conselho de Segurança Nacional* (National Security Council) – which was to replace the Council of National Defence. A brief comparison between two institutions reveals the status attained by the armed forces under Vargas. It also sheds light on how the phrase 'national security' aimed to invert civil–military relations. The CSN established that each federal ministry and each department of public service was to have its own in-house CSN cell. Even though the CDN had previously established a similar policy, their cells were limited to the federal ministries, and legislation was not clear on what sort of information to collect. Under the CSN, their mandate was to keep in check 'the civil state of individuals and morale of the population in what regards National Security and the surveillance of the political and moral behaviour of public servants' (Brazil-DOU 1934: 4,249). In the CSN, the military staff on the council were reserved the highest and most decisive posts. This further jeopardized civilian input on the council, since they could not directly advise the president nor have their votes account for anything beyond the status of advice. Furthermore, in the absence of the president at the meetings of the council, the Minister of War or the Chief of Military Staff could act in his name, including delegating task forces and the implementation of policies.

From the signing of the 1934 constitution onwards, military strategy in government aimed to impose the scrutiny of civilian life in political and moral terms by the armed forces. This way, the surveillance of the morale of the population as well as the political and moral behaviour were the aim of a series of institutions set up in the late 1930s. The Law of National Security (LSN; Brazil-DOU 1935: 6,857), introduced in 1935, created a separate, more rigorous legislation for political crimes (previously under the jurisdiction of common justice). Penalties were from 1 to 10 years of imprisonment and included repeal of military rank, the closing of unions and censorship of radio and newspapers (Fausto 2001: 196–7). The communist-oriented uprisings of that year opened space for tightening of the LSN to include further penalties to public servants and military staff who promoted public disturbance with political goals. It also paved the way for the creation of a special tribunal that would prosecute political crimes – which came into existence the following year under the jurisdiction of the military justice; the Tribunal de Segurança Nacional (TSN, Tribunal of National Security). In practice, the TSN was a military tribunal created by the government to prosecute political dissidents away from the jurisdiction of civilian rule. It reduced the rights of defendants and dramatically shortened its procedural process (cases could last no more than 10 days between accusation and prosecution). The judges in charge of the tribunal (always two civilians and four military judges) could choose what evidence to consider and were able to prosecute based on their own political convictions (Campos 1982: 103; Faoro 1975: 340). For civilians in power, perceived to be corrupt, selfish and inadequate for public service, the 1934 constitution also established the *mandado de segurança* (in Common Law, the 'writ of mandamus'). In Common Law, the writ of mandamus is issued by a superior court to compel lower authorities to perform mandatory and ministerial duties correctly (Campos 1982:

103; Faoro 1975: 340). Between 1934 and 1945, the Tribunal of National Security was in charge of issuing *mandados de segurança*. Since judges in this court could act in accordance with their own political view and no further witnesses or proof could be provided after the issue of the *mandado*, such a document became the fastest legal action against political dissidence within public and military service. National security was not taking the place of national defence in Brazilian legislation. Rather, they each served different purposes for the militarization of the state proposed by General Góis Monteiro. National security was the politics of the army – as Góis Monteiro had himself suggested in 1934. He had himself drafted the first Law of National Security, and his was the organization and regulation of the Council of National Security (Coutinho 1956: 267–9), where he was also its vice-president and could act in the name of Getúlio Vargas if he was not present at discussions. By inscribing 'national security' into the institutional arrangements of the country, General Góis Monteiro and his political supporters submitted the civilian realm to the scrutiny of the military through a string of institutions (Fragoso 1975: 9). Such institutional arrangement included an intelligence-gathering institution (Council of National Security) and its surveillance cells, a law that delimited political participation (Law of National Security) and a special jurisdiction to deal not only with political dissidence but also anything that could be considered a 'moral crime' against the nation (Carvalho 2005: 52). This was the key to the conceptual difference between 'national defence' and 'national security' in the mid-1930s: the former established a niche of military policy-making that would define their modernization platform and separate it from civilian scrutiny, while the latter was used as the means to make that platform possible by submitting social and political relations to military inspection. In essence, 'national defence' and 'national security' as used in legal vocabulary post-1934 were intimately connected to Vargas' growing dependence on the armed forces. As the power and influence of General Góis Monteiro grew in the aftermath of the 1930 coup, so too did his ability to dictate the set up of institutions that would submit public life to the surveillance of the military and leave military issues to the scrutiny of only the highest rank of the armed forces. By 1936, all of the aforementioned institutions were already in place and had already, if not officially at least in practice, made the country a de facto military regime. As such, the set up of surveillance and ad hoc tribunals, as well as the growth and spread of framing of issues as matters of 'national security', further politicized the very act of evoking these phrases. It is relevant to call attention to this politicization of the use the terms 'national security' and 'national defence' as authoritarian military perspectives determined who got to think about security and defence. The use of 'national security' and 'national defence' signposted any discourse as a military one and predeterminately marked it as authoritarian. This, in turn, pre-emptively marked anything relating to 'national security' and 'national defence' as the realm of the discourse and practices of the military. Furthermore, it also prevented any form of democratic dialogue between civilians and the armed forces in the decades to come. The aim of this chapter was two-fold. First, it sought to uncover the political meanings of thinking about security in Brazil during the first Vargas government. Second, it attempted to explain its political relevance by intertwining the narrative about security in relation to the rise of the most conservative anti-liberal sector in the post-1930 era. The chapter examined the development of thinking about security put forward by conservative actors in an authoritarian regime – the first of the three contexts making up the structure of this book. By focusing on the rise of the armed forces as a political actor, the chapter analysed how the conceptualizations of national defence and national security were fundamental in two areas: first for gatekeeping policy areas outside civilian jurisdiction and later for submitting civilian affairs to military scrutiny. By guaranteeing internal order through the various institutions of national security, the armed forces and Vargas also dramatically curtailed the spectrum of political projects that would shape the state-building enterprise of the 1930s and 1940s. Furthermore, the use of national defence and national security as concepts under the competence of an institution that pragmatically implemented and ran the dictatorship politicized the very use of those terms; excluding their discussion (and use) from the civilian political agenda.

In analysing the alliance between Vargas and the armed forces during the *Estado Novo*, McCann (1980: 115) stated, 'Vargas promised that if the military gave him order, he would give Brazil progress'. As I have tried to analyse in this chapter, the military gave Vargas more than just order; it imprinted the militarization of society into the institutions that were set up even before the establishment of the *Estado Novo*. In this sense, what General Góes Monteiro gave Vargas was, in fact, the politics *of* the military – a modernization platform that not only freed the armed forces from civilian scrutiny but also put civilian public life under the surveillance of the military. As for the progress Vargas would give the country, it was much more fitting to the armed forces than it was for Brazil as a whole. By the end of the *Estado Novo*, the armed forces enjoyed a level of development and modernization that was unmatched by any other sector of society. Furthermore, they successfully imprinted militarization, exclusion and authoritarianism into the institutional structures of the entire country. Out of the series of institutions put in place at that time – including the Brazilian civil and penal codes – only the Tribunal of National Security and the constitutions issue in 1934 and 1937 are no longer in existence. Neither of the democratization governments of 1945 and 1985 dismantled these institutions. Up to this day, Brazil has still not come to terms with a great part of the institutional heritage that was created during the *Estado Novo*.

In relation to the TEA, the analysis of thinking about security strengthens arguments proposed in Part I and which aimed at factoring in the role of intellectuals in Souza's critique. Although the developments analysed here roughly refer to the same time that the works of Freyre and Buarque de Holanda were published, they highlight a few relevant points. First, the works of Freyre and Buarque de Holanda may be understood more comprehensively if one contextualizes them within the two great academic and political debates of their time, namely, the relationship between race and development (or lack thereof) and intellectual dissidence from the liberal republican system. *Casa Grande & Senzala* is an intellectual response to the former, whereas *Raízes do Brasil* is deeply indebted to the latter. Likewise, authoritarian actors' response to those debates was to propose and enforce the militarization of society and the rigid differentiation between irrational, venal, racially weak civilians and rational, honest, hierarchy-driven armed forces. As discussed in the following chapters, this need to divide society between those who govern and those who are governed also pervades later developments of thinking about security. It is characterized not only by a continuous reification of the role of intellectuals in bringing about development in the country but also, and most importantly, the association of rationality with leadership aptitude and whiteness, and of irrationality with lack of agency, pre-modern and emotional behaviour. In this sense, Freyre's *Casa Grande & Senzala* provided grounds for perceiving race positively. However, there is an underlying hierarchy of race in which the social category of white is more highly regarded than others (this is discussed in Chapter 4). In what concerns *Raízes do Brasil*, the idea of the cordial man offers a sort of discursive sensibility that was missing before the publication of Buarque de Holanda's 1936 volume. If one takes the examples provided in this chapter, the 'tumultuous masses' were addressed plainly as racially weak, uneducated, irrational. The concept of cordial man allowed the rephrasing of those terms as 'amorous, sensual, cordial, friendly, etc' as a kind of moral compensation that replaced the more negative discourse previously used. Chapter 4 examines the development of thinking about security as pursued by conservative actors, both military and civilian, under a democratic regime. It starts by arguing that, upon the return to democracy in 1945, the conservative sectors of society had to compete with other development platforms which had been coercively silenced during the *Estado Novo*, and it importantly moves to examine how 'national security' was developed and how it can be understood within the framework of Souza's TEA.

4 Security as state development

This chapter develops a critique of the DSN by establishing the links between the TEA and the development of thinking about security between 1945 and 1985. It starts by exploring the continuities in the power of the military after the end of the Second World War and the ousting of President Getúlio Vargas from the presidency, and uses this analysis as the framework for the historic context in which the establishment of the *Escola Superior de Guerra* (ESG) took place.

From there, it moves on to analyse the Brazilian Doctrine of National Security by dividing it according to the three tenets of the TEA proposed in Part I: being, becoming, and method. The TEA highlights important aspects in relation to thinking about security in this context. First, being uncovers how the essentialization of Brazilian identity allowed the ESG to determine who was to be made secure. Second, becoming allows one to think about how the emphasis placed on development through rationalization enabled ESG intellectuals expand the reach of their thinking about security to include an outward look at the world. Through method, this chapter argues that the DSN constituted the method of development proposed by the ESG. Lastly, worlding Brazil allows this chapter to explore how these ideas were put into practice through governmental policies.

The armed forces in post-1945 politics

Throughout the *Estado Novo*, Vargas and his supporters in power had given signs of sympathy for the Axis and inter-war authoritarian regimes (Seitenfus 2000: 104–8). Examples of this range from the very name of the Brazilian dictatorship – which was copied from the Portuguese *Estado Novo* (1933–74); passing through the 1937 constitution – authored by the most renowned advocate of corporatism in Brazil, Jurist Francisco Campos; to the anti-Semitic policies pursued by the government (Levine 1968; Carneiro 1988). Despite the authoritarian nature of the *Estado Novo*, Vargas negotiated Brazil's entrance into the war on the Allied side in 1942. In exchange for the right to build US military bases in the north and northeast regions of Brazil and on the island of Fernando de Noronha, US President Franklin D. Roosevelt agreed to finance the Companhia Siderúrgica Nacional (National Steel-making Company) (Rogers 1968). The *Força Expedicionária Brasileira* (FEB, Brazilian Expeditionary Force) was sent out to join the fight in

Italy in 1944 (McCann 1980: 116–18). Military participation in the Second World War affected not only the way the top military command perceived its own deficiencies with respect to training, education and equipment, but also influenced them to rethink the validity of the *Estado Novo* in Brazil. Officers expressed concern that the country was fighting alongside democracies in Europe while holding an authoritarian regime in Brazil (Pandolfi 1999: 11). Back home, the continuity of the *Estado Novo* was being challenged through a succession of strikes and protests. Thus, aided by the general intellectual discontent with the *Estado Novo*, the top rank of the armed forces colluded to oust Vargas from power through a coup in October 1945. In sum, the armed forces brought down the regime they had themselves put in place. They promoted the democratization of a regime they had themselves put in place in 1937. By doing so, they not only survived their own regime but were also able to choose which areas of politics should be returned to civilian control (Zaverucha and Pereira 1998: chap. 1; Zaverucha 2000: chaps. 1 and 2). Furthermore, they retained control over specific policy areas, especially security and defence. The apparent return to democracy left intact the most comprehensive authoritarian institutional apparatus established in Brazilian history. The military-sponsored 1945 redemocratization of Brazil paved the way to the prominent position the armed forces had in Brazilian politics in decades to come. They retained not only its central status in politics after the end of the regime, but also the series of institutional privileges they had gained under Vargas. The election of Marshall Eurico Gaspar Dutra – one of the most powerful men of the *Estado Novo* for the term 1946–50 – was a further sign of the unscathed reputation of the armed forces. The armed forces also led the redemocratization process in 1985 and ended the regime they had themselves put in place. This was done through a system of gradual return to democracy in which the military closely chose which areas would return to civilian control. As a result, the armed forces were never fully discredited as political actors in the country and, furthermore, they were able to retain control over specific policy areas (such as security and defence). Compared with other countries in the Southern Cone, this is one of the most distinctive characteristics of the Brazilian military. Whilst some of the consequences of this specificity are further analysed in Chapter 5, for the moment it is important to highlight that, despite the institutional power the armed forces held after the end of the *Estado Novo*, the 1945 democratization opened up space for political projects that were silenced during the regime. It is within this context of political competition between different intellectual sectors in the aftermath of the *Estado Novo* regime that one can understand the establishment of the ESG – to which we now turn.

The ESG and the anti-Vargas coalition

The initial plans to set up the ESG date back to 1942. The institution was initially conceived as a centre of military training for army generals and colonels, precluding even the enrolment of officers of the other armed forces (Arruda 1983: XXI). This project, however, was never fully implemented. Upon the return of the FEB to Brazil, war veterans were adamant about pushing for continued military assistance from the US government. As part of his official visit to the USA, president Dutra (1946–50) was shown the recently created National War College in Washington DC and became interested in the possibility of setting up a similar institution in Brazil (Gurgel 1978: 30). A programme of military assistance, signed in 1946, included provisions for US officials to come to Brazil and help set up the ESG as an equivalent of the US National War College (Dreifuss 2008: 386). Although the initial purpose was to establish a Brazilian institution that mirrored the National War College, the political context in Brazil led the armed forces to change the institutional arrangements of the ESG (Arruda 1980: 20). Instead of being a training institution for high-ranking officers of the army, it was established as a military think-tank that held courses for both civilians and the armed forces. The ESG would also accept middle-ranking staff of all the three forces and had an official policy of attracting civilians to its courses as a way of influencing political outcomes in the state bureaucracy. Even though the ESG was based in Rio de Janeiro and its main audience was composed of sectors of the federal bureaucracy, its teachings percolated down to lower levels of civilian and military service through the establishment of local branches that would hold courses for the non-federal civilian bureaucracy. On this subject, General Juarez Távora, the second commander of the ESG, stated 'as a commander, I intended to increase civilian representation [at the ESG]. I thought the objective of the school was not only to train military men but also to train all of those who could influence the government' (Stepan 1975: 130). Such a shift in objectives and audience cannot be understood outside the need to compete against political platforms that had been silenced during the *Estado Novo* and against Getúlio Vargas (who had announced that he would return in 1950 as a democratically elected president). Once censorship of the regime was lifted, projects sponsored by other sectors of society came to the forefront of political debates and intellectual practices in Brazil (Trindade 2005; 2007; Svartman 2006: 33–4). The authoritarian state project of the military, which had been the rule of engagement of the armed forces in politics throughout the *Estado Novo*, now had to face competition (and opposition) of those political alternatives that had been silenced since the mid-1930s. Unable to rely on censorship and authoritarian means to assert their practices, the high command of the armed forces understood that they were now dependent on the adherence of other sectors of society to their project. At the same time, if Vargas did return as a democratically elected president (as he did in 1950), it was obvious that he would now come to power in open opposition to those who ousted him in 1945. Anti-Vargas sectors, of which the military elite was a key part, were aware of the need to unify their efforts against him (Levine 1968: 82–5; Skidmore 1989, 135–9; Rogers 2006: 228–31). Given the political stakes at hand (countering Vargas with a political project that reassured and maintained the centrality and relevance of the armed forces), the ESG was founded as a governmental military think-tank, where the conservative and authoritarian sectors of Brazilian society reconvened and relaborated their modernization project to suit the change in regime. In doing so, they maintained security as the key discursive element through which their political platform would be understood. This dictated the development of thinking about security in the following decades. The future Brazilian Doctrine of National Security was the political statement of the conservative actors about their project of modernization. In a 1981 interview, Antônio Carlos Murici (1993: 255), a member of the ESG's original group, recalled the thinking behind the doctrine:

> At the end of the school year of 1952 came the definitive moment of the school. We had to prepare the curriculum for 1953 and we were quite embarrassed. Ideas were vague, disconnected. We felt that for the school to be more politically relevant we needed to tackle Vargas' populism, we needed to design our own grand strategy for the country.

Murici's testimony clearly identifies the political goal behind the design of the doctrine: countering Vargas with a sort of master plan intended to guide politics and to push forward the agenda of the anti-Vargas coalition. Concerning these two objectives, one of the official historians of that institution noted: 'the makers of the ESG felt that there was a need to elaborate doctrinaire concepts in order to harmonize knowledge, to establish a common understanding on essential issues, and to maintain their political project of security and development' (Arruda 1980: 9). Instead of having its initial activities in 1952, President Dutra ordered the inaugural lecture to take place while he was still in office, avoiding the possibility that Vargas (if elected) would prohibit its establishment altogether (Dreifuss 2008: 76–8). Between 1950 and 1985, about 45 per cent of the ESG graduates were civilians. Up to the present day, the ESG produced some 5,000 graduates. These numbers, however, are considerably higher if one takes into consideration the work of the *Associação dos Diplomados da Escola Superior de Guerra* (ADESG, Alumni Association of the *Escola Superior de Guerra*) which was set up in 1951. ADESG holds local offices in each state where former ESG graduates teach courses on the Doctrine of National Security (Oliveira 1976: 13). By 1979, ADESG had over 35,000 course attendees (Montarroyos 1979: Annex 3). By 2012, that number had risen to nearly 75,000 graduates (ADESG 2013: 1).

The fundamental principles of ESG (1948)

As part of the works that led to the creation of the ESG, the Joint Chief of Staff designated a study commission in 1948. In January 1949, the commission issued the *Princípios Fundamentais que Orietaram a Criação da ESG* (PF, Fundamental Principles that guided the set-up of the ESG), a half-page-long document composed of seven bullet points which are not followed by any explanatory remarks. Together with a 1953 lecture by General Juarez Távora, the PF is the most reprinted document in the history of the ESG. These two documents contain what the ESG scholars believe to be the main ideas that inform the DSN. Before moving on to the analysis of the document itself, there are two points relating to the language used in the DSN that need to be raised. These concern the challenges faced by anyone reading those texts. The language of the DSN is difficult to understand even for native Portuguese speakers. It requires a concerted effort to grasp its meaning. In the case of writings by ESG intellectuals, language standards are also often compromised. Not only is there overuse of long and far-fetched sentences and metaphors, but poor grammar and style are not uncommon. To cite an example, a 1958 volume by the ESG's main intellectual, General Golbery do Couto e Silva, published in English, received the following review: '[the book was made up of] incompletely digested matter often resulting in cloudy paragraphs built around undefined and imprecise terms. A certain diffuseness and wordiness in the text is aggravated by bad punctuation and poor editing' (Evans 1958: 200). The original text in Portuguese is no different. I have attempted to address these issues by providing additional explanations of some passages and to the best of my knowledge I have provided reliable translations of these documents, keeping the capitalization and the bold formatting of the original texts. The translation of the *Princípios Fundamentais* follows:

I   National security is more a function of the general potential of the nation than it is of its military potential.
II   Brazil has the indispensible requirements (area, population, resources) to become a great power.
III The development of Brazil has been delayed due to factors that may be addressed.
IV   As in every task, the orientation of this acceleration requires the use of a driving power and a process of application of this energy.
V   The existing impediment against the emergence of national solutions to Brazilian problems is due to the adopted process of application of energy and the lack of habit of group work.
VI   It is urgent that the method of opinions be substituted by other methods that may allow for harmonious and balanced solutions.
VII The tool to construct and disseminate the new method to be adopted includes the creation of a National Institute of Higher Studies which will work as a permanent centre of research.

The next three sections explore the PF in relation to the TEA. The focus is to provide a clearer understanding of how the TEA both informs the views expressed in the PF and provides a structure of thought in the form of a map to development. This structure entails not only the essentialization of identity but is also charged with specific meanings for development and the path to its attainment. Since the PF does not provide any further commentary regarding the meaning of its statements, whenever possible I use statements and comments on the PF provided by scholars associated with the ESG.

Principles I and II

As discussed in Part I, the breakthrough offered by the works of Freyre (1933) and Buarque de Holanda (1936) helped Brazilian intellectuals move away from turn-of-the-century racial theorization. The delinking of racial miscegenation from the possibility of development was a discursive advance deemed impossible not long before. In practice, this meant that instead of perceiving the people as genetically incapable of becoming 'developed', one could now see them as potentially the greatest resource of the country. It is thus important to explore how this affected social theorizing. Principle I and Principle II provide a positive understanding of the people of Brazil and their relationship to the wealth of the country. 'Nation' in Principle I and 'the population' in Principle II appear as contributing factors to Brazilian development along with the country's national resources. In Principle II the geographic resources of the country appear alongside population as one of the basic requirements for becoming a great power. If one thinks back and compares it with that 1913 editorial of ADN which talks about the tumultuous masses (Chapter 3), the people/nation in the PF have a much more positive role as they are no longer an obstacle to development but one of its sources. With respect to thinking about security, Principle I introduces a meaning not previously associated with the concept. In the post-1945 period, part of the production of the ESG utilizes national security to mean 'development'. Often they are used interchangeably – which led some authors to call the DSN the 'Doctrine of National Security and Development' (Alves 1984). In Principle I, for instance, the reference is to development. Two underlying meanings can be discerned from this principle. First, it means that the Brazilian armed forces are the most developed national institution and, as such, the military should be one of the agents to take on the task of realizing the potential of the people. Amaral Gurgel commented on Principle I of the PF, stating that

the document starts from the assertion that the general development of the country is the way to national security. In accordance with this assertion, the institutions that are responsible for the security of the nation must have the role of ensuring the development of its potential. (Gurgel 1978: 31)

The underlying argument of Gurgel's statement is that the armed forces ought to be the sector that leads the effort of modernization, since it is the institution that has been historically responsible for the security of the nation. Tellingly, there is no mention of the fact that such a role was the result of the ultraconservative sector of society imposing militarization on the rest of the country by setting up a series of institutions, legislation and political arrangements in the name of security. However, if compared with the *Estado Novo* context, post-Second World War politics demanded that the armed forces recognized they needed to rely on both like-minded military and civilian elite to lead their modernization project. Thus, the pedagogic role ESG intellectuals took upon themselves – teaching the bureaucratic elite of the country the 'project of national security'. The way this plays out in both policy and intellectual practice will be further explored later. The second idea underlying Principle I is that the country as a whole should take part in the effort of development. As argued above, this is a direct effect of the positive understanding of identity of the 1930s. In the inter-war years, policies of development were taken to mean the establishment of national heavy industries, roads and ports to aid the development *of* the armed forces. In post-*Estado Novo* politics, development (as this chapter argues) meant rationalizing society and political processes in order to become a world power and enter the select group of Western Christian democracies.

Principles III and V

One of the key tenets of the TEA is the essentialization of Brazilian identity around the ideas of *personalismo* and *patrimonialismo*. The former invites the disqualification of class struggle, minority rights and difference, since it denies the existence of racism, political exclusion and power relations within different sectors of society (Souza 2006a: 12). It masks prejudice and exclusion while also rebuffing the possibility of the recognition of politics outside Brazilian identity. The reproduction of this attractive idea of 'Brazilianness' hinders processes of exclusion in favour of the reification of national identity. *Patriomonialismo* is the spill-over of the character of the people to the state – governance through personal rather than public interest. This is perceived to be the main source of underdevelopment. The general argument is that the lack of rationality in public relations both produced and reinforced the underdevelopment of the state. In order to clear the state of its *patrimonialismo*, it is necessary to promote the rationalization of the *cordial man* – the same cordial man who is cherished and celebrated as a cultural trait. Thus, cordial men serve a dual purpose: they are celebrated in face of antagonism, but scorned when it comes to having agency in the institutional apparatus of the state. Hence, the drafting of Principle III – 'the development of Brazil has been delayed for reasons that may be removed' – and *Principle V* – 'The existing impediment against the emergence of national solutions to Brazilian problems is due to the adopted process of application of energy and the lack of habit of group work'. The driving logic behind these statements is that the culture of *patrimonialismo* has been the main impediment to development. The 'lack of habit of group work' relates to the perceived inability of cordial men to work for the public interest. The 'adopted process of application of energy' relates to the way the culture of *personalismo* spills over into state structures and renders them inefficient. In other words, the way to change the 'current process of application of energy' is to promote the rationalization of the cordial man and of his *patrimonialista* state. It is with respect to the creation of national solutions that a former commander of the ESG, General Bina Machado, stated that the knowledge produced at the ESG sought to 'neutralize deformations promoted by personal points of view that are not rational in the search of common denominators and possible consensus' (cited in Gurgel 1978: XII). By 'personal points of view' he means the *personalista* attitude of Brazilian culture that hinders development. Another former commander of the ESG, General Lyra Tavares (Lyra Tavares 1958: 29) used the same anti-*personalista* argument to talk about the provision of national solutions: 'the fundamental condition of affirmation and vitality of a national community is the existence of a national conscience that stands against the impact of emotions, [a national conscience] that is settled and enlightened'. Essentially *Principles III* and *V* can be traced to the immanent character of Brazilian culture as revealed in TEA. They work with the assumption that the aim of political praxis is to realize the immanent potential of the Brazilian people and state.

Principles IV, VI and VII

The analysis of the PF has so far pointed towards a contentious relationship between what the country and the people are and what they ought to be. It is the idea of realizing this potential that anchors the remaining principles. As discussed by Souza (2006b: 100), the TEA relies on the existence of one counterpoint to Brazil's 'emotionally driven' culture: the rational characteristics of countries that exemplify a culture of individualism, emotional control and discipline. It is against the background of the perceived rationality of the West that the TEA develops prescriptions about Brazil. In this sense, 'becoming a great power' (Principle II), realizing the potential of the nation, attaining 'national security' and/or development, all carry the underlying assumption of *becoming* rational and leaving behind the pre-modern cultural traits that characterize Brazilian identity. Take, for instance, General Cordeiro de Farias' comment about the differences between the ESG and the US National War College:

> The American school was embedded in a developed place. It could afford to be entirely dedicated to war issues and not worry about the solution to the national problems – since they were under the umbrella of an elite that had been educated in a system of known efficiency.
>
> (Camargo and Goés 1981: 9)

Cordeiro de Farias' words are a clear example of the essentialized views on the USA that dominated Brazilian thinking. Rationality meant development and efficiency. In this case, he used these notions to justify the necessity of educating the civilian elite in Brazil – who, in his opinion, have not been brought up in a system of efficiency. Thus, in his view, the role of the ESG was also to correct this deficiency in the education of the Brazilian elite in order for them to pave the way to modernization. It is not for any other purpose that General Juarez Távora (1983: 19) stated that the ultimate end of the studies conducted at the ESG was to 'inculcate into the conscience of our elite, without distinction between civilians and military men, an ample and uniform understanding of the problems of National Security'. This pedagogical aim of the doctrine in relation to the elite is anchored on the idea that there is a 'true elite', one whose conceptualization General Golbery borrowed from Toynbee's idea of spiritual elites (Birkner 2002: 58, 154). He makes use of Toynbee's conception of the elites that lead the historical progress of their time and applies it to the Brazilian reality as *elites verdadeiras* (true elites):

> For such duty, for the unequivocal comprehension of its meaning as well as for its prudent planning and dedicated execution, the country requests, the nation requires, and the people demand the vigilante effort and the enlightened intelligence of its true elites, conscious that the problem of national security, for its complexity, for its amplitude, for its implications of all sorts, concerns all citizens.
>
> (Couto e Silva 1959: 446)

ESG intellectuals took up the idea of the rationalization of societal and political relations to a great extent and, through the DSN, proposed the de-politicization of politics. It is in this context that Principle VI finds its meaning: 'It is urgent that the method of opinions be substituted by other methods that may allow for harmonious and balanced solutions'. The 'method of opinions' is what the armed forces perceived to be the nature of civilian politics: opinionated discussions that were seldom able to resolve anything. The comments of ESG's Antonio Gurgel provide further clues as to what the armed forces held to be the civilian method of opinions: 'it is pervaded by the study and solutions of individual connotation, visibly *personalista* and not uncommonly contradictory. This way, public administration proves to be static and undefined' (Gurgel 1978: 32). As for Principle IV, it states that 'the orientation of this acceleration requires the use of a driving power and a process of application of this energy'. The general idea was that the armed forces would join together with 'influential civilians' to provide the road map to development. As stated in Principle VII, 'the tool to construct and disseminate the new method to be adopted includes the creation of a National Institute of Higher Studies, which will work as a permanent centre of research'. However, and still according to Principle IV, it is not only a 'driving force' that is needed, but also a 'process of application of this energy' that shall bring about 'harmonious and balanced solutions'. The road map, their *method* of modernization, was the DSN produced by the ESG. In this context, it is relevant to look at the critique of the PF offered by Joseide Montarroyos (1979: 59–71). The idea is to read her critique as an example of a work that is critical of the PF but still works within the TEA . Her basic contention with the seven principles is the right of the armed forces to invest themselves with the responsibility to lead the modernization effort (Montarroyos 1979: 60–2). In her critique, she proceeds to partially agree with six of the seven Principles. She argues that area, resource and population are indeed 'incontestable' principles for the foundations of a great power, but that one needs to look at the prescriptions to bring the country to the group of developed nations in order to analyse its legitimacy (1979: 62). The same line of argument is provided for the third and fourth Principles, in which she ponders on 'whom and what would be considered an obstacle to be removed' (1979: 65–6) and the legitimacy of the 'elite that would get to choose which of the said obstacles were to be removed, and when' (1979: 67). As for the fifth Principle, again, her arguments concern who gets to choose what the impediments are and how to remedy them (1979: 68). In relation to the last two Principles, she questions whether the armed forces would be the best candidate to either apply the 'necessary method for development' or 'to hold a research institution' (1979: 69–71). In sum, Montarroyos' line of argument in criticizing the PF does not rely on what the Principles state, but in who is saying it. Her criticism is not against the idea of rationalizing society by removing the obstacles to development, but against who gets to name the obstacles. She is not against the development of a method of work, but against the imposition of the specific method of the armed forces. She is not against the elitism inherent in the principles, but against the legitimacy of that specific elite. She does not directly denounce the statements, but the authoritarian and conservative elites that enunciate them. In sum, she is not countering the axioms (or the 'deep structure', in Booth's phrase). She questions the validity of a conservative method and the legitimacy of the sector of the elite that represents them. I would like to use her critique to clarify two points about the nature of social theorizing within the paradigm of the TEA. First, the TEA is above political and professional affiliations. It works by pre-defining the departure point of social theorizing and by establishing development – or the rationalization of society – as its ultimate goal. As a result, political and intellectual debates are reduced to the analysis of different methods of modernization. In this sense, Montarroyo's critique of the PF is an example of the sort of thinking produced by investigations that work within the TEA paradigm. It only goes as far as asking the legitimacy of a particular method. It does not enquire into formative processes of exclusion, nor is it interested in unveiling what development means, for whom and by which means. It steers away not only from these issues, but also from self-questioning – this is my next point. Second, there is no room for self-reflection within the TEA paradigm. Since the political place of intellectuals as agents of modernization had been already clearly defined in previous decades that was seldom challenged (for scholarship that has challenged it, see Franco 1978 and Chauí 1983). Instead, debates have focused on the legitimacy of different sectors of intellectuals. Daniel Pécaut (1989: 128–31) examined this issue amongst anti-military works and left-wing intellectuals. He explored how discussions on the role of the intellectual elite in the country were presented through dichotomies – good/bad elite or true/false elite – and their legitimacy in translating their will into the acceleration of development. He compared the writings of Nelson Werneck Sodré, a Marxist military officer, to that of Theotônio dos Santos, one of the key figures in Development Theory, and Wanderley Guilherme dos Santos, a renowned geographer. Note the following:

> The great lairds, the high bourgeoisie and middle-classes are those compromised with imperialism. . . that bad elite ought to be excluded from the people, now and forever
>
> (Sodré 1962: 5)

> On one side, the forces of progress, the overwhelming majority of the people, and, on the other, the retrograde and the anti-popular elite...
>
> (Santos 1962: 30)

> On one side, those who desire to alter the fundamental structure of the country so that social requirements may be fulfilled, and on the other, the false elite, those who consider that the structure should not be altered, who wish to keep [Brazil] as a capitalist nation, dominated by imperialism
>
> (Santos 1962: 8)

These three excerpts work with the same idea of legitimacy that General Golbery do Couto e Silva does when proposing his own conceptualization of elites in order to legitimize the armed forces and the like-minded conservative sectors grouped around the ESG as the true elites of the country. In this sense, political and academic arguments put forward by the Left and the Right, and by civilians as much as the military, are charged with an underlying political struggle for legitimization. This additional internal struggle amongst different sectors of intellectuals further impoverished social theorizing, since discursive legitimization takes precedence over other aspects. It is these underlying aspects of any political debate that are often more important than the arguments on paper. Thus, analysing this discourse involves not only the analysis of what the discourse says, but the identification of that which, after some time, did not need to be said anymore. Silences speak the longest. On this aspect, historian Francisco Wefffort has criticized Brazilian intelligentsia for:

> Gaining more influence the less it says about real people living in the concrete reality of the present and the more it insists on the proposal of myths for the future which are but a desperate defence of their own past.
>
> (Weffort 1972: IV, 2)

The connection Weffort established between past, present and future only gains meaning through the pen and words of intellectuals interested first and foremost in the fabrication of a national unity that is dependent on these spokespeople of the state. This is the authoritarian utopia of the Brazilian intelligentsia. The will to be the agent of modernization and to speak in the name of national unity without reflecting on how they themselves are a part of the processes that normalize the exclusion of most of society. Before analysing the DSN, the next section addresses the influence of US thought and geopolitical thinking in the doctrine – often perceived as discursive changes in comparison to the way that security had been thought in the previous context.

US thought and geopolitics in the doctrine of national security

Before 1945, the use of 'national security' and 'national defence' was connected to the legal and institutional set up of the *Estado Novo*. Once the thought that informed these authoritarian assumptions had to be presented in another format, the references to the USA and geopolitical authors started appearing in texts. The arguments I proposed in relation to the emulation of the USA is that their intellectual influences on the DSN were much more in terms of what it allowed ESG intellectuals to say and teach about their own role in politics and their own project of development than a specific will to engage with theorizing outside Brazil. By this, I mean that there is no evidence of a pragmatic attempt or methodological approach in the use of those texts. Early studies on the DSN and on post-1945 Brazilian military thought were particularly keen to present the doctrine as simple emulation of US realism and military thought (see: Stepan 1971; Comblin 1978; Chiavenato 1981; Schilling 1981; Alves 1984). According to these writings, the influence exercised on the doctrine took shape through a series of interconnected instances of the USA–Brazil bilateral relationship. Some works place emphasis on the training of Brazilian officers in the USA (see: Schoultz 2000: 68; Braga 2002: 51; Silva 2006: 106). Others focus on the deployment of US officers who worked as consultants during the establishment of the ESG and their presence in that institution until 1970 (Dreifuss 2008: 80). My objection to these arguments is two-fold. First, US writings served as examples of the content – and the approach to writing this content – the original ESG group wanted to propose. While there should be no doubt that ESG intellectuals had access and often made references to foreign literature in general, this does not seem to have been done in any methodologically oriented manner. In fact, there seems to have been very little self-conscious 'method' in the evolution of the doctrine during this time. Antônio Carlos Murici remembers it this way:

> At that time [1952] we were studying and we realized that we needed a basis to justify what we were saying. We already had some conclusions but they were fluid. This was when one of those wonderful things happened. Rodrigo Otávio was in charge of collecting the data that would structure the formulation of a doctrine. When the school day was over, each one of us went to a bookstore to buy whatever there was that might be of interest. We were looking for ideas that that would give us the basis to say what we wanted.
>
> (Muricy 1993: 254–5)

His account sheds light on how ESG intellectuals worked to formulate the doctrine. It seems they already knew what they wanted to say but were studying *how* to say it, that is, they were researching a way of structuring their thought in ways that would be accepted as authoritative knowledge. In this sense, the influence of US realism and/or military thought on the ESG lies in what it allowed that intellectual group to claim. It gave them licence to claim that the method of rationalization they proposed was an authoritative form of knowledge production. Furthermore, a closer reading of the text of the doctrine together with the references makes it clear that quotations from other authors are only used inasmuch as they corroborate what the ESG intellectual sought to say. In this sense, the theoretical approaches of the original authors are neither discussed nor relevant to ESG texts. The 1953 lecture by General Juarez Távora is a good example. He cites Brazilian Ambassador Raul Fernandes to talk about sovereignty; the (then) Commander of the US Navy Ralph Williams to say that national security is a social condition; Simmons and Emeny (1935) to talk about the antagonism between great nations and poor ones and, later on, to mention the 'art of governing'. Likewise Edward Earle is used to introduce national strategy; Brazilian Lieutenant-Colonel J. Campos to talk about national objectives; Brazilian Colonel J. Magalhães to talk about the idea of 'total war'; and, Brazilian Judge Levi Carneiro to talk about international law. As General Távora's foundational lecture of the DSN suggests, they were as likely to use Edward Earle, a classic book on the history of strategic thinking in the USA, as they were to use the end-of-term essays written by former ESG attendees such as J. Campos and J. Magalhães. This seems to be in tandem with Murici's statement that the texts were used to selectively authenticate what the ESG intellectuals wanted to say. Seen in this light, it seems difficult to argue that these men were simply emulating US thought. The second objection is based on an argument put forward by Markoff and Baretta (1985: 186). They propose that the revolutionary wars waged by armed forces in Indochina, Cuba, China and Algeria caused disquiet in the West – to say the least – and that led them [the USA] to support conservative armed forces in the periphery, as part of Cold War strategy to contain the 'Communist threat'. Western countries, and especially the USA, came then to endorse internal surveillance as part of the role of the armed forces in peripheral states. Given this context, Markoff and Baretta suggest that this was much more of a novelty to the military of developed nations than it had been for the armed forces in Latin America. In the case of Brazil, it only further legitimated a long state of affairs for the army. They argued that the US support of this old role of the armed forces 'enabled Brazilian officers to talk and write and teach without embarrassment about their actual concerns, which had always been present but often regarded as unprofessional' (Markoff and Baretta 1985: 186). The arguments presented here suggest that the kind of influence exercised by the USA – be it through the literature or endorsement of the political role of the armed forces – was much more about legitimizing what ESG intellectuals wanted to say and the conservative sectors wished to continue doing. On the one side, this legitimization drew sustenance from US fears that other armed forces in Latin America would support revolutionary wars, and on the other, it justified and gave international license to the violent practices against political dissidents of the regime. The advent of the Second World War in Europe was directly responsible for the discrediting of nineteenth-century geopolitical writings, especially those linked to Nazi Germany (Hepple 1992). However, as the interest in deriving nationalistic expansionist policies from the geographic landscape declined elsewhere, in South America – and more specifically the Southern Cone (Dodds 2000) – Western geopolitical thinking at the turn of the century started playing a large role in influencing Brazilian authors to look at the interplay between geography, national and international power (Child 1979; Hepple 1992). In Brazil, those studies legitimized the idea that the country had a natural blueprint for international power. In this sense, the extension of the territory, the Amazon basin and forest, the long coastline, the South-Atlantic geostrategic location and the possibility of encountering resources to fuel industrialization worked as basic canvas on which Brazil was to become a great power. Early geopolitical thinking in Brazil set out to provide policy prescriptions intended to make the country occupy the power position correspondent to its natural greatness (Meira Mattos 2000: 60). Such instructions ranged from territorial integration through railroads, ports and roads (Travassos 1930,1941) to populating the largely uninhabited areas of Brazil's land frontier (Backheuser 1948), including the establishment of a new capital in the mid-west (Rodrigues 1947). As Hepple (1992) reminds us, these prescriptions gave a new perspective on areas of the country that had been historically neglected, including the primordial political and economic importance of the coastal line, the Amazon borders with other South American countries (Meira Mattos 1980; 1984; 1990), the unpopulated areas in the west of Brazil (Hepple 2004: 161), the navigation of rivers (Child 1979: 95) and territorial claims to Antarctica (Kelly 1984: 450). Tying these largely unpopulated and often neglected territories to the modernization project became official state policy still during the *Estado Novo*. It included the programme *Marcha para o Oeste* (March to the West), intended to populate the uninhabited areas of Brazil (Brazil 1943); the protection of the Amazon (Monteiro and Coelho 2004); the development of railroads, roads and ports (Couto e Silva 1959: 20–32), as well as the establishment of the *Conselho Nacional de Geografia* (National Council of Geography) in 1937 to collect data and information on the vast unpopulated territories (Anselmo and Bray 2002: 117). Therefore, geopolitical writings and policy prescriptions by geopolitical authors were not novel in post-1945 Brazil. The novelty was the use of geopolitical ideas as the foundation of security thinking. In post-1945 Brazil, geopolitical writings were almost exclusively authored by ESG intellectuals. The metaphor of the state as an organism that needed to be protected against internal maladies and external threats was met with great excitement at the ESG. Indeed, the reverence with which the most prolific of the Brazilian geopolitical writers – General Golbery do Couto e Silva (henceforth, Golbery) – spoke about this strand of geopolitics is evident in the following: 'It [geopolitics] is robust in perspective, admittedly partial, always incomplete, schematic even, and at times fanatic. In the end it unifies and clarifies, and imposes on our complex reality its imperative and its will to plan and to act' (Couto e Silva 1957: 28). Such emphasis on the role of geopolitics had an underlying purpose. It placed geography at the centre of historical narratives and 'interpreted and portrayed a political landscape in an apparently detached manner' (Hepple 2004: 365). By emphasizing the geographical landscape as the source of power, it depoliticized that very landscape, making it subject to strategy rather than dialogue, to rationality rather than politics. These tenets went hand in hand with the modernization project proposed by the ESG. It reduced political realities to a contiguous territorial space. If Brazilian identity was one and indivisible, so was the state-organism to which it corresponded. In this sense, geopolitics provided intellectuals with the organic metaphor of the state and the idea of tempering with the environment to influence political outcomes. This, in turn, went hand in hand with the idea of rationalizing the country into its potential. The tempering of geographical landscape to serve the development of the country became a metaphor of what could be done to society and politics as a whole. Geopolitical writings became the backdrop against which one could imagine the method of development proposed by the ESG. With the establishment of the ESG, geopolitical thought became an integral part of 'worlding' Brazil. Geopolitical thought influenced not only the armed forces, but also charged all understandings of the place of Brazil and its role in the world. Let us now look at the DSN.

The crystallization of the DSN (1953)

Until 1973, the DSN was scattered among a voluminous stack of around 10,000 documents, which was the ESG's knowledge production (Miyamoto 1987: 77; Miyamoto and Gonçalves 1995: 12). It consisted of lectures, reports, papers, interviews and a few books produced by ESG scholars which were loosely referred to as the DSN. It was a body of thought but not a doctrine as the name suggests – but those who were in favour as well as against its assumptions and claims knew exactly what was being invoked by the phrase 'Doctrine of National Security'. This further strengthens two of the arguments proposed here. First, the basic views that inform the doctrine had been established before the Doctrine itself and were, in fact, a re-adaptation of the old desire to subject civilian life and politics in general to the principles of military organization. Therefore, in this respect, national security retained the underlying role it had during the *Estado Novo*. The innovation was to extend that role to include like-minded civilians who shared the principles of modernization of the armed forces. When commenting on the doctrine, Dreifuss (2008: 14) stated that the terms of the doctrine were 'not up for discussion, they precede the institution'. In this case, the dogmas had indeed preceded the institution. Much of the arguments defended were based on authoritarian thinking of the *Estado Novo* period.

The second argument concerns what the doctrine actually said or claimed was of secondary importance in relation to who got to say it. In itself, the doctrine was a dry, poorly written, ill-thought and inconsistent road to development. However, those who advocated it had the power and means to dictate political currents and violent practices in the state. The simple mention of 'national security' in any speech was politically charged with the memory of the military's desire to silence dissidence, to censor difference and to make use of the state apparatus to persecute any sort of diversity in the name of its modernization project. Murici stated that the original idea was to have a course taught on the subject of national security and let the Doctrine emerge from group discussions in class, but 'there were too many ideas and we needed something systematic' (Muricy 1993: 254). This was especially relevant because the group eagerly sought to structure a grand development strategy under the guise of national security which would both preclude and do away with Vargas' populism. Thus, the group decided to systematize their thoughts into what would become the DSN. General Juarez Távora, the then Chief of Military Staff, presented the results in the opening lecture of the 1953 school year at the ESG. The paper was later published as *A Segurança Nacional, a Política e a Estratégia*, one of the two most reproduced documents of the DSN. Instead of being taken as a brief introduction of the concepts around which ESG attendees would develop their studies, the paper became *the* DSN. By this I mean that it not only contained the basic aspects of all later versions of the DSN (Gurgel 1978: 37), but also that updated versions of the DSN never went beyond what that first lecture stated. About that same lecture, Proença Jr noted 'what had been but a first attempt at a common language became the irredeemable Doctrine of National Security' (Proença Jr and Diniz 2007: 57). For this reason, the focus of the critique presented here is on that specific lecture, although reference to later versions of the doctrine and other writings by ESG scholars provide the sources for triangulation and support of the arguments presented here. As previously argued, the doctrine was part of the attempt to do away with politics by reducing the political process to management tasks of the state apparatus.

Thus the DSN acquired the appearance and structure of a manual that attempts to explain every aspect of societal, political, economic, moral, religious and military life through descriptive axioms. In a 1988 interview, Hélio Jaguaribe commented that the concepts used by the ESG had no 'organizing conceptual structure'. The ESG was a collection of entries (Kumasaka and Barros 1988: 16). Jaguaribe could not be more correct. Going through the doctrine resembles reading a dictionary, but one that is not in alphabetical order and extremely confusing. ESG scholars prided themselves on claiming that the doctrine was constantly changing and that new conceptualizations were introduced with each graduating class of the institution – which presumably gave the doctrine a democratic aspect (Arruda 1980: 19). The very form in which the DSN presents concepts – in ways that resemble a technical manual – was taken very positively by its scholars, since it gave a sign of the level of rationalization of the studies conducted at the ESG (Meira Mattos 1973: 65; Távora 1983: 11). See, for instance how General Meira Mattos spoke of the doctrine: 'it is a rigorous process of scientific reasoning: divided into a system, a structure, and a technique that constitute the instruments of an ordered and consistent rationale leading to policies and strategies that will efficiently achieve the desired goals' (Meira Mattos 1975: 12). In fact, the practices of conceptual innovation of the doctrine are best summarized in the phrase 'changing to remain the same'. This occurred in two ways. First, concepts in the doctrine were simply reworded each year – always in ways that did not alter or challenge their informing ideas. Take, for instance, the concept of 'national politics'. In 1957, it was defined as 'the art of the government in conducting internal or external affairs taking into consideration the supreme interests of its national objectives' (Secco 1957: 14). In 1960, the concept was changed to 'the governance of the State with the objective of attaining and safeguarding National Objectives'. Then, in 1963, it became 'the art of formulating, attaining and maintaining National Objectives through the application of National Power' (ESG 1978: 18). The following year it was reformulated as 'the integrated set of norms, guidelines and plans organized and adopted by the Government to give body and life to National Objectives, conquering and preserving them' (Campos 1964: 23). Language tweaks were common to all other concepts of the doctrine, but they never represented meaningful changes in ESG thinking. Still, they provided the justification for ESG scholars to claim continuous studies, reflection, research and, thus, constant conceptual innovation of the doctrine. What is important to highlight here is that these were reworks of the original 1953 lecture. This is why one seldom needs to analyse different versions of the doctrine: the basic structure presented by General Távora in 1953 works in any given edition of the doctrine. Second, on trying to sum up the norms that run through political life, there was an ever-increasing need to specify and further enhance the scope of each concept. That is, the need to de-politicize political processes and to re-work them as management tasks affected the way in which each concept would be extended to cover an aspect that had been left out the year before. Let us examine the conceptualization of 'national power'. In his foundational lecture, General Távora (1983: 10–11) defined national power as 'the integral expression of all means which the Nation effectively has, at the considered moment, to promote in the international field and in the internal scope, to attain and safeguard national objectives despite existing antagonisms'. Later versions of the doctrine subdivided the concept into: *actual* national power, *potential* national power and *future* national power. Each of these was then subdivided into different *characteristics* (integration, relativity and sphere of practice) and *structural aspects* (fundaments, factors and expressions). Then, each structural aspect gained further subdivisions: geographical, political, economic, psychosocial and military aspects. Pragmatically, this meant that, once it was decided which type of national power one was dealing with (actual, potential or future), there were still forty-five variables left to examine under each sub-concept. Not only was there no room for political creativity, the doctrine also did not explain how or if different variables interacted or how the relationship between them might be configured. To be fair to ESG scholars and their institution, it is very important to highlight some conceptual breakthroughs briefly introduced in the DSN and which were not part of the 1953 lecture. Even so, as the following paragraphs demonstrate, the ideas that informed the doctrine were so deeply crystallized in the conservative and authoritarian thinking of the institution that when new conceptualizations did not conform to the overall structure of the doctrine they were rapidly dismissed. Let us examine the conceptualizations of *individual security*, *communitarian security* and *collective security*, introduced in 1972 (Arruda 1980: 27). The text that introduces individual security states:

> The **Nation** is the human substance of the **State**. In its turn, it is a duty of the state to allow the **individual** to feel endogenously secure. That is, to have solved his problems of health, education, means of subsistence, and social opportunity. Furthermore, he [the individual] must feel exogenously secure. That is, the **State** must guarantee rights such as property, the right of movement, and the protection against crimes of all forms.
>
> (Arruda 1980: 137; bold in original)

Communitarian security was presented as:

> Man is essentially a gregarious being. It is not enough to have Individual Security guaranteed. Thus, the State must also guarantee those aspects that give stability inside the communities to economic and social relations, preserving property, capital and work in the social interest.
>
> (Arruda 1980: 137)

As for collective security, it was initially presented as 'the type of security that should be provided by the state to different groups of the national collectivity in order to ensure their cultural and societal rights' (Arruda 1980: 137). Taken together, the concepts of individual, communitarian and collective security promote the same principles as that of 'human security' decades before its time. The 1994 report of the United Nations Development Programme (UNDP), in which the original concept of human security was devised, described the concept as 'safety from chronic threats such as hunger, disease and repression' and 'protection from sudden and harmful disruptions in the patterns of daily life' (UNDP 1994: 22–4). While this conceptualization of human security still works with a Westphalian perspective (Booth 2008: 321), it seeks a shift from the security of the state to the security of the people (UNDP 1994: 22). Individual security, as presented by the ESG, presented the same Westphalian-based shift in security by stating it was the duty of the state to make the individual feel secure. Likewise, Caroline Thomas's regard for 'participation in the life of the community' (Thomas 1999: 3) as an aspect of human security resembles the concept of 'communitarian security' of the ESG. In both cases, there is an explicit advocacy for the shift in focus from the state to other referent objects. Although working within a state perspective, the three aforementioned concepts inverted the logic of the DSN. The doctrine advocated the education, the surveillance, the policing of society in order to derive power from it. From this perspective, the state is the referent object and the recipient of the benefits provided by the DSN. These three conceptualizations turn that perspective around and state that the nation (the individual, society and the collectivity) should be the recipients of this power and, as such, have their basic civil, social and political rights guaranteed by the state. Furthermore, since ESG scholars did not preclude authoritarian measures to enforce national security and development, some of these ideas (especially concerning the right of movement and the protection against all forms of crimes) went against the basic assumptions of the doctrine. The conceptualizations of individual and communitarian security maintained that not only every individual but also the communities of which they were a part should be made secure. Furthermore, they put into question the basis of the doctrine by arguing that the state ought to provide – instead of attain – security. This is a breakthrough, especially since such a large part of the doctrine is about discussing, producing and reproducing the national community, while excluding what did not conform to a specific idea of national identity. Not long after they were proposed, individual and communitarian security were dropped from the doctrine altogether, whereas 'collective security' was adopted with a different meaning: 'collective security is the strengthening of National Power through the mutual support established with other centres of National Power'. That is, the original concept of collective security was altered to mean the collective security of Western capitalist countries. This shows that the DSN was conceived to correspond to a closed and crystallized set of ideas. Once there were developments on the way security was thought of, they were quickly discarded because they did not conform to the founding principles of the doctrine. The next three sections examine the DSN in the light of the three analytical tools of the TEA.

TEA: 'Being'

As explored in Part I, the works of Freyre and Buarque de Holanda provided the solution to the perceived idea that the country could not develop due to its high miscegenation. The writings of these two authors influenced both civil and military realms in no small measure – to the extent that it became *the* informing view of Brazilian identity in political discourse, state policies, intellectual debates, party politics and common sense. These assumptions about Brazilian identity populate ESG writings and inform the conceptualizations of the most basic principles from which that institution derived its method of modernization. In his 1953 lecture, Juarez Távora (1983: 1) defined three concepts that composed the necessary understandings for an introduction to the DSN: society/nation, state and national power.

Society, nation and security

For the DSN, society and nation are the basic forms of collectivity in one country. The difference between them is that the nation is a later stage of the evolution of society. The two are conceptualized below:

> Society: every human group that lives together under certain structure of social phenomena, connected by common interests under the influx of certain historical and cultural processes.
>
> (Escola Superior de Guerra 1978: 102)

> Nation: society in an advanced stage of evolution in which common solidarity takes society to project itself onto the future, preserving acquired values.
>
> (Escola Superior de Guerra 1978: 102)

It is the idea of rationalization that supports the assumption that the nation is a later stage of the development of society. In this case, 'nation', as the advanced stage of society, has the underlying meaning that only a society that works in a unified manner, free of 'the method of opinions' and engaged in the process of development can be deemed a *nation*. A nation projects itself into the future, while a society is lost in arguments and in the wrong 'process of application of energy'. For the ESG, it is not society that must be made secure, it is not the irrational, passion-driven, pleasure-seeking pre-modern cordial man that needs to be defended. Rather, only those who conform to their specific idea of nation are entitled to security. It is in this context that one can understand the perennial preoccupation of ESG scholars in determining the Brazilian *national character*. The intent was to define and differentiate between the character of society (pre-modern and cordial) and the character of the nation (modern and developed). National character is the embodiment of what/who needed to be made secure through development. With that objective, Freyre and Buarque de Holanda were constantly invited to give lectures on this specific subject at the ESG. Other nationally renowned intellectuals would also hold talks on national character throughout the academic year (Lima 1953; Madeira 1955; Mota Filho 1958; Guerreiro Ramos 1960; Carneiro 1966). Invariably, guest lecturers were invited to come up with a list of good and bad character traits in Brazilian identity as if to help the ESG community identify what or who should be made secure. In 1967, the ESG published a list of the basic and complementary qualities of the Brazilian character. The 'basic characteristics' were those that they wished to preserve, while the 'complementary attributes' were to be eschewed from the national character. The former included 'exuberance, idealism, adaptability, improvisation, communicability, sense of humour, pacifist vocation' (Arruda 1967: 7–9). Lecturers at the ESG then proposed many complementary characters, such as superficiality, sentimentalism, impatience, inconstancy, sadomasochism (!), corruption, *personalismo*, weak convictions and lack of motivation among many others (Arruda 1980: 165–200). Antônio Arruda provides another example where an attempt is made to secure the traits that are perceived as Western/rational while excluding those that simply are not. He asks himself 'what are the future perspectives of the Brazilian National Character?' and responds with 'concerning some characteristics of negative connotation, those culture traits inherited from the Native Indians and the Africans, they correspond to a stage of economic or social evolution and there is a possibility of change. This is the case with carelessness and mysticism, etc' (Arruda 1980: 198). That is, national security, as the security of the rationalized nation, was based on views and meanings that placed black and indigenous peoples on the pre-modern end of the spectrum (in the TEA terms), whereas the white/Western archetype figured as rational, and hence within the parameters of national character that needed to be made secure. Such hierarchy of cultures and the allocation of 'national' to traits perceived as being rational/Western/white were not novel in Brazilian politics. D'Ávila (2003) has shown how the modification and rationalization of race and men were central to education and health policies throughout the first Vargas government. He wrote:

> Schools would provide the resources of basic health and culture that could earn children, regardless of their colour, the social category of white. Educators, social scientists, and policymakers spared little energy or expense in building a state role in mediating Brazil's escape from the determinist trap of blackness.
>
> (D'Ávila 2003: 7)

'Being black' was a social category rather than a racial one, and the first Vargas government threw itself at the possibility of making the marginalized classes – whether black or white – escape their blackness. The novelty in the post-1945 era is that the possibility of socially undoing the blackness of the population was now within the scope of national security. National security implied a requirement of class status (both economic and racial) in order to qualify as the subject of security. Hence Távora's assertion in the 1953 lecture concerning national security: 'It should be conceptualized, before anything, as a social condition, something that national leaders believe necessary to the well-being of the nation' (Távora 1983: 12–13). His assertion also implied that the 'national leaders' stand outside the pre-modern condition of society. Leaders are *national*, thus rational, Western and socially white. Theirs is the role of proposing prescriptions that will set the population free of its blackness and lack of development. This builds on the idea of blackness being a non-permanent condition and, as such, remediable through policies that can promote the social category of being white (D'Ávila 2003: 6–8). In this context, the first classes of graduates of the ESG – grouped at the ADESG – proposed a series of conferences entitled *O Problema da Recuperação Moral do País* (The Problem of Moral Recovery of the Country). The central concern of the conferences was to 'thoroughly review many social sectors on the moral plane and propose appropriate measures to mend them' (ADESG 1955: 1). From 1955, the ESG held these conferences yearly, since 'the preservation of spiritual, moral and national values of the Brazilian character constitute one of the Permanent National Objectives of the doctrine' (capitalization in the original Fragoso 1975: 192). Some of the policies that were influenced by these conferences will be explored in the following sections.

State, national power and security

The conceptualization of the state in the DSN is 'an entity of a political nature which exercises jurisdictional control over the nation and whose resources it has to achieve and maintain National Objectives' (original capitalization; ESG 1978: 103). It is necessary to highlight that it is the resources of the nation (and not of society) which enable the state to maintain its national objectives. In this sense, it is the existence of a nation with specific traits worthy of being made secure that ultimately gives the state the national power. Another point deserving of further exploration is that the state is the only concept that is not subdivided into other categories such as actual/future or potential/real. This is due to the state being perceived as a sort of barometer of rationality both inside and outside the country. Again, the *personalista* culture of cordial men transcends the realm of personal relationships into public governance and renders the state its *patrimonial* characteristic. The DSN perceives the same sort of relationship between the nation, the state and the international. That is, if society is not rationalized enough, the state suffers from the same general character flaws. The state is the reflection of the nation. Therefore, the state is only as strong as the rationalized/Western/ white nation that it makes secure. Following from this line of reasoning, the status of the state vis-à-vis other like-units (thus, the 'international') is the ultimate test of the level of rationality attained by the nation. The state is, at the same time, a reflection of what is 'national' (white/Western/rational) and a source of comparison of one nation with others in the 'international'. That is, the state is a mirror of modernization. This explains not only the need to make the nation (and not society) secure – prioritizing those who ultimately give the state its positive rational traits – but also reveals the fetishization of becoming a great power that has dominated Brazilian political and academic discussions for decades. In this sense, becoming a great power, or a rationalized state, is the ultimate proof of the country's successful modernization. This is where the third pillar of the basic concepts of the DSN, national power, finds reasoning. Unlike the state, one can tamper with and enhance national power, since it is 'the integral expression of all means the Nation effectively has to promote in the international field and in the internal scope' (Távora 1983: 10–11). That is, national power does not come from the state but from the nation; the state is but a reflection of national power. Furthermore, Távora (1983: 11) asserts that national power depends on 'political, psychosocial, military, and economic factors of the nation'. His further division of national power into four major characteristics is not only a dramatic search for signs of development, but it also provides the basis for exclusion, since the aim of the doctrine is to 'properly counter irrationality and inefficiency'(former president General Castello Branco cited in Arruda 1980: XI). Thus, *being* concerned primarily the pedagogic role attributed to national security and, as such, it looked inwardly (to the people) as the potential source of power. It used bodily metaphors for the state and referred to political dissidence as 'cancerous cells' (Couto e Silva 1958: 30) that needed to be removed, and it proposed to mend character deviation and disruptive moral values. The DSN implies the acceptance of authoritarian measures to rationalize society. It was thus overtly concerned with policing, scrutinizing, educating, mending and tampering with the people in order to obtain the rationalized source of power it perceived to be necessary.

TEA: 'Becoming'

The second tenet of the TEA refers to two ideas. The first one is the endpoint of social theorizing – the development of the state. The second one is the constant comparison with states perceived to be rational/Western/white. *Becoming* then adopts an outward perspective on the world. It is driven by an aspiration to be part of the select group of Western Christian democracies. As a project, becoming means being politically included in the West through rationalization, which was summarized by Golbery as:

> The only West that is lasting and coherent, the West that can actually and clearly be distinguished from other civilizations and cultures, is the West as an ideal, the West as a purpose, the West as a program. What is this ideal, this purpose, this program that impels, galvanizes and supports Western civilization? Let us summarize it in its essential terms: Science as a tool of action, Democracy as the formula of political organization, and Christianity as the supreme ethical standard of social coexistence.
>
> (Couto e Silva 1958: 231)

Becoming part of the West implied looking out to the international environment and displaying the strength gathered from national power. As such, the side of the DSN associated with becoming is preoccupied with the place that Brazil occupies in the world. Take, for instance, the term *inserção internacional*, widely used to mean the strategies pursued by one country in order to insert itself in the group of developed nations. The phrase started to be used in the 1950s (Lessa 2005a: 38), in both civilian and military literature, regardless of political orientation or professional affiliation. Used throughout South/Latin America, its literal translation to English is 'international insertion'. *Inserção internacional* is both reflective of and charged with this idea of *becoming* developed. This outward look derives from the perception that the signs of development and power are awarded by the international environment. This is where the West as a project finds its place. In the DSN, 'becoming' the West is a teleological goal that is perceived as a sign of development and greatness, the ultimate objective of social theorizing. One can apprehend this underlying meaning in the DSN through some of the 'Permanent National Objectives' (PNO) of the doctrine: sovereignty; strengthening of international prestige; international respect; international projection of Brazil; and affirmation of hegemony in South America (Arruda 1980: 87). In a 1954 paper, Távora (1983: 10) expanded the list of the PNOs to include 'political independence, consolidation of the unity of the national group through the effective occupation of the territory and better political, economic, and social integration, the strengthening of economic structure and prestige of the Nation in the international realm and sovereignty'. However, the DSN never clearly provided any detail as to how Brazil is supposed to attain these objectives or how one can check whether they have been attained. In this sense, the PNOs are much like the concept of the state in the Doctrine – they are supposed to be taken as a reflection of a successful method of modernization.

Becoming in conflict

When it comes to the outward gaze of *becoming* in DSN writings, an interesting discursive conflict develops. The establishment of the TEA as the political and academic common sense added another layer of concern for Brazilian identity: thinking about the international. This required social theorizing to include the comparison with states perceived to be rational (Souza 2006b: 104). Furthermore, it required thinking about Brazil's place in the international system, the place it ought to occupy and whether the system was fair. Therefore, if on the one hand ESG intellectuals defended the West as a project, on the other they had to grasp the consequences of the West and the power relations it imposed on others. Lest we forget, most of the theorizing done in relation to underdevelopment is expressed through moral exhortations by intellectuals who claim to speak in the name of the subaltern when, in fact, there is no place for agency *of* the subaltern. Thus, when speaking of the international realm, ESG intellectuals resorted to a moralizing discourse in the name of the underdeveloped peoples. The discursive conflict of becoming arises from the fact that the endpoint of theorization is to become an equal to those states which they simultaneously argue are the source of unfairness in the world. At times, like the aforementioned 'the West as a project', it is clear that the objective of becoming is to be a Western Christian democracy. At other times, the international system in which these countries are hegemonic is portrayed as the very source of underdevelopment of other countries. Let us look at some examples in the 1953 lecture. Távora presents a view of a world system composed of sovereign/independent nation-states in which international relations constitute 'the sum of contacts among the national politics of these states' whose conflicting interests have negative effects on the system as whole (Távora 1983: 11). The greatest consequence of these negative effects is *um mundo sem lei* (a lawless world) in which 'only the great powers are able to successfully apply their national politics by manoeuvring their own power and attaining real projection in the international realm' (1983: 11–12). Following his argument, Távora criticizes the differentiation among countries through the establishment of permanent seats on the United Nations Security Council (1983: 12). At times, his idea is to become a great power alongside the West, since 'in this world only the great powers are in a condition to apply their national politics with any real impact on the international realm' (1983: 12). In another passage of this lecture, Távora (1983: 14) comments on the role of Brazil in denouncing certain international practices:

> Externally, and on one side, the restraint of imperialist greed that poisons the relationship between developed States and underdeveloped Nations through the war against the international trusts and its political links; and, on the other side, the definitive abolition of the colonialist anachronism which is generating structural crises among the colonized people.

From the passages above, one can perceive the inconsistency in approach presented by the ESG. On the one hand, there is a latent wish to become a Western Christian democracy, on the other, the lecturer himself recognizes the need to change the practices of that same group of countries. Significant here is the lack of engagement in changing the very status quo that he perceives to be cynical (Távora 1983: 12).

Another example can be also found in the writings of Golbery – the same intellectual who proposed the West as a project. Here is another passage by him:

> And, in the framework of this creative and affirmative politics of peace, Brazil cannot, in face of a world populated by misery and hunger and by expansionist ambitions that are neither insignificant nor remote, deny itself a role in the concert of nations in favour of the redemption of the social-economic periphery of which it is part and which tragically extends from the Andes to the whole of Africa, from the Middle East, to the Indian peninsula and to Southeast Asia until the confines of the Indonesian world.
>
> (Couto e Silva 1959: 96)

The picture of the world provided by Golbery in the excerpt above seems certainly very disconnected from the 'West as a project'. Both types of moral exhortations found in these quotations are symptomatic of the kind of thinking about security provided by writings within the TEA paradigm. Beyond emotional and moral judgements, they reveal very little concern with how political and social processes affect the lives of those they claim to represent.

TEA: 'Method'

The TEA is based on the epistemology of Brazilian identity in which social theorizing is reduced to a specific point of departure and an endpoint (rationalization of Brazilian identity). Thus political and academic debates are circumscribed to the legitimacy of different *methods* of modernization. But after having analysed its concepts and assumptions, it is high time to look at how the DSN would bring about development. For ESG scholars and supporters,

> the importance of the doctrine is vital to any state, in the present stage of international relations, but ever the more essential the greater a **nation's potential resources** and the more reduced its actual power and its **ability to mobilize** those resources.
>
> (Távora 1983: 19; bold in original)

The bold in the original text implies that Brazil is a country with great resources in terms of land and natural wealth, but that society is not developed enough to make use of them. The doctrine then aimed to prescribe solutions to the discrepancy between the country's wealth and its power. It starts from the three basic pillars: society/nation, state and national power and then provides a chain of growing importance in which every concept encompasses the previous one in ascending order. Once the basis of national power (nation and natural resources) had been asserted, the rest of the doctrine was to be put into practice by the bureaucratic elite of the country. It was their role to identify national interests, turning them into national aspirations and finally define national objectives. The two following steps of the doctrine concerned the projection and integration of national interests into the national consciousness. That is, once the national interests were formulated, they needed to be planted back into the people in order to make them share the same objectives as the elite. This is how General Távora defined national objectives:

> Realities or aspirations, related to the geographic, political, economical, or social integration of a nation which, embodied in the spirit of the elite, is transmitted to the sensitivity of the people [*povo-massa*] as habits or unanimous or general necessities of the national collectivity
>
> (Távora 1959: 4–5)

There was an explicit step in the method that sought to educate the people about what their interests ought to be. National policies and national strategies were conceived in relation to national interests. It also implies a circular logic. On the one hand, national power is the starting point of the doctrine, what the nation 'has' at a given moment. On the other, the very purpose of the doctrine was to attain national security which would, in turn, give the country more national power so it would have more resources to attain more national security. As demonstrated by this brief explanation of the doctrine, the DSN was not only simplistic in its conceptualizations; it was also confused and confusing, not to say superficial in its attempt to grasp and deal with political processes. It was a thinly disguised attempt to put forward the limited set of ideas that have been explored in this chapter. So far, this book has discussed the contingencies and the interconnected nature of the relationship between intellectual thought and the various modernization waves in

Brazil since the nineteenth century. By doing so, it has unveiled the exclusionary elitism, the essentialization of identity and the meanings of 'becoming developed' that were common to both civilian and military literature. It has also analysed the relationship between the armed forces and the state, and the conservative coalition formed to support the militarization of the state during the *Estado Novo*. However, this chapter is yet to look at how these writings have affected the *worlding* of Brazil. The next section explores how those ideas were materialized into policies.

Worlding Brazil I

Worlding concerns the way in which intellectual work has been a formative part of how Brazil is represented by intellectuals both inside and outside the country. This section explores specific cases which reveal the mutual relationship between ideas in the TEA and perspectives on security. The cases of *worlding* explored here were chosen because they display the relationship between national identity and security in policies pursued at this period of Brazilian history.

At the ESG, national identity was a central aspect of national security. Only those who had the desirable traits of national identity were entitled to be made secure. As such, praising and sponsoring national identity became an inclusive part of thinking about security, of teaching Brazilians how to be Brazilian and of reproducing ideas about a form of *inserção internacional* that would make Brazil a great power. Thus, each of the policies analysed here are related to one of the aforementioned elements. The first case (the introduction of a series of obligatory subjects in schools and universities throughout the country) highlights the pedagogical tenet of the doctrine, whereas the second case (the main lines of foreign policy and its *inserção internacional*) uncovers the relationship between security, national identity and the outward look of the doctrine.

Securing national identity

Along with the educational reforms that took place after the 1964 coup, a 1969 piece of legislation established the obligatory inclusion of three additional subjects in the national curriculum at all education levels (including postgraduate studies). These three new subjects were: *Educação Moral e Cívica* (EMC, Moral and Civics Education), *Organização Social e Política Brasileira* (OSPB, Brazilian Social and Political Organization) and *Estudos Políticos Brasileiros* (EPB, Brazilian Political Studies). In order to devise and implement the national curriculum in these three new subjects, the government hired six members of the *Conselho Federal de Educação* (CFE, Federal Council of Education) and nine members of the *Comissão Nacional de Moral e Civismo* (CNMC, National Commission of Moral and Civics) (Cunha 2006: 5,095). The latter was a commission created by the aforementioned ADESG conferences on *O Problema da Recuperação Moral do País*. Pragmatically, the majority of the seats were given to ADESG members in order to make sure that national curricula on the three subjects would correspond to and follow the principles of national security

(Miranda 2004: 4). The establishment of these obligatory subjects is connected to the idea that there are certain traits of the national identity that need to be preserved and/or apprehended by Brazilians. They also made reference to the idea espoused by the most conservative sectors that Brazilian youth was perceived as the most susceptible to subversive influence. The young age of the guerrilla fighters who opposed the government led ESG scholars to claim that young people's innate passivity and irrationality made them prey to communist activism. Citing a 1969 lecture at the ESG on the bio-psychosocial youth problem, Cowan (2007: 467) commented 'only functionality in the role of the heterosexual adult could effectively resolve the violent, hysterical emotiveness that caused adolescent's proclivity for revolutionary politics'. The response to this issue was the establishment of subjects in Brazilian schools that would teach Brazilian students how to steer away from the 'communist seduction and enticement tactics' (Pereira and Medeiros 1965: 11). The decree that established the three new subjects as obligatory stated that they sought to 'maintain the strengthening of values and the projection of spiritual and ethical principles of nationality, improve one's character, and prepare the citizen for civic activities supported by moral values, patriotism and constructive action aimed at national security' (Brazil-DOU 1939b: 7769) – principles that were in tandem with the idea of selecting the traits of national character that would serve the modernization effort. These books were published in Brazil right up until the early 1990s – long after the end of the dictatorship – when a reform in education left them out of the curriculum. They contained not only a sort of diluted Doctrine of National Security but also primarily aimed at teaching Brazilian youth how to be and behave as rationalized Brazilians. In this sense, this pedagogical strategy was *worlding* the character it perceived Brazilians should have in order to serve the project of national security and development in the country. School books approved by the commission were thoroughly infused with moral and Christian values, of Brazilian identity and its connection with the effort of development. Their pedagogic practice also included equating blackness with lack of rationalization. The CNMC vetoed any extra material or mention of African and indigenous religions (Miranda 2004: 12). Let us now turn to analyse some of the manuals authorized by the commission. One of the books sought to explain the aim of development with the following passage: 'You, me, all of us are subordinated to Brazilian laws. The State has the purpose of conquering and maintaining national development. That is our fight for national security' (Hermógenes 1977: 64–5). This other passage asks each citizen to surrender to the love of the *pátria*: 'the more we love our *Pátria*, the more democratic we are. Voters and politicians must, before anything, seek the interests of the *Pátria* and to make it secure' (Correia 1976: 128). The part each pupil should play in the effort of development appeared in another book as 'the construction of Brazil may become reality tomorrow if each young person accepts the task of self-rationalization and joins in the collaboration for the development of the whole Brazilian people' (Galache *et al.* 1971: 10). The preface of this same book comments that the heroism and virtues it sets out teaches 'students to live in the rhythm of a great Brazil, to live together with all Brazilians and to accomplish with them fascinating discoveries of our *inserção internacional* from where we shall irradiate our vitality and our idealism' (my emphasis, Galache *et al.* 1971: 7). Another book gives the recipe of happiness:

> A word to the young student:
> You dream of your future and in your noble aspiration, you want to be somebody that fulfils a mission. In order to reach your ideal, you need to form you character with perfection. You need profound convictions that show you how you relate to God and with your next. You can forget neither your family, to whom you owe so much, nor that *pátria* that cradled you. There is no other way to be happy: happiness only exists to the good of character.
>
> (Correia 1976: 140)

In relation to love for the *pátria*, Braz recommends:

> the greatness of a country is not built only through the wisdom of those who command but, also, with the humility of those who follow. The great honour is not that of commanding but of commanding with rationality. Therefore, may all our hours be of service: service to the family, to society and to the *pátria*. Our *pátria* needs us to be examples of the great Brazilian character. It is only by loving our *pátria* and by making our identity a resource of security that we can break the chains that stand in the way of development.
>
> (Braz 1979: 95)

The passages referenced in this section demonstrate the guiding ideas introduced in the educational system in the early 1970s. Teaching Brazilian youth how to be Brazilians of character, permanently striving for the development of the country, was one way that the regime kept youngsters aligned with the idea of national security. The irrationality and hormonal fragility of the youth and women and the need for heterosexual male adults to guide them away from communist permissiveness meant that these sectors of society literally and figuratively coincided as those 'most likely to form the security state's soft and penetrable underbelly' (Cowan 2007: 466). Hence the insistence in these books on the role of the family and of women in that scope:

> The woman who is prepared for marriage must seek to be an expert in domestic labour and to collaborate with her husband and stimulate him in his profession and his superior ideals. It is necessary that the youth prepare themselves for marriage and for children. Children are the link between the past and the future: in one word, they are the Nationality in which the family is the main basis and vital principle.
>
> (Salgado 1971: 27)

Women are only present in these books in a supporting role to the father or as supporting actors in the education of children. Another book states 'A lot of what grandpa says comes from what grandma thinks. I have already noticed this: some think and some command. I think my turn to command will come when I am man, a father, a kind of boss' (Garcia 1972: 55). Thus the adoption of these books in schools and universities throughout Brazil not only implied that there were character traits of Brazilian nationality that were important to the modernization effort, they also sought to teach society those traits. By doing so, these books celebrated specific traits perceived to be white/rational/Western while excluding from political processes those who did not conform to those ideal traits.

Securing Brasil potência: on becoming a great power

The first example of worlding Brazil dealt with the essentialization of Brazilian culture and the assignment of roles to the national effort of development. The present case deals with another scope of that project. It explores how geopolitical ideas informed and united intellectuals and practitioners around a common goal: to determine the main principles of Brazilian foreign policy. It does so by analyzing common themes in both civilian and military literature and exploring how these are informed not only by geopolitical ideas but also the established 'Permanent National Objectives' of the doctrine. The chapter has argued that what the ESG proposed was a method of development whose ontological parameters were informed by the TEA. This teleological aim of developing the state has cemented a consensus about policy matters such as the relationship to the West, Brazilian sovereignty and *inserção internacional*. Let us go back to the geopolitical prescriptions for foreign policy. Both General Meira Mattos (1973, 1975, 1977, 1980, 1990, 2000) and General Golbery (Couto e Silva 1957, 1958, 1959, 1968) wrote extensively on geopolitics and strategy. In terms of the internal geography of the country, they identified two main areas of policy. The first was the integration of Brazil, connecting the coast to the borders with other South American countries, especially in relation to the Amazon and the Pantanal basins. The second prescription was to populate these areas in order to economically exploit them (Meira Mattos 1984: 52). As for the geostrategic importance of the country, prescriptions consisted of (a) protecting the borders with other Latin American countries, (b) protecting the Amazon, (c) strengthening bilateral and multilateral relationships with Southern Europe and Africa for the protection of the South Atlantic and, later, (d) staking a claim to Antarctica. What developed out of that, according to both civilian and military literature on foreign policy, was the necessity to construct Brazil's identity in the international realm. (The literature on Brazilian identity in International Relations has produced a plethora of studies and will be further analysed in the next chapter.) Here, I look at what became known as *Brasil Potência* (Brazil World Power) – a catchphrase of the regime that indicated that Brazil was on the path to becoming the world power it was destined to be (Couto e Silva 1957: 21). *Brasil Potência* was infused with ideas of the manifest destiny of the country and this was the point of agreement among the various sectors of intellectuals in the country (Miyamoto 1999: 85). *Brasil Potência* was in part the result of the *milagre econômico* (economic miracle) when the Brazilian economy grew on average more than 10 percent a year, spurred by massive investments in staple industries, import substitution, and the reformulation of the national financial system, including the creation of a central bank (Prado and Earp 1984; Singer 1972: 19). Such growth rates led the regime to conclude that these were signs of Brazil's rise to international power. In a 1967 lecture at the ESG, President General Costa e Silva stated:

> It is time that Brazilian identity made a statement in the international realm. As our recent history shows us, the effort of development that the Brazilian people have made is returning to us as national power. Brazilian sense of justice and love for peace shall work to bring change about, to help the less fortunate of the international system, to change the status quo and the ambitions of the great powers, to share knowledge and development, to work past the degrading conditions of a bipolar system that freezes international power in the hands of a few. The Brazilian custom of cooperation among friends shall show the world that development, not greed, is the key to the future.
>
> (Costa e Silva 1968: 4)

Thus, in the international realm, Brazilian identity was purported to be normative and ethical and, as such, granted the world the real meaning of development, of cooperation, of change in the status quo. *Brazil Potência* was a time of intense participation in multilateral forums. At the United Nations Conference on Trade and Development (UNCTAD), Brazil sought to adopt resolutions that would demand better terms of access to manufactured goods and better terms of exchange on raw materials (Cervo and Bueno 2002: 401). In 1971, it denounced the idea of 'collective security' and proposed the idea of 'collective economic security' for it

> [t]ook the problem away from the bipolar confrontation and sought to move towards the possibilities of international peace. If the rich did not want to remedy the unfair international status quo by helping the underdeveloped, at least they should not stand in the way of other people's efforts and they should eliminate the obstacles to development.
>
> (Pinto 1967: 12)

This excerpt was taken from the 1967 speech by the Ministry of Foreign Affairs, Sérgio Correa da Costa, and which introduced the foreign policy of *Brasil Potência*, the *Diplomacia da Prosperidade* (Diplomacy of Prosperity) of General Costa e Silva's government. The Diplomacy of Prosperity sought to engage in bilateral economic relations with African countries (Saraiva 1994: 305) as well as with non-aligned states (seeking to represent them in G-77) and Eastern European countries. The idea of 'economic collective security' was used to justify the refusal to sign the Non-Proliferation Treaty in 1967 and in its place the signing of the Treaty of Tlatelolco which made Latin America and the Caribbean the first region of the world to ban nuclear weapons (Wrobel 1993: 27). On that issue,

Brazilian diplomat and director of political planning of the Ministry of Foreign Affairs of the time, Paulo Nogueira Batista, stated in a lecture:

> The superpowers, in name of the preservation of a peace that they believe is only possible through the conservation of nuclear monopoly, ask us to waive that prerogative. The Brazilian government is not willing to accept that. *Our Brazilian identity* in the world leads us to believe that other fairer arrangements may be possible for the common good of all.
>
> (Martins 1975: 70, my emphasis)

Throughout the military regime, the inscription of Brazilian identity in foreign policy became commonplace both in civilian and military literature. In these texts, Brazilian identity is portrayed as being fair, legitimate, working for the greater good, and in opposition to the status quo. While it is undeniable that *Brasil Potência* was indeed a time that Brazilian diplomacy was not only assertive but also anti-establishment, there are some points that need to be raised in relation to *worlding* Brazil. In a 1976 interview, General Cordeiro de Farias, a former commander of the ESG, commented on the establishment of that institution: 'in 1948 we harvested oaks. We did not plant cabbages. Cabbages grow fast, but only once. Oaks take a long time but are solid. When the time came, we had the men, the ideas, and the means' (Dreifuss 2008: 116). The DSN is the oak to which the general referred while 'the time' was a direct allusion to the military coup that initiated the dictatorship in 1964. It is undisputable that the armed forces had the men and the means to impose the 1964 dictatorship, but the ideas they had could be summarized as a pseudo-scientific method of rationalization whose platform subsumes all aspects of societal life to the concept of national security. Their ideas involved the essentialization of both Brazilian identity and the drive to inscribe Brazil into the realm of Western Christian democracies. The conceptualization of Brazilian people as *personalista* and the Brazilian state as *patrimonialista* were charged with assumptions of pre-modernity and irrationality that only served to justify and naturalize exclusion within society – since the disenfranchised are perceived as 'pre-modern' rather than subjects of various exclusionary processes. These ideas are still present everywhere in political and academic discourse. These are the true oaks that were planted in Brazilian culture. They were not buried with the dictatorship that advocated them. The true oaks have been harvested for eight decades and have been central to the way Brazil has been worlded.

5 Security as foreign policy

The aim of this chapter is to explore the development of thinking about security in Brazilian IR between 1985 and 2010. Before that can be attempted, however, there is a need to establish the framework within which this form of thinking about security took place. The institutional and political context of the development of thinking about security in academia differs from that examined in previous chapters. As much as policy-advising power may be claimed by academic circles, Brazilian IR intellectuals are not able to legislate and/or establish state institutions (as was the case with the authoritarian sector of the armed forces in Chapter 3). They also do not have a closed body of thought that is concentrated and produced in one institution alone (as was the case of the ESG in Chapter 4). Thus, as part of an academic discipline, thinking about security needs to be contextualized within the general conditions of development of the discipline of Brazilian IR, the academic establishment that has harboured it and the historic conditions of its establishment. The chapter starts by exploring the development of the education system in Brazil and its relation to the ideas of national security. It then explores the history of IR as an academic discipline in Brazil as a way of politically contextualizing the place of IR intellectuals in the country. Finally it explores the idea of Brazilian identity in International Relations, laying the groundwork for the analysis of IR through the tenets of the TEA and worlding Brazil.

Brazilian authoritarian regimes and higher education

Chapter 4 briefly explored some of the consequences of the interplay between national security and identity in the educational system. It examined how the perceived need to make certain character traits and behaviours secure was materialized as new subjects were introduced to the education system. The textbooks analysed then represented a single policy within a much wider strategy that was introduced by the *Estado Novo* dictatorship and then reintroduced by the 1964 regime. The overall project was to inscribe the educational system within the modernization effort by socially engineering its rationale, embedding it into society through education (D'Ávila 2003: chap. 2). This section argues that this objective guided reforms at all levels of the education system, from primary school to postgraduate research. The institutionalization of the contemporary university system and academic disciplines was deeply indebted to the authoritarian projects of the *Estado Novo* and the military dictatorship. In the 1940s, the *Estado Novo* established its basis and, nearly three decades later, the 1964 military regime expanded it to other states of the federation. This produced not only the political place of the university and academic research – aiding state development – but also charged these activities with preconceived notions of identity, development and rationality. The establishment of the higher education system was also accompanied by the severe exclusion of debates and progressive intellectuals. This had long-term consequences for the way that disciplines developed and staked their claim to authoritative knowledge, since it was within this perspective that, with rare exceptions, most of the social sciences developed in Brazil. For example, in the 1930s, the regime not only shut down the (for that era) innovative *Universidade do Distrito Federal* (UDF, University of the Federal District) in Rio de Janeiro, but also promoted a witch-hunt in academic departments, cancelled programmes in the humanities that incentivized research and had links with the local community, and then absorbed surviving programmes and staff into the more regime-compliant *Universidade do Brasil* (UB, University of Brazil) (Bonemy 1999; Fávero 2007). As the model for future federal universities around the country, the UB was set up to be a centre of formation of Brazilian civilian bureaucracy. Given its main objective of providing the state-building project of *Estado Novo* with an educated labour force, there was seldom any interest in sponsoring research in the social sciences. Until the end of the regime, research in university remained outside the agenda. In this context, universities fit the purpose of development. After the Second World War, the return to democracy provided new opportunities to the social sciences in Brazil. The lift of censorship, the relaxation of the Law of National Security, the end of the Tribunal of National Security and proposals of university autonomy from the central government led to greater productivity in the area and to collaboration opportunities with institutions outside Brazil (Filho 2005: 387, Oliveira 1995: 261–72, Trindade 2007: 75–91). Still, the university system remained untouched and there were no incentives to conduct research in universities. In São Paulo, research sponsorship was granted by the local state, while in Rio research sponsorship was reserved for governmental think-tanks such as Instituto Superior de Estudos Brasileiros (ISEB, Higher Institute of Brazilian Studies), ESG and other national institutions of specialized knowledge in areas of policy interest (Morel 1979: 50; Lamounier 1982: 416; Trindade 2007). Since funds were only available for governmental think-tanks and policy-advising specialized agencies, research channels were developed outside universities' state-induced demand. This promoted further alienation of research by universities and as such students were seldom in contact with research-oriented academia (Forjaz 1979: 14–15; Morel 1979: 60–3). A similar process to that of the establishment of the higher education system took place in the late 1960s and early 1970s under the military regime. After the initial process of persecution and repeal of political dissidence in the country (Morel 1979, 60–3), the regime put forward a new reform in the education system that encompassed primary, secondary and higher education. As it had happened during the *Estado Novo*, prior to the university reform, entire research teams were dismissed and prohibited from working due to their political affiliations. Between 1964 and 1973, many intellectuals of research institutes and university professors were expelled from the education system, while many others went into exile (Morel 1979: 62–3). Both processes of institutionalization and professionalization of academic social sciences were not only highly guarded by the regime, but also very restricting concerning the kind of authoritative knowledge it aimed at producing. Regarding the shape of the institutional setup of higher education, Gustavo Capanema (Minister of Education) wrote in a 1941 letter to Getúlio Vargas:

> there is a need to think carefully about what sort of university system we need to have. Knowledge may be dangerous for the system if it is not used for development in the national cause. Sometimes it is better to have *technicians* who can operate machines than educated ones who wish to destroy them.
>
> (Capanema 1982: 50; my emphasis)

Twenty-five years later, the then president Marshall Castelo Branco made reference to the higher education reform that his government was going to implement:

> No country can attain prosperity without the foundations of science and technique, without counting on technicians who are able to respond to the growing demands of progress. There is an intimate relationship between national wealth and the proportion of *technicians* in any collectivity. It is of utmost importance that we promote the education of *technicians* who will be responsible for national development in our own universities, institutes, academies, and laboratories.
>
> (Castelo Branco 1966: 3; my emphasis)

The lapse of a quarter of a century seems to be the only thing separating the first statement from the second. In each one of them, the word 'technician' appears as a central concept for the intended purposes of higher education. The word in Portuguese, *técnico*, describes a person who has specialized knowledge and uses it to implement solutions, without questioning the assumptions and basis of their work. Thus the university system in Brazil was set up and later reformed with the same purpose: educating individuals who would support the reform without questioning its principles. The overall project was to inscribe the educational system within the modernization effort by socially engineering its rationale (D'Ávila 2003: chap. 2).

The institutionalization of the federal university system (set up by Capanema in the 1940s) sought to 'prepare the elites that will take on the state bureaucracy and to integrate them in the life of the state' (cited in Prado 2001: 16), since it was to be 'maintained and directed by the state, with a view to have an important function in the national character and development' (Brazil 1935: 29). This refers back to the recurring ideas of rationalization of society and depoliticization of political processes analysed in previous chapters. It is therefore from this perspective that, with rare exceptions, most of the Brazilian social sciences were developed. This produced not only the political place of the university and academic research in the country – aiding state development – but also charged the practice of social sciences with preconceived notions of identity, development and rationality. Although the overall aim of the establishment and expansion of the higher education system in Brazil has had an effect in the kind of social science (and scientist) that the country has produced, there are multiple layers to this process that also need to be investigated. How can one account for the emphasis not only on state development but also on the widespread adoption of the terms of the TEA in the production of authoritative knowledge? Here, the work of intellectuals who lived under the last regime may shed light on this issue. Forjaz (1989: 82) comments that, under constant persecution, universities became highly politicized as the place of intellectual resistance to the regime and that was reflected in their research choices. Reflecting on the development of political science in her generation, Forjaz (1997: 1) stated that, even though the state had historically been the main referent in Brazilian social theorizing, 'post-1964 there was an accentuation of that tendency' due to the perceived need among intellectuals to 'understand the conservative mode of modernization that had maximized state intervention'. She goes on to say:

> Slowly, the 'primacy of the state', the 'prominence of the state', became the norm of sociological and political production in Brazil. It was around the 1970s that statism became fully dominant. It was around that time that it became fashionable in Brazil to read Gramsci. It was exactly because of his criticism of economic determinism and his ideas concerning the place of intellectuals in the state.
>
> (Forjaz 1997: 1)

Being educated under the regime, Forjaz speaks about the mindset and the political questions faced by her generation. The will to resist and apprehend their time and place as intellectuals led that generation to focus even more vehemently on the state as the main referent of social theorizing. Where Gramsci sought to transcend Marxian economic materialism with the idea of culture, Forjaz's generation perceived in it a way to criticize the regime's propaganda about the *milagre econômico* (Singer 1972; Prado and Earp 1984: 210). Where Gramsci explored the place of intellectuals in the state, this generation perceived themselves to be in a war of position over the state against the regime (Coutinho 2009: 39–40). Sorj (2008: 66–9) perceives the dictatorship to have engendered the mode of research imposed on this community. The state-commissioned studies that would serve to support policy-advising and policy-making thus employing a large proportion of these social scientists in the state bureaucracy (Sorj 2008: 69). That is, if, on the one hand, there was a perception that intellectuals were waging a war of position against the regime, on the other, it was the dictatorial regime which ultimately employed and provided the conditions for the development of academic social sciences in Brazil. In turn, social scientists were dependent on the regime for jobs and research funding. Both sides worked with a common understanding that there was a development imperative guiding their role in the country (Morel 1979: 60; Sorj 2008: 72). On this aspect, Sorj asserts that he finds the growth in decision-making power of anti-establishment intellectuals and their peaceful coexistence with the dictatorship quite impressive (2008: 69). This 'peaceful existence' should perhaps not be so surprising. As previously argued, it was the discourse of a strong national state and the need for economic developments that prevailed and were common to both sides. That is, the level of disagreement in Brazilian politics has more often than not been restricted to the *method* of modernization, while the *being* and *becoming* of the state are commonly shared assumptions among the many political sectors. It was in this context of expansion of the university system and the perceived need for providing the state bureaucracy with technicians with knowledge of 'the international' that the first IR undergraduate programme was established at the University of Brasília.

Brazilian IR

Before 1973, university programmes regarding the 'international' were restricted to a few modules taught around the country scattered in different undergraduate programmes – most commonly history and law (Almeida 2006: chap. 1). Outside the university system, few research centres and journals displayed an interest in international themes (Soares de Lima and Cheibub 1983: 4–48; Almeida 2006: 94–110). Publications of studies on international relations were confined to a few journals of small circulation, some papers in non-specialized journals and non-academic research centres (Almeida 2006: 94). Censorship and lack of funding are generally cited for the great discontinuity in the teaching programmes, journals and publications aimed at international politics (see Almeida 2006). Of the two journals strictly dedicated to international politics that were set up between 1930 and 1973, only one remains active – *Revista Brasileira de Política Internacional* (RBPI) – while the other – *Política Externa Independente* – was shut down by the regime within the first year of the 1964 coup. The institutionalization of IR in Brazilian academia followed the same principles of rationalization applied to the state bureaucracy and education of specialized staff (*técnicos*) to aid the development effort. At the height of *milagre econômico*, there was a consensus in government that Brazil would soon need more *técnicos* prepared to deal with the impending *inserção internacional* of the country. Thus, the government sponsored the establishment of the first undergraduate course of International Politics in Brazil in 1974. Antônio Lessa's account on the 'birth' of academic IR at the University of Brasília in 1974 states:

> The aim of the program was to train professionals that would be able to engage with the activities of the state related to the internationalization of Brazil. The idea that guided the creation of this course came from the perception that the official institutions (beyond the Ministry of Foreign Affairs) needed to

create and prepare administrative structures that were able to engage with policy-advising and policy-making of public policy that were greatly connected to the possibilities opened by Foreign Policy. The professional formed in this new degree could aspire to a peculiar career that would be developed in the State bureaucracy and in the external interfaces of private and public economy. S/he would exercise new functions that arose from the new international profile that Brazil was acquiring: taking part and giving support to the programs of expansion of foreign trade in the diverse governmental agencies that dealt with the subject.

(Lessa 2005a: 35–6)

Being a member of staff at the University of Brasília, Lessa seems to have little doubt about what concerns the birth of academic IR in Brazil. Its main objective had little to do with the encouragement of research in this area and was clearly focused in training state bureaucracy for the 'development effort'. Lessa was not the only one to put forward that argument. Myiamoto supported the same assumption when he stated:

The growth of the field of IR, academically speaking, takes place when the country projects itself in the international stage. The greater the position enjoyed by the country, the more the study [of IR] will also grow in a directly proportional manner, making it possible to even set up institutions outside the country which are concerned with studying the Brazilian reality, e. g. the Centre of Brazilian Studies at the University of Oxford.

(Miyamoto 1999: 96)

The literature is quick to make the connection between the period of *Brasil potência* and/or *milagre econômico* and the need to develop an area of research that was able to meet the country's international needs. Anyone reading the history of Brazilian IR as told by its academics is seldom faced with the political issues that surrounded the institutionalization of the discipline (see Miyamoto 1999; Herz 2002a; Lessa 2005a). Another example of this connection drawn between the development of IR as a discipline and the needs of the state is found in a 1977 government report in which Brazilian Political Sciences are reviewed. It is through this report's analysis that one can understand the assumed relationship between the state and the need to develop specialized knowledge. The report states:

The abandoned condition of the area of 'international relations' in Brazil is due to two processes. The first one concerns the fact that interest in this area is greater in countries that have an active role in the international system – which has not been the case of Brazil. The second reason is due to the distinctiveness of the Brazilian diplomatic body. Studies about the international had been confined to the diplomatic service and, thus, had been established outside the university system.

(Schwartzman 1977: 1)

According to the report, this tendency was bound to change once 'the participation of Brazil in the international stage increases and the internal relevance of the international system becomes the object of general attention' (Schwartzman 1977: 1). The reasoning in the 1977 report are shared by contemporary scholars of IR (see Miyamoto 1999; Herz 2002a; Santos and Fonseca 2009; Lessa 2005a, 2005b, 2005c). The institutionalization of the discipline did not aim to promote research but to produce *técnicos* who would be familiarized with the interface between national and international in the conduction of state affairs. That is, academic and governmental circles both shared the assumption that the development of IR studies in Brazil was strictly connected to the wider state project of *inserção internacional*. In sum, the perception of a connection between the increased participation of Brazil in the international realm and the institutionalization of IR as an academic discipline reflects an underlying idea that the role of Brazilian academic intellectuals is to aid the state and the development of the country. Furthermore, as discussed in the following sections, the coupling of this specific birth of Brazilian academic IR with the TEA had severe consequences for knowledge production put forward by the discipline since then. It produced a discipline that specializes in thinking and theorizing about the international but whose primary focus is to discuss Brazil's *inserção internacional*. Take, for instance, the place of theorization in Brazilian IR. Let us start by going back to the 1977 report. According to its author, there were no researchers working on the topic of political theory. The report goes on to justify the lack of research in political theory:

> Traditionally, political theory does not have a tendency to be a line of research *per se*. It is either conducted by the researcher as an individual activity or it is connected to theorization concerning empirical research in another area. In Brazil, there is not the idea that a study in political theory may become a project of research for its own merits. It is also possible that this area is destitute due to the young age of the majority of these professionals since theorizing in social sciences requires a high level of intellectual maturity.
>
> (Schwartzman 1977: 1)

The idea that political theory is enough to justify research on its own merit relates back to Souza's critique of the contemporary state of social theorizing in Brazil. The lack of interest in theory has led academic discussion to a nearly pre-Kantian state in which there is a commonly shared idea that reality can be apprehended by sensible and immediate observation without the need for abstraction and conceptualization (Souza 2006a: 118). The assumption that empirical and relevant knowledge does not need theorization paves the way for social theorization being little more than common-sense ideas structured in an academic fashion. As this chapter argues, this is still one of the main tenets of Brazilian IR. The 1977 report highlights the grim state of the art of IR in the late 1970s. It listed only two practising researchers in the field of international politics (Schwartzman 1977). One was Maria Regina Soares de Lima, at the *Instituto Universitário de Pesquisas do Estado do Rio de Janeiro* (IUPERJ, University Institute of Research of the State of Rio de Janeiro), who worked on foreign policy. The other was (future president of Brazil) Fernando Henrique Cardoso, who was working on Dependency Theory at *Centro Brasileiro de Análise e Planejamento* (CEBRAP, Brazilian Centre of Analysis and Planning) in São Paulo. That is, 4 years after the institutionalization of the first IR programme in Brazil, there were only two people conducting research in IR: one was in the USA (undertaking her PhD studies) and the other was not employed by a university and, therefore, did not train other researchers. In the 40 years since the institutionalization of the first IR undergraduate programme in 1973, Brazilian IR undergraduate and postgraduate courses have multiplied around the country. Well over one hundred undergraduate degrees in IR have been officially recognized by the Brazilian Ministry of Education (INEP 2010). Three-quarters of these courses started their activities after 2000. Figure 5.1 is a comparison of the growth of undergraduate and postgraduate programmes in IR.

From Figure 5.1, one can see that the growth in research programmes is far more modest than undergraduate degrees. Of the ten PhD programmes presented here, only two are degrees offered specifically on IR. The others offer IR as a line of research within a political science programme. Until the early 2000s, fewer than twenty MPhil theses in IR were secured per year and, even as late as 2010, the number of successful PhD theses completed yearly in IR had not increased. The majority of programmes are located in the southeast of Brazil, which makes contacts, meetings, conferences and networking relatively contained in one area even though the country is of continental proportions (Santos and Fonseca 2009: 357). Although no official numbers about students and/or professors are available for the specific area of IR (since it is subsumed under political science), the small number of programmes and theses completed each year may give an idea of the limited scope of this area in Brazil. Concerning professional associations in the discipline between 1980 and 1994, there was an IR working group at the *Associação Nacional de Pós-Graduação e Pesquisa em Ciências Sociais* (ANPOCS, National Association of Social Sciences Post-Graduation and Research). However, due to its limited number of participants, the group was excluded from the

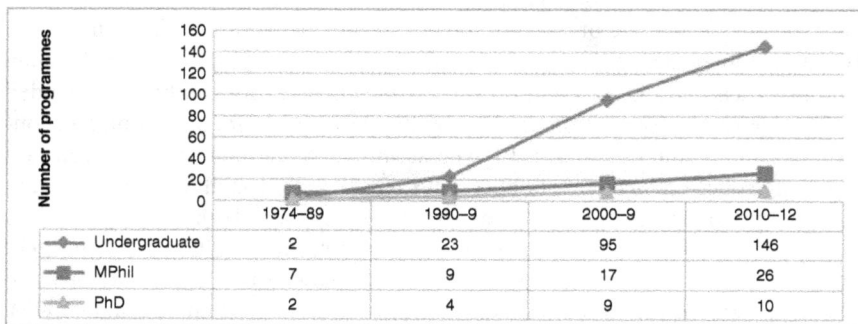

	1974–89	1990–9	2000–9	2010–12
Undergraduate	2	23	95	146
MPhil	7	9	17	26
PhD	2	4	9	10

Figure 5.1 IR programmes offered in Brazil, 1974–2012.

association in 1994 and was only allowed to return in 2000 (Miyamoto 1999: 90). In 2005, the group established the *Associação Brasileira de Relações Internacionais* (ABRI, Brazilian Association of International Relations), which has held biannual meetings since 2007. During fieldwork, I attended the first meeting of ABRI in Brasília at the end of July 2007. I took the opportunity to have informal conversations with panellists and attendees. I was especially interested in those who composed the discipline of IR in Brazil and how they perceived its development in recent years. The first issue that stood out was the strong sense of community that pervaded most of these conversations. In talking about IR, these scholars talked about *we*, the Brazilian IR community, which comprises not only scholars but also military staff, diplomats, journalists and a few politicians. I found strong resistance to the idea that the IR field in Brazil was composed only of its scholars. For most of its history, 'community' has been the word used by Brazilian IR intellectuals themselves in reference to those who share the same broad research interests in international issues. The phrase *Comunidade Brasileira de Relações Internacionais* (Brazilian Community of International Relations) is often used in the literature to describe the wider range of diplomats, military officers and academics who work in the field (for some examples, see Almeida 1998: 49; Cervo 2001: 14; Lessa and Almeida 2004: 2; Soares de Lima 2005a: 10; Souza 2008). To that end, I was often corrected and reminded that Brazilian IR was not a discipline, it was a general field or area of knowledge that also included non-academic members around which an internally coherent *field* of International Relations was created (for a work that uses the same definition of 'field', see Schmidt 1998: 245). Despite their different professional affiliations, the community has no rifts between members of the armed forces, the diplomatic body and academics. Most importantly, members of this community share particularly homogenous views about not only what the discipline is, but also its history, its agenda and their political role as intellectuals in Brazil. Having been a member of that community, I knew this before I went to Brazil on fieldwork. However, the extent to which ideas about the role of intellectuals and the development of Brazil were ingrained and ossified amongst its members (from early postgraduate students to senior researchers, high-ranking officers and diplomats) only began to dawn on me during my fieldwork. With close colleagues with whom I had previously shared the nature of my research, I could discuss my views on the discipline in Brazil. I clearly remember one of them telling me what I should and should not mention about critical security in my interviews. His/her words were:

> Well, you cannot mention you are looking at security thinking in Brazilian IR from a critical perspective. You need to rephrase that as the history of the concept of security in Brazil. Just drop 'critical', drop it. Seriously. They will say you were paid by the Brazilian government to take a PhD and now you are turning against them with these foreign perspectives that only serve other powers. And you know how it is, once one of them drops you, word will go around and you might as well just give up your fieldwork.

It was the first time I could not openly speak my mind. From my family, I had learned that to voice my ideas was one of my most important rights. I had learned that one should speak truth to power and, until then, I had only been in positions where I needed not be afraid of doing so. But those 6 months in my own country, speaking my own language, amongst people I had known, read and looked up to, were a constant exercise of silence, of holding myself back from speaking truth to power in my discipline. The fact that ideas were so crystallized and widely shared in the discipline made me realize early in my fieldwork that, outside biographical differences, each ensuing interview would be the same as the one before and that I would have to continue to exercise restraint and constantly rephrase my words in my mind before I could speak. Upon sharing these thoughts with a friend in São Paulo, they said, jokingly, 'you should have just done one interview and made fifty copies of it. . . less costly and just as accurate'. The following sections will make this statement more obvious. Let us move on to the main IR journals in the country.

Revista Brasileira de Política Internacional and Contexto Internacional (1985–2010)

In order to provide an overview of knowledge production in Brazilian IR between 1985 and 2010, this section explores work published in the two most prestigious IR journals in Brazil, namely, the aforementioned RBPI and *Contexto Internacional* (CI). These journals offer a consistent sample of the main debates, discussions and research agenda in Brazilian IR. First, they are published by the two main IR departments in Brazil. The *Instituto de Relações Internacionais* (iREL) at Universidade de Brasília (UnB) publishes RBPI, while CI is published by *Instituto de Relações Internacionais* (IRI) at Pontifícia Universidade Católica do Rio de Janeiro (PUC-Rio). Second, both of these journals have published consistently and regularly since their first issue more than half a century (in the case of RPBI) and more than 25 years (CI) ago. They both have the highest grade given for a national journal (A2) by the Brazilian Ministry of Education's ranking system. Third, RBPI was also the first journal specifically dedicated to thinking about the 'international' in Brazil. It was derived from the *Instituto Brasileiro de Relações Internacionais* (IBRI), set up in 1954 in Rio de Janeiro. IBRI was established outside the university system in post-Second World War Brazil. In this sense, it followed the logic of other think-tanks established during the democratic interregnum such as the ESG and ISEB (Debert 1986: chap. 3). In 1993, the University of Brasília incorporated both think-tank and journal, where they remain active (Almeida 1998: 45). As for CI, it has been published since 1985 by IRI. IRI was established in 1979 as an institute of research within PUC-Rio. Its masters programme dates back to 1987, while the PhD programme was established in 2001. Table 5.1 refers to the total number of papers published in the two journals and the country of origin of authors.

Table 5.1 Breakdown of papers published by RBPI and CI. Data divided according to authors' nationalities and geographic subject of paper

	Brazilian authors		Non-Brazilian authors	
Subject	Brazil	Other	Brazil	Other
Number of papers	*413*	*244*	*7*	*126*

Table 5.2 Papers on security published by RBPI and CI (1985–2010)

	Brazilian	Non-Brazilian
CI (1985–2010)	22	19
RBPI (1985–2010)	32	4
Total	54	23

As may be perceived from the numbers presented in Table 5.1, the focus of Brazilian IR has been much more on Brazil than on the international. If one examines only works authored by members of the Brazilian IR community, more than 63 percent of all papers published between 1985 and 2010 were on Brazil whereas the total number of papers on other geographic areas and theoretical issues accounted for 27 per cent. Of the 413 papers published by Brazilian authors on Brazil, nearly 80 per cent (or 329 articles) were primarily on Brazilian foreign policy. That is, the main object of Brazilian IR is specifically the state and its foreign policy. As such, it is not the state that takes political precedence over other referent objects. It is the *Brazilian* state that is at the centre of intellectual reflection in Brazilian IR. Let us now look at papers on security published by RBPI and CI between 1985 and 2010. Table 5.2 shows the number of papers published by Brazilian and non-Brazilian nationals in both RBPI and CI between for that period.

As presented earlier, the total number of papers published by RBPI and CI for this period was 790, of which 657 were written by Brazilian authors. If one takes into consideration Table 5.2, about 10 per cent of these were specifically on security. If we subdivide the papers published by Brazilian authors into geographic and issue areas (where each paper was assigned one area in each of these labels), we can get a better idea of the security agenda (see Figures 5.2 and 5.3).

In terms of geographic areas, Brazil is placed first at the top of the agenda, providing the main focus with twenty-four papers. Concerning issue areas, foreign policy had twenty-one papers. That is, Brazil and foreign policy had more scholarly attention than their respective second and third place combined. What do these numbers reveal about Brazilian IR scholarship on security? The preferences of geographic and issue areas show that the knowledge production on security closely resembles that of IR as the focus is also on Brazil and foreign policy.

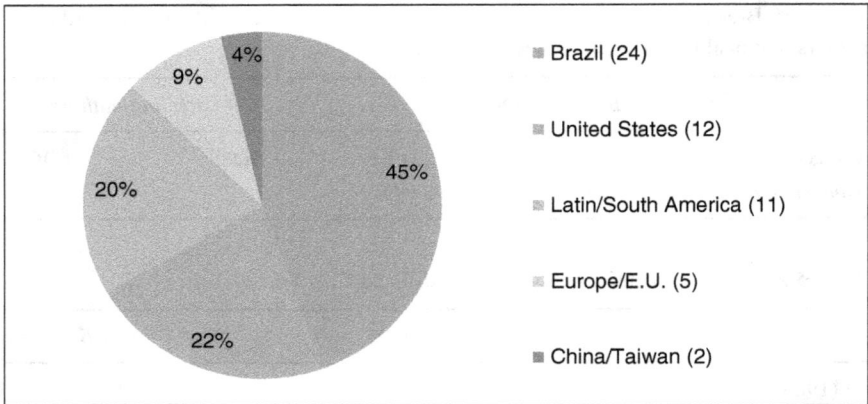

Figure 5.2 Papers on security published by RBPI and CI, 1985–2010, divided by geographic areas.

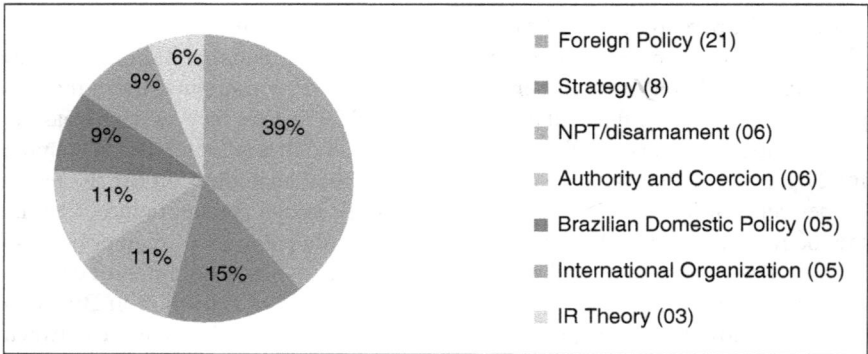

Figure 5.3 Papers on security published by RBPI and CI, 1985–2010: issue areas.

As will be argued in the following sections of this chapter, Brazilian foreign policy is the defining constitutive part of what legitimizes the role of IR as a discipline in that country. The rest of the agenda closely relates to issues that have been historically perceived as vital to the development of Brazil, namely, the relationship with the USA (Costa 1989: 55–66; Moura 1986; Miceli 1990; Souto Maior 2001; Braga 2002; Villa 2002; Proença Jr and Duarte 2003; Hirst 2006), Brazil's cooperation with (mainly) South American countries to resist US influence (see Bocco and Hirst 1989; Costa 1989; Barbosa 2002; Moniz Bandeira 2002; Souto Maior 2003; Soares de Lima 2005b; Vizentini 2007) and the European Union (EU) as an example of international cooperation (see Bernal-Meza 2000, 2005; Oliveira and Onuki 2000; Miyamoto 2002). Before analysing the security agenda in Brazilian IR, the next section explores how security has been conceptualized in the discipline.

The concept of security

When the Ministry of Defence was being established in Brazil in the late 1990s and early 2000s, the federal government sponsored a series of meetings, conference cycles and policy discussions between the armed forces, the Ministry of Foreign Relations and members of the Brazilian IR community. In 2003, one of these events – a cycle of conferences – aimed at gathering knowledge and reflecting on security and defence. The proceedings were later published as a collection of essays in four volumes, entitled *Pensamento Brasileiro Sobre Segurança e Defesa* (Brazilian Thought on Security and Defence). When interviewed, one of the organizers commented:

> The idea was to get the armed forces, diplomats, scholars, people of the field of international relations and ask them to discuss and work together. . . to think about security and defence together and also to think in different ways than had been proposed before. One of the obstacles to thinking about security in Brazil is due to the dictatorship. Putting civilians and the armed forces together to think about it has always been an issue. . . but with the establishment of the Ministry of Defence, that situation had to be overcome and we took the opportunity of the cycle of debates to do that.
>
> (Interviewee A)

The difficulty referred to by the interviewee was the way that the last wave of democratization took place in Brazil. The military's early embrace of the concepts of security and defence in the 1930s safeguarded its use for the armed forces and the authoritarian conservative politics they represented. As argued in Chapters 3 and 4, it was the concept of security that discursively accompanied and justified the rise of the armed forces as a central political actor in Brazil. Thus the word 'security' became strongly associated with experiences of violence, censorship and the lack of civil and political rights that characterized both the *Estado Novo* and the 1964 regime. By 1985, when José Sarney took his oath as the first civilian president since 1964, the armed forces had been responsible for Brazil's security for over five decades. This long-held monopoly over security meant that there was a direct association between security, the armed forces and authoritarian state practices. Therefore, redefining the role of the armed forces in the country entailed not only asking who would be in charge of the area of security, but also opening the possibility of thinking about it in other, non-authoritarian ways. After the regime announced it would slowly give way to civilian rule (Mainwaring 1986: 150; Martins 1986: 36), a series of questions about security arose in political and academic debates (Stepan 1988: chaps. 4 and 5) such as military thinking, the links between security thinking and the violent practices of the regime, and the role of the armed forces in politics (see Diniz 1985; Diniz and Boschi 1989; Zaverucha 1992). Behind this debate lurked the question of the politics of security in Brazil. This process was not easy. On the one hand, the armed forces were not willing to let go of the privilege of defining and implementing security policies. On the other, very few civilians had any expertise in security, and those who did had strong connections with the military. The word 'security' was so politically charged that even just pronouncing it would be enough to identify someone as a friend of the regime. Reflecting on thinking about security during that period, interviewees often raised this issue. When asked about it, a high-ranking military officer pondered whether we should be talking about that. He then replied:

> The end of military government brought about a time of distance between the armed forces, academia and *Itamaraty*. There was a mutual distrust that could be described as 'pragmatic distance'. We did not interact because there were too many unresolved feelings. Only very recently have we been able to sit side by side during conferences.
>
> (Interviewee C)

I then asked what the mutual distrust was about, and he replied:

> Well, there was the Amnesty Law. . . we [the armed forces] wanted to turn the page and move on. In a sense, I think that is what they [non-military members of the Brazilian IR community] wanted to do as well. . . just talk about what was best for Brazil and leave political discussions to politics. But every time anyone said 'security', it was like saying a forbidden word. To be honest, we [armed forces] didn't even want to talk about security. We wanted to talk about defence but security kept coming back. It would be years before enough time had passed by so we could discuss it again.
>
> (Interviewee C)

The same sort of disengagement surrounding discussions on security was analysed by another interviewee:

> There was a general discomfort on both sides. The scars were still too recent on our side. On their [military] side, it was like raising a big flag of *mea culpa*. The word security had serious implications for everyone. It would be a long time before we could all talk about it.
>
> (Interviewee C)

Following their answers, both interviewees were asked whether they thought there was any particular difference in the way civilians and the armed forces thought about security. One of the previous interviewees (B) replied:

> Back then there were some civilians who were my friends but they had very different views from me. I especially remember one civilian friend of mine. . . . When we talked about security and Brazil, we had the same views. . . you know, we both thought the NPT [non-proliferation treaty] was unfair, we

both thought Brazil needed to protect its borders in those uninhabited parts of the Amazon. He even told me once that after the Malvinas he understood that we needed to keep our armed forces. Deep down we had the same views about what was needed to defend Brazil and our interests outside. . . the thing was about the inside [the dictatorship]. He could not forget what had happened inside.

(Interviewee B)

Another Interviewee (C) replied:

These days we can talk about these issues and there are no problems. But look at it this way. The dictatorship had just ended. If we sat with them to talk about security policies, it would be as if we were forgetting everything that had just happened. We couldn't do that. It was [a] political [issue]. Now, if you look at the foreign policy of the regime, it wasn't bad. It was a lot better than Sarney, Collor, and FHC [Cardoso], wasn't it? It wasn't their international thought that was the source of disagreement. Like I said, there were scars.

(Interviewee C)

Two points emerge from their talks. On the one hand, the violent practices of the regime had left deep scars and these, not the subject of security itself, were the main source of contention. On the other, none of them thought that their thinking in terms of the international diverged very much. Rather, the source of the problem seems to have been that the word 'security' was so strongly stigmatized as 'authoritarian and violent' that discussing it was virtually impossible for both sides. In a 1988 paper in CI, Brigagão and Proença Jr (1988: 85) pointed out the reluctance of academics to get involved in security discussions due to the political implications entailed in 'speaking security'. Still, as recent as 2010, the then Minister of Defence spoke about the distance between academia and the armed forces when it came to discussing security in Brazil:

The association of the idea of security with political repression during the military regime cramped the ability of both the state and academia to think about it. The national social imaginary always identified those who spoke of security with political repression. I say this because I remember. During the process of drafting the 1988 constitution, if anyone ever mentioned security or defence, [everybody] immediately identified that person in connection with political repression.

(Jobim 2010)

Thus, that 2003 conference on security and defence aimed to overcome political differences within the broad IR community in Brazil in relation to the dictatorship. However, as interviewees also stated, there were not many differences in the way security was actually thought about in the realm of the international. This becomes clearer when one examines the security concepts that came out of those meetings. An academic who took part in the discussions commented:

> We needed to come up with a concept of security and another one of defence. We had a sort of guiding idea, it needed to be something that was practical and realist and that could help us think about the agenda. We opted for thinking that security is a state that can be attained and defence is the measures taken by the country against external threats to guarantee the attainment of security.
>
> (Interviewee D)

One of the keys to his reply is that they were looking for concepts that were practical and 'realist'. As shall be argued in later sections, realism is not directly concerned with the IR theory that goes by that name. Rather, it refers to the idea that assessing 'reality' and its political implications to different actors does not entail the use of abstraction or theorizing. Tellingly, the concept of security offered by the conference – 'a state that can be attained' – is neither practical nor realist. As a concept, it does little to overcome the two decades that it took them to sit side by side without bringing up the dictatorship. In addition, according the interviewer's statement one of the objectives of the meetings was to think about security in different ways than it had been done before. However, if we look back to the concept of security established by the ESG we find striking similarities: 'Security is a state and defence is an act or a set of acts. Defence has the aim of stopping a foreseen threat and security is established as an integral doctrine against any threat' (cited in Arruda 1980: 20). Apart from the clear reference to the Doctrine of National Security, the concept above is no different to the one proposed in 2004. Stating that security is a state that can be attained is what paved the way for the violent practices of the state in the first place. Likewise, concerning defence, the difference between the ESGian concept and the one established during the conference was that defence was not an act 'against *any* threat' but 'against *external* threat'. That specific change in words was made to mean that the armed forces could no longer act internally and ought to be concerned with the defence of the territory. Thus, conceptual change was made regarding the role of the armed forces in a democratic regime – a political advance in comparison to what had been the role of engagement of the armed forces in politics since the 1930s. As was the case with the concept of security, defence continued to be thought of in the same terms presented by the ESG. These two brief conceptualizations of security and defence were the same as those provided by most of the interviewees during fieldwork. Furthermore, they are the same conceptualizations presented in many articles published on security post-1985. Here are a few examples:

> Security is a state that can be attained not only through military consideration but also through the consideration of the social and economic structure of society.
>
> (Costa 1994: 109)

Security is the relative condition of protection in which threats are neutralized.

(Cepik 2001: 2)

Security is the state in which the existence, independence, sovereignty and territorial integrity of the state are not under threat.

(M. Santos 2004: 118)

Security is an ideal state to be attained and defence is the set of planned policies to obtain that state.

(Santos Filho 2002: 3)

On the concepts of security and defence, the panellists shared the idea that, even though these are complex concepts, there is a consensus around the fact that defence is basically an 'action' and security is a 'state'.

(Vidigal *et al.* 2004: 124)

The general perception I gathered from interviews was that conceptualizing security was not an important task. Below, the replies of three members of the Brazilian IR community when asked about the need for further discussion on the concept of security illustrate my point:

Academics are not interested in 'making things work'. They get too lost in the world of ideas and evaluation of foreign policy instead of trying to grasp how things work in practice. We are all trying to work for what is best for the country, its defence and security. We all view national security as the same.

(Interviewee D)

Diplomats and military men think much alike. We try to put security and defence into practice. If we relied on academics to think about security, we would still be discussing it.

(Interviewee E)

I do not see why the concept of security should be so complicated. It all depends on the foreign policy the country adopts.

(Interviewee F)

In all three interviews, as was the case with at least four others (Interviewees A and G–I) there were three important issues on the security agenda. First, the need to make the concept easily understood. Second, the assumption that security was an inherent part of the foreign policy agenda and, as such, needed to be thought of in terms of the strategies of the Brazilian state. Third, there was a desire to make the concept of security practical enough to be utilized for foreign policy-making.

For many, it was important to develop a security agenda which countered US interventionism. That, according to one interviewee, was partly the case with research on security in Brazil:

> There are two reasons why we went back and started looking at security again. The first one was the issue with the armed forces and their role in the country. The second one is. . . well, blame it on the Americans. . . [laughter] or the Taliban. We are a peaceful country, there was no need to securitize anything, to bring security to the agenda. But then, after the attacks, there was this return to framing things as matters of security. . . which is just another excuse for intervention.
>
> (Interviewee H)

A paper published in RBPI referred to the same idea expressed by Interviewee H:

> The 9/11 terrorist attacks brought terrorism to the centre of the international agenda – this will frame all issues concerning security. Nothing changed in regard to the relative power and position occupied by the EU, Japan, China and Russia. What changed was the attitude of the US to the world. The US will influence the international efforts concerning security by pressuring other states and the United Nations to act in conformity with their desires. After 9/11, those themes that were of greater interest to Brazil – commerce and development – had to make space for the issue of security. In the internal and external agenda, security has more weight than in the past.
>
> (Barbosa 2002: 82–5)

Both examples show that security had not been a priority issue in the agenda of the Brazilian IR community and had to be rescued from its secondary status of concern. One interviewee reflected on the issue the following way:

> They [the Cardoso administration] had set up the Ministry of Defence in a hurry, just to tick the box in 1999. The Ministry was left to its own devices, nobody really knew what would happen with it, then the [9/11] attacks happened. And who had always been interested in security, became suddenly necessary and famous. Nowadays, everybody is a specialist on security. How is that even possible? If you wanted to have a conference on international security in this country in 2000, there would be X, Y, Z, the armed forces and me. Now, everybody is a specialist on security and they have no idea what they are talking about.
>
> (Interviewee I)

This interviewee and the others she/he cited were part of a group who have held an interest in security and defence since the 1980s. During the interview, she/he stated that there had not possibly been time enough for Brazil to develop a solid basis for thinking about security. She/he said:

> At the ESG, they are very excited about this. [In the 1990s,] They were nowhere near the status they once had. Then the [9/11] attacks happened. Then. . . who has thought about security in Brazil? Who has the minimum know-how on the subject?
>
> (Interviewee I)

It is helpful to look at the publishing history of works on security. Figure 5.4 shows a survey of papers on security published by RBPI since its first issue in 1958. It demonstrates that between 2001 and 2010 RBPI published more papers on security than it did in the previous 43 years put together.

Why was there a rising interest in security studies? Some interviews reveal scholars' motivations are often linked to the US security agenda:

> The greatest concern of the Brazilian agenda is to promote our international insertion through multiple channels so as not to remain overtly dependent on the US or to have any sort of automatic alignment with them. It is the same for the area of security. For example, establishing an area of regional security that understands the problems of the Amazon borders, drug-trafficking, illegal weapons and opposes these threats in other ways instead of those established by the USA.
>
> (Interviewee J)

> In terms of security, Brazilian discussions have aimed at promoting security differently from the US. Before 2001, there were not many discussions in this area but now the international agenda requires us to think in terms of security. The US is enforcing an agenda that is very detrimental to Latin America. They are securitizing the agenda, and we have to respond to that.
>
> (Interviewee A)

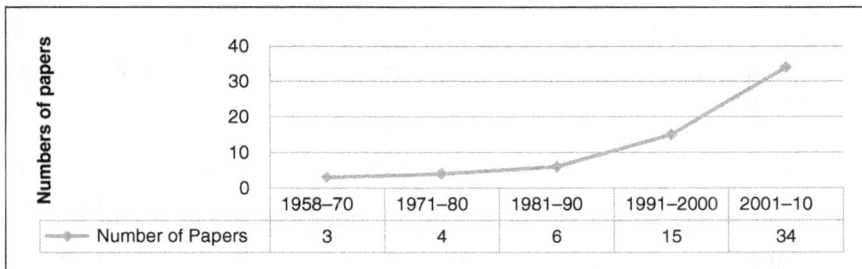

	1958–70	1971–80	1981–90	1991–2000	2001–10
Number of Papers	3	4	6	15	34

Figure 5.4 Papers on security published by RBPI, 1958–2010.

Interviewees conveyed a general assumption that once the USA demanded that the agenda be set in terms of security, it elicited reactions in Brazil. These reactions concerned resistance against the idea of discussing the relationship with the USA through 'security'. As analysed in the previous section, the concept of security had been stigmatized as authoritarian and conservative, and this left deep political wounds concerning the very act of speaking security. Thus, once the US agenda started using security even more emphatically in its foreign policy – and especially in its relationship with Latin/South America – different reactions emerged within the Brazilian IR community. On the one hand, scholars denounced the militarization of the US security agenda as a veiled attempt to breach the sovereignty of other countries in the name of security (see Lessa and Meira 2001; Barbosa 2002; Proença Jr and Duarte 2003; Penna Filho 2004). On the other, some Brazilian scholars expressed suspicion of critical approaches to security, since they were perceived as Western and, as such, sought to compromise 'Brazilian intellectual sovereignty' (see Amorim 2004; Sorj 2005). In order to understand this suspicion of critical approaches to security, we need to go back to the contextualization of the word 'security' and its implications. After redemocratization, not talking about security was a political stand. Not thinking about it, rarely publishing anything on it or producing knowledge on it was a political act. It sent the armed forces the message that security had no place in a democracy (even if civilian and military thought about the international did not differ). As one military officer explained in his interview, the armed forces were not inclined to use the term 'security' either – also due to the political weight it carried. They preferred to discuss defence, which was much more narrowly defined and would concern only the defence of the territory. In this sense, the strategy before the 9/11 attacks was to not discuss security. After the attacks, when the international environment required this security debate, that demand was met. However, the perception that 'security' could be used to legitimize US military practices and, ultimately, compromise Brazilian sovereignty, set the terms in which 'security' was to be used. Thus, while critical approaches to security elsewhere sought to politicize the concept and to propose a progressive agenda, Brazilian IR refrained from deepening and broadening the concept. This refusal to accept either the US foreign policy position or critical approaches to security cannot be understood without taking into consideration the legacy of denial of political and civil rights, of violence, torture and death bequeathed by decades of security rule in Brazil. Bernardo Sorj offers a similar argument on his paper on 'human security':

> The majority of NGOs that deal with human rights as well as the academic community have criticized the concept of human security. The perspective of human security is perceived to be an attempt to inscribe social life into the doctrine of national security by transferring social problems to the sphere of security. Furthermore, the concept of human security causes discomfort in intellectual and military circles because it was developed in opposition to the view of international relations based on national sovereignty.

The foreign policy of Latin American countries is based on the idea of national sovereignty, which is understandable given the latent apprehension against the US.

(Sorj 2005: 45–6)

This contextualized political interpretation is what underpins the argument made by former Minister of Foreign Relations Celso Amorim, when he stated that 'new approaches to security may be used as a legitimizing discourse for intervention in other countries' (Amorim 2004: 135). He goes on to say:

We have serious doubts about notions such as 'human security' or 'individual security'. If they were to be implemented by an international institution – and even so, not a security institution – they would have to make explicit the notion of the right to development.

(Amorim 2004: 151)

Ramalho da Rocha was also dismissive of the use of the term 'security'. He has commented:

The great problems of the country concerning security are about public security and thus the responsibility of the police, not the armed forces. In terms of traditional geopolitics, the place of Brazil has changed little in the last decades, except concerning the greater acceptance in the region of its leadership, and its peaceful and constructive character.

(Rocha 2005: 102)

His comment implies that Brazil has no direct security concerns in the international realm since all the problems in that area are internal. In stating this, Rocha lets slip his conservative view even on security concerns deemed strictly 'national'; 'it is the responsibility of the police, not the armed forces'. By arguing that it is an issue for the police, Rocha sought to argue that the armed forces could not intervene in society like they had once done – but at the same time, he only changed one means of repression for another, thus weighing military perspectives of repression against civilian ones. What is relevant in his quotation, however, is that even though he affirms that Brazil's geopolitical position has not changed much, his discourse goes back to reifying Brazilian leadership as having peaceful and constructive characteristics. The constant reification of Brazil's 'natural characteristics' bears striking resemblance to the most basic informing idea of the TEA. It is an exercise in reducing politics to an issue of identity and, in doing so, naturalizing essentialist views of Brazilian identity. This leads to the second issue concerning the need to make security practical for foreign policy: establishing and conceiving security in ways that promote the *inserção internacional* of Brazil. It is to this element of becoming that this chapter now turns. This close correspondence between the Brazilian foreign policy agenda and academic research is discussed in more detail in the following sections, where I examine what the TEA can reveal about Brazilian IR thinking about security. Being

The most basic step of the TEA lies in the essentialization of Brazilian identity. The present section focuses on the purpose of that essentialization in Brazilian IR. The overall argument is that there are considerable differences in the way IR has presented and reproduced Brazilian identity. Since IR is perceived as being removed from and above national politics (Soares de Lima 2005a: 4; Huelsz 2009: 78), the discipline has refrained from thinking about national identity. Instead, it has helped itself to the idea of 'Brazilian international identity' – the anthropomorphization of the state and its foreign policy. Let us first examine the original common ground between the national and the international identity of Brazil and explore what sort of image intellectuals have sought to promote and identify with Brazil. As previously discussed, the starting point of the TEA is the perceived natural disposition of Brazil to become a world power. A 1978 paper asks 'Is there a pragmatic reason beyond emotional grounds to defending the idea that the Amazon should remain Brazilian?' The author's own reply is:

> we need to add other more immediate and objective [reasoning] to this issue. Those [reasons] that represent the contribution [of the Amazon] to the process of development so that we can attain in the near future that leadership position that we ought to attain. In the issue of its participation in the Brazilian rise [to power], the Amazon has a great role. The Amazon means land, it is an area of natural resources.
>
> (Reis 1978)

Another paper commented on the Brazilian continental platform:

> We need to convince ourselves that a country like ours, having one of the most extensive coastlines in the world, cannot live eternally divorced and disconnected from the wealth of its underwater resources, we can easily understand the imperative and urgent need for policies that are capable of bringing us to our destiny as a continental and world power.
>
> (Castro 1972)

This assumed predisposition to become a great power was one of the core assumptions espoused by the ESG. This is in tandem with the first tenet of the TEA, *being*, in which the geographic landscape of the country is perceived as a source of unrealized power. However, in contradiction to the other two contexts analysed in this book, in Brazilian IR being has not been concerned with the irrational, emotional and pre-modern character of the Brazilian population. In fact, IR has seldom developed any sort of thinking about the people at all. Unlike the preconceptions of the pre-modern or irrational tenets that have defined social theorizing in Brazil, Brazilian IR has adopted notions of the Brazilian state as peaceful, law-abiding, legalist and normative in its behaviour. Here are some examples the dimensions of the country, its importance in the geographic space, gave Brazilian foreign and defence policy clear specificities. The extensive border, the nonexistent border issues, the common Iberian character it shares with its neighbours, its geographic position in the south, its Atlantic coast. All of these contingencies are principles that have guided the international behaviour of Brazil and, therefore, its policies. Issues other than geographic principles must also be debated, such as history and culture, which became part of the body of ideas that have informed and inform the international insertion of Brazil. Brazil was always averse to confrontation, was always a law-abiding country, was always realist and became pragmatic.

(Costa 1999: 144)

Brazil's extensive territory, the thousands of kilometres of coastal line and borders shared with other Latin American countries, the ecological wealth of not only diverse environments but also the diversity of its natural resources, have given the country an advantageous initial position in its geopolitical setting. Furthermore, Brazil's international position as a peaceful country, the lack of bellicose disputes in the area and its international position as a follower of international agreements give it a favourable position it its *inserção internacional*.

(Miyamoto 2000: 440)

Historically, Brazil, with its continental dimensions and borders shared with 10 neighbouring countries had its political and diplomatic dimension translated into the search of peaceful negotiations and solutions to international conflict. In general, borders are an inexhaustible source of interstate disputes but Brazil was able to preserve national unity and maintain the balance of power through its diplomacy and developed over the last 150 years a peaceful culture with its neighbours.

(Brigagão and Seabra 2009: 75)

In every quotation, the perceived grandiosity of the country matches its peaceful, law-abiding, war-averting nature. In this sense, the excerpts above are examples of this permanent attempt to inscribe essential identity traits to the Brazilian state as peaceful, law-abiding and a follower of agreements. Authors perceive these traits as part of Brazilian international identity, a term that has become a watchword in Brazilian IR (see Lafer 2000; Santos Filho 2002; Santos 2003; Soares de Lima 2005b; Almeida 2006; Galvão 2009) and which refers to a set of traits that are understood to permanently describe Brazil's behaviour in the international arena. In the same way that Brazilian national identity is often portrayed as unique (whether through the myth of racial democracy, *personalismo/patrimonialismo* or Brazilian cordiality), its international identity is also perceived to be the result of a unique set of permanent characteristics of its foreign policy-making. Emphasis placed on particular aspects of Brazilian international identity varies depending on the issue under consideration, but the general traits may be summarized in these aspects: self-determination and sovereignty, binding multilateralism and the duty to represent developing countries, and realism and pragmatism. Various IR scholars have adopted the idea of Brazilian international identity in their work (see Moura 1982; Fonseca Jr 1989; Lafer 2000; Lessa 2005b; Parola 2007; Vigevani and Capaluni 2007; Vidigal 2010). Instead of discussing them separately, I have opted to focus on the work of Cervo (Saraiva 1994; Cervo 2008: 26–31). I do so for four reasons. First, Cervo is perhaps the most renowned contemporary Brazilian IR scholar and has co-authored the single most adopted IR textbook in Brazil (Cervo and Bueno 2002). Second, he is not only well-connected but also well-respected in military, diplomatic, journalistic and academic circles alike. He has taught at the Brazilian diplomatic academy and has lectured both at the ESG and at the University of Brasília. His books are reference to the armed forces, academia and members of Brazilian diplomacy. Third, in interviews conducted during fieldwork in Brazil, some IR scholars referenced his work as the most important theoretical contribution developed in Brazilian IR (especially Interviewees A, D, F and I). Lastly, he has explicitly explained how he understands the connection between identity and foreign policy:

> Throughout its evolution, Brazilian foreign policy has adopted principles and values in diplomacy in ways that these values become a part of its behaviour. These patterns have two functions: first, they give predictability to our foreign practice and, second, they frame the state's behaviour in foreign affairs, giving it an aspect of continuity to foreign policy. In sum, they contribute to giving *rationality* to state policy.
>
> (Cervo 2008: 26)

I have italicized 'rationality' because it is central to his concept of state policy. Where the ESG sought to rationalize the people and politics in general, Cervo advocates the rationalization of foreign policy through the 'prevalence of continuity over change, of causation over rupture' (Cervo 2008: 26–7). However, what follows in the narrative he offers on the guiding principles of foreign policy is a system of pick-and-choose, where he selects what fits into those principles. He identifies nine patterns of behaviour in Brazilian international identity. His original list includes: self-determination, non-intervention and the peaceful solution of controversies; legalism; normative multilateralism; cooperative and non-confrontational external action; strategic partnerships; realism and pragmatism; official cordiality in the treatment of neighbours; development as a direction; and independence of international insertion (Cervo 2008: 27–31).

From this classification, Cervo demonstrates patterns of linearity in Brazilian diplomatic history which, in retrospect, confirm already established assumptions about Brazilian international identity. Brazilian scholars – of which Cervo is a leading example – use episodes of past Brazilian foreign policy, *ex post facto,* to confirm Brazilian patterns of behaviour. As an example, Brazil's participation in the Second World War is taken to be a sign of its cooperative external behaviour – since Brazil cooperated with allies in Europe (Cervo 2008: 28–9). However, that episode is forgotten when it comes to justifying the trait of peaceful solution of controversies, when the signing of border treaties with neighbouring countries in the early nineteenth century is evoked (Cervo 2008: 30). The other characteristics of Brazilian international identity are analysed below. Cervo (2008: 30) refers to Brazilian behaviour in international politics as realist and pragmatic. By realism, Cervo does not mean the branch of IR theory that has traditionally dominated post-war US academia, but rather 'the sensible observation of reality for what it is' (Cervo 2008: 29–30). That is why Cervo puts it as 'realism and pragmatism' – the view that once reality is apprehended from sensible observation, one can make pragmatic choices conducive to *inserção internacional*. For him, pragmatism is 'the evolution and advanced state of realism, for it displays the prevalence of diplomatic acuity over the deeper forces of economy, society and decision-making process of other governments' (Cervo 2008: 30). Cervo's analysis of 'realism' as a characteristic of Brazilian international identity is well within the overall state of social science theorizing in Brazil. The realism Cervo claims as a tenet of Brazilian international identity is but a fetishization of what 'immediate knowledge' may have to offer academia (Souza 2006a: 120). What Cervo presents is an anti-theorization platform. His perception that pragmatism is the evolution of realism obliterates the need for any form of theorization because it implies that the political ability to derive gain from difficult situations can be apprehended through the sensible perception of reality. His concern with Brazilian international identity and its representation in foreign policy leads him to create fitting patterns. Cervo is not alone in his thinking. The assumption that knowledge production does not necessarily entail the systematization of concepts, abstraction or even a structure of analysis has been the default perception in Brazilian academic social sciences (Souza 2006b: 99). Such assumptions are also a reflection of what has been practiced as social science in Brazil: the art of quickly saving Brazil. Since academic thinking is reduced to the purpose of realizing the potential of its national identity and the development of the country through the sensible apprehension of reality, efforts to theorize are perceived as being of secondary importance. Another trait associated with Brazilian international identity is what Cervo calls the 'official cordiality in the relationship with neighbouring countries'. He dates this characteristic back to the time of the Baron of Rio Branco (and of his father, the Viscount of Rio Branco) as Minister of Foreign Relations. Cervo argues that both of them 'valued friendship and trade with neighbours in order to maintain peaceful coexistence' (Cervo 2008: 30). Relevant here is his use of the word cordiality and its connection with Buarque de Holanda's 'cordial man'. Cervo uses 'cordiality' to mean friendly and close relations with neighbouring countries, but distances himself from Buarque de Holanda's idea of the imposition of the personal sphere over public interest. In this aspect, Vidigal (2010) published a paper entitled 'Brazil: a cordial power?' in which he sought to set a distinction between Buarque de Holanda's cordiality and the above meaning intended by Cervo:

the notion of cordiality applied to foreign policy distances itself from Sérgio Buarque de Holanda. The Brazilian chancellery prizes technical competence, international dialogue and its forums. However, it must be recognized that both Fernando Henrique Cardoso's presidential diplomacy and Luís Inácio Lula da Silva's *personalismo* sought informal dialogue and fluid personal relationships with great international authorities – motivated more by passion than reason.

(Vidigal 2010: 34)

Vidigal promptly distances the notion of the cordial man from the idea that the Brazilian chancellery could act on 'the basis of feelings which spring directly from the heart, without the mediation of rationality, treating friends and foes differently and restricting the space for abstract norms and rules to function' (Vidigal 2010: 34). At the same time, he admits that former Brazilian presidents Cardoso and Lula da Silva have used *personalismo* to foster informal dialogue with great international authorities. Vidigal thus creates an opposition between presidential diplomacy – which may be *personalista* and stem from passion rather than rationality – and Brazilian foreign policy. Thus, in Brazilian IR the essentialization of identity hardly resembles the overtly emotional character of the people and the country which have been central to social theorizing in other disciplines. This discrepancy between the 'national' and 'international' identity of Brazil is infused with the same elitist ideas that for so long informed the differences between the people and the elite in social writing in Brazil. At the ESG, the differentiation between the 'people' and the 'elites' was vital not only to the way in which the Doctrine of National Security ought be executed, but also in setting out what (or who) needed to be made secure by the state. As discussed in Chapter 4, the elite possessed the rationalized/modern character traits that made up the nation, whereas the people were deemed to be irrational/pre-modern beings. In Brazilian IR, the Ministry of Foreign Affairs is the very personification of rational elites and technical competence. Professor Amado Cervo spoke of the role of statesmen, intellectuals and diplomats in the following way:

When statesmen or intellectuals conceive the fate of the nation – its project and its role in the international arena – they are establishing the guidelines of foreign policy, and when diplomats shape their actions based on them they are fulfilling their role. In the absence of said guidelines, what often happens is that the decision-making process of foreign policy becomes subservient to the values, interests and rules of [foreign] others. In this context, the nation remains in its political infancy and falls under the tutelage of others.

(Cervo 2008: 10)

This perceived superiority and rationality of Brazilian diplomacy is the source of all other characteristics assigned to Brazilian international identity: its normative conduct, pragmatism and legalism. What is the overzealous pride this community holds for the Brazilian Ministry of Foreign Relations if not the same sort of fetishicization of the elites as the sole agents of politics outlined in the ESG writings? What is the complete silence concerning non-elite societal sectors if not the same disregard for the pre-modern irrational Brazilian people so latent in the works of the ESG? These claims to an international identity are not only elitist but also exclusionary. By accepting the corollary that Brazilian foreign policy is above and removed from the state, and by reinforcing and reproducing its practices and discourses, IR scholars only further reify the idea that agency in IR derives from the ruling elite.

Becoming

The *becoming* tenet of the TEA relates to three aspects of social theorizing in Brazil. First, the TEA informs the relevance and the centrality of Brazilian identity to social theorizing. Therefore, knowledge production in the social sciences in that country has been underlain by the need to rationalize the *personalista/patrimonialista* traits of Brazilian identity and thus to adapt the people and the state to modernity (Souza 2006a: 125). Second, and stemming from the rationalization of the people, there is an underlying need to develop the state as a condition for rationalization. Development, thus, means the realization of the potential of the Brazilian state. This is the teleological endpoint of social theorizing in Brazil, and IR has not gone unaffected (Muñoz 1980: 340; Tickner 2003: 342). As an academic enterprise, Brazilian IR does not spell out a platform of development as was the case with the ESG. However, the certainty with which the IR community approaches the idea of aiding the development of state is neither unique to the discipline nor novel in the history of social sciences in Brazil. Souza (2006a: 125) argues that development has been the central concern of Brazilian intellectuals since the mid-1930s. As this section argues, a particular path to development can be apprehended from the underlying themes and arguments present in its knowledge production. First and foremost, development means countering US influence. For every issue on the IR agenda, the need to escape US influence is what determines the security agenda for Brazilian IR. Second, and as a consequence of the first theme, Brazil is presented as a counterpoint to US power – as a benevolent and natural leader that seeks to improve security conditions in the world. Investigating *becoming* then is also a way to assess how this community envisions not only the development of the state, but also resistance through foreign policy.

In April 2000, former Minister of Foreign Relations, Luiz Filipe Lampreia, announced that the project *Brasil Potência* was to be put on hold. The next day, the most widely circulated paper in the country had an eight-page editorial entitled *Adeus Brasil Potência* (Goodbye Brazil World Power). The editorial, run by *Folha de São Paulo*, stated:

> The dream is over. Minister Lampreia discarded the idea of transforming Brazil into a world power. This is an extraordinary shift in discourse and praxis of the last decades. Though this should only mean that it is not through military efforts that Brazil will pursue its global insertion. Brazil can still increase political and commercial participation in the world.
>
> ('Adeus Brasil Potência' 2000: 1)

The excerpt above still shows the resistance to accept the end of *Brasil Potên-cia*. It had been nearly three decades since the height of *Brasil Potência*. Still, the Minister's official statement about the implausibility of carrying on the project resonated as the end of an era. Despite Lampreia's statement, the firm belief that Brazil will achieve the status of a world power is still very much alive in political and academic debates. Members of the Brazilian IR community do not use the phrase *Brasil Potência* – due to its association with the 1964 dictatorial regime – but instead they speak of 'development'. Attaining the status of world power, or becoming developed, or even the *inserção internacional do Brasil*, have the same discursive value in IR academia. It is the all-encompassing solution to the problems of the country. It is the teleological aim that has underlain social theorizing in Brazil. Here, we go back to the work of Cervo. Regarding development, his argument is that the policies of *desenvolvimentismo* (developmentalism) pursued by Brazil between 1930 and 1989 are the main pattern of Brazilian international identity (2008: 31). This platform of development resembles one of the arguments raised by Souza (2006b: 107) in relation to the TEA, where he argues that Brazilian cordiality (its benign nature) is used as a moral compensation for the lack of development and rationality of its people. Much in the same manner, Brazilian international identity in Brazilian IR is presented as a moral benevolent counterpoint to US power. The result of this is a sort of knowledge production that is based more on moral exhortations about good (Brazil) and evil (USA) than on political enquiry. The earlier survey pointed towards some key issue areas: foreign policy, strategy, the NPT and disarmament issues, authority and coercion in international politics, and international organizations (especially the Security Council at the United Nations). All of these issues relate, either directly or indirectly, to Brazil's relationship with the USA. Reflecting on the production of IR in Latin America in 1980, Muñoz (1980: 340–1) argued that political autonomy and economic development were the main underlying goal of IR writing in the continent. In the context of the 1970s, autonomy had two interrelated meanings. The first one concerned the attempt to navigate as a non-compliant state through world politics during the Cold War (Kramer *et al.* 1985: 36–7; Hirst 2006: 99). The second meaning of autonomy concerned the influence exercised by the USA in the continent, which was thought to limit the political and economic options of South/Latin American countries (Muñoz 1980: 340; Vaz 1993: 71). Although the word 'autonomy' is rarely used in contemporary IR writing, it is the possibility of greater autonomy from the USA that largely continues to define the IR agenda in Latin America (see Schoultz 2000: chap. 4; Petras 2005: 197). Interviewees made reference to this aspect of the discipline in the following ways:

> I believe our greatest challenge has always been how to balance the relationship with the US. Brazil is a country of great potential but our opportunities are always curtailed by the many US impositions. It is not a question of cutting relations but of preserving our sovereignty.
>
> (Interviewee J)

We need to use the principle of sovereignty as a shield against the influence of the US. Why is it that every time a Brazilian government seeks to establish a close relationship with the US, it is never to our own benefit? Isn't it enough that they get to dictate the international system?

(Interviewee N)

Our international insertion is also guided by the need to diversify our agenda and establish links so as to guarantee diversification and sovereignty in our national choices.

(Interviewee M)

For these members of the Brazilian IR community, the key to a successful *inserção internacional* is to pursue policies that enable greater autonomy from the USA. Thus, *becoming* a developed country is infused by the general aim of resisting US influence.

Two recurring themes emerge from the arguments proposed by Brazilian IR. The first regards the justification of these policy concerns in relation to Brazilian international identity. The second concerns the relationship with the USA. In both cases Brazilian IR generates a sort of academic writing that is not concerned with understanding or exploring political processes, and it does little more than legitimize Brazil's foreign policy. Much like other forms of social and political theorizing in Brazil, Brazilian IR academia's desire to reduce politics to national identity has crippled not only political imagination, but also academic diversity. Take, for instance, the issue of the reform of the United Nations' Security Council (SC). Although its reform has been a talking point in the Brazilian Ministry of Foreign Affairs since the 1980s (Fonseca Jr and Lafer 1994; Amorim 1996), Brazil only officially put forward its bid for a permanent seat on the SC in 1994. Since then, the issue has been referred to as 'the obsession of the permanent seat' (Arraes 2005: 154). It led ambassador Amorin (then Minister of Defence) to state, in words reminiscent of the ESG, that the bid for a permanent seat on the SC was a 'true national objective' (Amorim 1999: 93). This is linked to the policy asserted by the Brazilian government that a reform of the SC should involve giving a permanent seat to countries that are regional leaders, thus making Brazil the strongest candidate for Latin America (Silva 1987; 1992; Hirst and Pinheiro 1995: 12–15; Mello 2002: 41; Almeida 2004: 165–6; Arraes 2005; Saraiva 2007). When I asked why a permanent seat on the SC was such a central concern in Brazilian IR, two scholars responded thus:

Two issues deserve attention. First, the reform of the SC. It needs to reflect the changes in international relations that have occurred since its establishment more than 60 years ago. Second, Brazil is a natural candidate for one of the permanent seats. . . . It has all the necessary credentials for the post and Brazil could bring discussions and points of view that are different from those of the US, for example.

(Interviewee C)

To put it bluntly, it is an issue of power. Why do we want to be on the Security Council? Because whoever has that seat has decision-making power in the region and influence in the world. Now, at the same time, it is not just about power – it is about what sort of power. Brazil is a benign power – we do not have nuclear weapons, we are peaceful, we do not support military missions as a cover-up for economic and geopolitical interests, we can speak in the name of the developing world, we can push an agenda of development and social justice. This is the sort of power we speak of, not what Americans make of it [having power].

(Interviewee H)

The first interviewee did not elaborate further on his statement. Tellingly, these were well-established ideas that need not to be further discussed or analysed. The second one was clear in his convictions about the SC – blunter than anyone else I interviewed. His statement was quite a surprise, though, given that no one else spoke about Brazil gaining power or having power. More often than not, for the Brazilian IR community, other countries, regions and institutions either have or seek power, but not Brazil. Brazil has 'natural' leadership (Amorim 1999: 92; Arraes 2005: 153; Saraiva 2007: 47), influence (Oliveira and Onuki 2000: 118; Almeida 2004: 172; Galvão 2009: 68), and respectability (Sardenberg 2005: 365; Lessa *et al.* 2009: 95). Another interesting aspect of the practice of IR writing in Brazil may be apprehended from the case of knowledge production on the issue of the signing of the Non-Proliferation Treaty (NPT) in the 1990s. For more than two decades, Brazilian foreign policy had voiced its opposition to the signing of the NPT as 'the incarnation of the paradigm of international injustice' (Herz and Wrobel 2002: 281). Opposition to the NPT was justified in four ways. First, the signing of the Treaty of Tlatelolco had already made Latin America the first Nuclear-Free Zone in the world since 1967. Second, the NPT promoted greater Brazilian dependency on the USA, in case of a foreign threat to Brazilian territory; it would not have the military capability to defend itself and thus would have to rely on the USA (Rosenbaum and Cooper 1970: 80). Third, it perceived the NPT to be detrimental to its development project, since it required the abdication of all forms of nuclear technology, which would result in foregoing benefits deriving from the peaceful use of atomic energy. As President Marshall Costa e Silva stated, the signing of the NPT 'would mean our acceptance of a new form of dependence surely incompatible with our aspirations for development' (Brazil 1967: 3). Fourth, it was seen as a way to resist the bipolar order and defy the USA (for papers in Brazilian IR that defend this point of view, Rosa 1985; Goldenberg 1987; Menezes 1987; Vidigal 1987; Wrobel 1993, 1996; Cavagnari Filho 2000; Duarte 2006; Flemes 2006; Rocha 2006). As Herz and Wrobel comment:

For more than 20 years it was difficult to find individuals or sectors that openly supported the NPT [in Brazil]. This vast and influential coalition of interest perceived the NPT to be a symbol of everything that was wrong and unjust in the international distribution of power. The expression 'disarming the unarmed' encapsulated the definition that the country applied to the regime.

(Herz and Wrobel 2002: 284)

Given the level of resistance to the signing of the NPT, it is interesting to consider how this discourse changed after the Brazilian government signed the treaty:

An important step that showed the world Brazil's willingness to cooperate and its respect for international regimes, a civilian and democratic form of making peace and including ourselves in the negotiations and benefits of the non-proliferation regimes.

(Brigagão 2004: 78)

Although not in favour of the signing of the NPT, Interviewee H also expressed that 'it would be contradictory to the principles of our political identity not to sign the [Non-Proliferation] Treaty'. His statement reveals one interesting point: from his perspective, political choices should be guided not by normative ideas and principles but by how they relate to Brazilian identity. This reflects the tenet *being* of the TEA and the need to constantly return to national identity as the starting point of political theorizing. In the 2004 cycle of conferences on security, a report of a round-table discussion stated: 'it was agreed that the signing of the NPT was also within the principle of Brazilian international identity that requires taking part in multilateral forums' (Vidigal *et al.* 2004: 200–1).

Such a statement highlights the central place that Brazilian identity occupies in thinking about security. Inscribing moral conduct to the Brazilian state and, thus, Brazilian international identity says more about the community of Brazilian IR than it does to explain the political contours of foreign policy. The themes in the agenda of Brazilian IR seem to follow a pattern of perceived resistance against US influence. The most prominent items on the regional agenda for both foreign policy and Brazilian IR are the Amazon and Andean regions (see Souto Maior 2003; Mathias *et al.* 2008) and the relationship with Argentina (see Vargas 1997; Miyamoto 2000; A. Oliveira and Onuki 2000; Pagliai 2006). For both the government and the Brazilian IR community, the subcontinent is the focus of policy concern for two reasons. First, Brazil is a 'natural leader' in the region. Second, because strengthening Brazil's relationship with its neighbouring countries is central to countering US influence in the region (see Vargas 1997: 44; Oliveira and Onuki 2000: 115; Macedo Soares 2004: 155; Viola and Leis 2004; Soares de Lima 2005b: 30). Out of these issues, interviewees displayed greater concern with the Andean region (see Oliveira and Onuki 2000), because of the so-called 'new threats' (see Procopio Filho and Vaz 1997; Santana 1999; Herz 2002b; Santos 2004; Martins Filho 2006). In the 6 months I spent in Brazil, 'new threats' was one of the buzzwords of the discipline and referred to the new priority that the USA was placing on drug-trafficking in the Andean region. On this subject, an interviewee commented: 'we need to work with their parameters because that is the sort of conceptualization that they use to militarize the Andean region, to impose their views on security, and to divide South America' (Interviewee F). His statement referred back to the framing of the foreign policy agenda as a reaction to the influence of the USA in the area, much in the same way that trafficking along the Amazon border was a new threat because the US literature on security 'says they are new'. That is, the Brazilian IR community not only depends on the US agenda to structure its own agenda, but it also legitimizes its research enterprise and political role in relation to that country. To cite another example of this, Oliveira and Onuki (2000: 111) have stated that the Brazilian security agenda in Latin America is aimed at 'countering US hemispheric hegemony and rejecting automatic alignment with US policies'. This drive to counter US hegemony in the continent was one of the most repeated ideas in every interview. Countering US influence was discussed almost as a solution to all Brazilian problems. As such, deeper tensions and security issues were not considered or reflected upon. I must confess that, during those interviews, I caught myself thinking that at the ESG there was at least a brief attempt to think about 'individual security' and 'communitarian security' (see discussion in Chapter 4). Brazilian IR intellectuals have not only refrained from such discussions, they have also frowned upon the intellectual possibilities opened up by critical approaches to security.

The method

Chapter 4 explored the method of development sponsored by the ESG. In that specific context, it was much easier to perceive practices advocated by that institution, since it had a clearly established map of development – the Doctrine of National Security. As such, the doctrine set out step by step how Brazil would attain security and development. As was the case with *becoming*, deriving *the method* from Brazilian IR academia is a different and more complex task. The method of development shared by this community is closely related to becoming. That is, it points towards a transposition of the need to counter the USA, but this time in the domestic political and economic realm. More explicitly, the neo-liberal economic prescriptions of the Washington Consensus are perceived to be an extension of US power and influence, which not only seeks to regulate international relationships but also domestic policy. Thus, the exercise proposed in this section – understanding method through intellectual practice and advocacy – allows me to argue that the majority of Brazilian IR scholars not only have an idea of what method to pursue (intellectual anti-neoliberalism), they are also politically committed to supporting and defending this method. In the case of Brazilian IR, the relationship with the USA has determined most, if not all, underlying themes of the agenda. In this sense, becoming had been related to the degree of autonomy from the USA. For this reason, the method of development espoused by Brazilian IR has been related to contesting US influence in Brazil's *inserção internacional*. Thus, I propose a different exercise in this section, namely one that concerns the place of intellectuals in Brazil and connects the first and last chapters of this book. As argued by Souza (2006c: 13), the USA has figured in Brazilian social theorizing as a counterpoint to Brazilian identity. Depending on the political context and the intellectual aim of different works, Brazilian knowledge production has perceived the USA variously as an example of rationalization (Souza 2006b: chap. 3), as an ideal to be attained (discussed in Chapter 4), or as the threatening other that holds back the development of Brazil. Part I introduced the leading political role of intellectuals during the crisis of the liberal republican system in the 1920s. It was argued then that the first decades of the twentieth century were characterized by an intellectual defence of the centralized state and activism against the liberal republic that denied political participation to those classes that ultimately ran the state (civilian and military bureaucracy). One of the arguments of Chapter 2 was that Brazilian intellectuals of the early twentieth century gave themselves the role of defending the centralization of the state and top-down forms of modernization. Since then, intellectual discourses have been confined to defining the method of modernization of the state. In a similar way, here I look at how the Brazilian IR community reacted to the civilian governments that sought to implement neo-liberal policies by rolling back the state and decentralizing the economy in the 1990s and early 2000s. Specifically I will examine how contemporary intellectuals, especially those in Brazilian IR, reacted to the perceived threat that neo-liberal policies pursued by subsequent governments posed to the state. The aim of this exercise is twofold. First, it provides further grounds for the argument that Brazilian academic debates are primarily concerned with different methods of modernization but never question the need for it. Second, it explores how the claim to resist the USA is extended to the national realm. In this sense, securing what is 'national' also suggests that there is a national 'other' that acts in the interests of the USA. During interviews, when asked to think about what Brazil had contributed theoretically to IR, scholars at UnB promptly referred to Cervo's *enfoque paradigmático* (a 2003 paper published by RBPI). It argued that neo-liberal policies pursued by Brazilian governments in the aftermath of redemocratization were a deviation from its international identity. For Cervo (2003: 15–22), postredemocratization governments were guided by the application of neo-liberal policies to the state which he called both the 'normal paradigm' and the 'logistic paradigm'. In his view, both of these constituted a deviation from the 'developmentalist paradigm' that had guided governments between 1930 and 1989. Thus, the supporters of the normal paradigm

> Put forward the destruction of the national wealth that had been constructed in 60 years of efforts. In Latin America, neo-liberalism became a fundamentalism typical of the late twentieth century. This fundamentalism had little science in it. It was more a form of catechism and church than a manual and academia. Its texts and political practice reveal their faith in conventional formulas of the neo-liberal creed. Devoid of a project of development and lacking any resources, the Cardoso era provoked the stagnation of the Brazilian economy and interrupted a cycle of 60 years of development.
>
> (Cervo 2003: 17)

Cervo also shows that there was resistance on the part of academia and within the Ministry of Foreign Relations to the policies being pursued by the Brazilian government. He calls the resistance to, and criticism of, neo-liberalism 'expressions of critical thinking'. Here is his account of the political dissidence offered by critical thinking at the time:

> Inside Itamaraty, the normal model of international insertion implemented by Cardoso was not unanimous among diplomatic thinking. Some of its intellectuals, such as Rubens Ricupero, Celso Amorim and Pinheiro Guimarães, expressed doubts about the decisions made in foreign policy. Samuel Pinheiro Guimarães promoted numerous meetings and published a series of books that criticized the paradigm that impregnated the decision-making process in international relations. In academia, a group of researchers of international relations at the University of Brasília disseminated severe interpretations, through seminars, lectures, books, and through the journal *Revista Brasileira de Política Internacional*. In this environment [UnB], there was the predominance of critical thought and we developed it [critical thought] with Luiz Alberto Moniz Bandeira, José Flávio Sombra Saraiva, Argemiro Procópio Filho, Antônio Carlos Moraes Lessa, Antônio Augusto Cançado Trindade, Alcides Costa Vaz, Estêvão Chaves de Rezende Martins, Antônio Jorge Ramalho da Rocha, Carlos Roberto Pio da Costa Filho. Critical thought did not endorse simple return to the developmentalist paradigm, although we were accused of that by Cardoso's group who called us nostalgic and *neostupid*.
>
> (Cervo 2003: 20, italics in original)

Regarding foreign policy, it was the first time since the presidency of General Eurico Gaspar Dutra (1946–51) in which academia and members of the Ministry of Foreign Affairs publicly expressed dissidence from the government. As may be perceived from the quotation above, the application of neo-liberal policies instigated not only resistance from the IR community but also led the community to organize against the neo-liberal wave of the 1990s and early 2000s. Interviewee F also spoke of the Cardoso office as years of resistance in academia:

> This is a delicate subject but. . . we can say what we may about the military governments but although the US played a part in putting them in power, they [the military] did not acquiesce to policies that were detrimental to our country like the civilian governments gladly did after 1985. Collor and FH [Cardoso] with the Washington consensus managed to undo whatever good things the armed forces had done. . . During FHC [Cardoso's government], we organized many seminars, workshops, publications, and talks concerning neo-liberalism, the Washington Consensus, and the dismantling of the state promoted by his government. That was an interesting moment in academia.
>
> (Interviewee F)

Interviewee H gave an interesting account of his perception of the growth of IR programmes in the country in the 1990s and 2000s. He thought it was

> tangentially due to the neo-liberal project of the state. Many students and researchers perceived IR to be a locus of dissidence. It was necessary to counter neo-liberalism and to protect the little development we had acquired prior to those governments.
>
> (Interviewee H)

Whether or not Interviewee H's perception was correct, it did strike a chord with my personal experience as an undergraduate in the late 1990s and early 2000s. During my undergraduate and postgraduate courses in Brazil, there was a joke among students of IR that said Cardoso was attempting something completely new: instead of 'international insertion', his government was pursuing 'international deletion'. What seems basic to interviewee H's argument is that Brazilian IR, as a discipline, was a place of resistance to the neo-liberal project, a place for critical thinking, in the words of Cervo (2003: 19). The deviation from Brazilian international identity was perceived as an attack on the vision of development espoused by this group. Cardoso's office was taken as a deviation from the state-centred modernization platform that Brazilian governments had pursued since the 1930s and was thus perceived as an attack on the vision of development espoused by this group. Cervo argues that the normal state sought to do away with 'national interest' and the 'national project of development' (Cervo 2003: 18) since neo-liberal policies were not pursued in the national interest or in the name of a national project of development. Rather, it was in the interests of the 'centre of command of capitalism' (Cervo 2003: 18). Thus, neo-liberal policies were taken to be a modified form of the breach of sovereignty and self-determination by Brazilian IR academia.

The aforementioned perception determined many lines of work and focused on two points. The first was the economic and political effects of neo-liberalism: the Washington Consensus (see Vaz 1993; Tavares 1994; Ianni 1998; Cervo 2000; Holanda 2001; Loureiro 2009), free-trade agreements (see Lipkin 1985; Melo and Costa 1995; Thorstensen 1998; Guimarães 1999; De La Reza 2002; Batista 2003), and international financial institutions (WTO, IMF, World Bank) (see Paulino 2002; Ricupero 2002). The second was the opposite move, a sort of search for alternatives to the model of international insertion promoted by neo-liberal policies. Thus, there was a new breadth of research on Latin American integration (see Carranza 1993), comparative studies between Mercosul and the EU (see Meyer 1999; Hirst 2001; Vizentini 2001; M. Saraiva 2004), cooperation opportunities with other Latin American countries (see Medeiros 1995, Martins 1997, Albuquerque 1998, Almino 2002), and multilateralism (see Vigevani 1999, Miyamoto 2000, Oliveira and Onuki 2000). These research areas contain an underlying praxis to them. By investigating the political and economic effects of neo-liberalism and by looking at alternatives that would serve to counter neo-liberalism, Brazilian IR scholars were actively pursuing their method of development. In doing so, their published papers left behind a trail of clues about what or whose development was at stake. As the research agenda and the statements provided by interviewees have shown, 'method' relates to the development of the state and to the defence of the strong centralized state. The next section analyses how these ideas are embedded in the way Brazilian IR community has worlded Brazil.

Worlding Brazil

As was the case with *becoming* and *the method* in Brazilian IR, *worlding Brazil* through security in the post-redemocratization period requires a different methodology than the one used to explore worlding under the military regime. In order to grasp the relationship between security and identity, sources other than legislation and policy had to be explored. Here, I use the aforementioned two cycles of conferences promoted by the federal government as sources for *Worlding Brazil*. They provide insight into how the armed forces, the Ministry of Foreign Affairs and academia have thought about security in the past decade. My analysis is presented in two sections. The first one relates to the essentialization and naturalization of Brazilian identity and Brazil's international role. The second looks at the connection between security and Brazil's international insertion. Both themes explored in this section return to arguments that have been made throughout the chapter: the essentialization of Brazilian identity and the overall project of international insertion.

Brazil: essential and natural

The great turn in social thinking promoted in the 1930s was based on the restriction and subordination of politics to the concept of Brazilian identity. Since then, the constant need to define Brazilian identity and derive from it strategies of development and rationalization have been the norm in Brazilian social theorizing. For Brazilian IR, the adaptation of the TEA to foreign policy thinking was accompanied by strategies that are perhaps unique to this discipline. While other forms of social theorizing find their political niche by perceiving Brazilian identity through the lens of *personalismo* and *patrimonialismo*, and the subsequent platforms of development, Brazilian IR has discussed identity through claims of fairness, rectitude, representation of the developing world, multilateralism and benign leadership. This is a very revealing strategy for Brazilian IR thinking. First, it is linked to the underlying assumption that Brazilian people may be *personalista* but the policy-making elite that conducts foreign relations is rational, well respected and assertive. This differentiation promoted by Brazilian IR has allowed the discipline to associate these characteristics with the Brazilian state, and thus essentialize Brazilian international identity with those same characteristics: *both* cordiality *and* rationality. When thinking about security, it is the naturalization of Brazil as a peaceful country that is endowed with natural leadership abilities that comes to the forefront of the discourse. In the 2004 conference, two panellists stated:

I am convinced that, through a solid and trustworthy policy of regional insertion, our country may contribute to increase security, its own as well as the regions'. Moreover, with the credentials it holds of being a mediator state with a vocation for peace, our contribution may be even greater.

(Rebelo 2004: 137)

Brazil is going to exercise a central role in any security effort in South America. That is almost [its] geographic fate: not only because of the dimensions of the country but due to the close contact that our borders have with almost every people in the continent. The fact that Brazil borders 9 of the 11 South American countries and that it has lived in peace with all of them for 130 years makes us share substantial interests with each of the nations of the region.

(Macedo Soares 2004: 154)

In the 2010 conference, statements by other members of the Brazilian IR community closely resembled the ones above:

We are at a very advantageous point of our international insertion. Brazil is constantly giving signs of its natural leadership in the region and it is not different in the area of security. Brazilian interventions through coalitions, and not through individual action, makes clear the disposition of the country to maintain the autonomy of the region in the area of security and to place itself as a counterweight to US hegemony.

(Garcia 2010)

Our international insertion in security has had very positive episodes, from the establishment of the Nuclear-Weapon-Free Zone to the relationship with Argentina. In recent years, we have sent troops to Haiti and, after the initial discomfort and resistance on the part of public opinion, the results have been positive.

(Rocha 2010)

Security is a very important area for the international insertion of Brazil. . . we have examples that contradict the American experience with security. We led the construction of a Nuclear-Weapon-Free Zone, we established a trusting relationship with Argentina and we cooperate with the Argentine government, we have sent troops to Haiti, we are seeking to create UNASUL.

(Salomao 2010)

From the statements above, one can discern the same discursive strategy used to legitimize Brazilian international identity using a wide range of different episodes and policy areas to justify the argument. However, they are deployed more for what they can assert about Brazilian identity than for what they can explain or highlight.

Security and 'international insertion'

In 2010, Antônio Patriota (the current Brazilian Minister of Foreign Affairs) introduced his presentation at the conference on security and defence by stating:

> Brazil projects itself on the international stage more and more each day. Among many reasons for this projection are its potentialities, its wealth, its people. We have a great territory, a great population and a vibrant economy. In this context, thinking about security and defence means thinking about our international insertion and [thinking about] how we are going to lead that effort. Brazilian identity in international relations demands that we think about multilateral, regional, constructive responses and steer away from unilateral perspectives.
>
> (Patriota 2010)

The above quotation encapsulates the arguments raised in this chapter in three ways. It starts by essentializing and reducing the place and the scope of politics to the Brazilian territory and identity. It then subjects thinking about security to state development. Following on from that, it equates multilateralism, regionalism and constructive measures to Brazilian international identity and it does so by immediately establishing an underlying counterpoint to this identity. In an interview, Jaguaribe spoke of the connection between security and the international insertion of Brazil this way:

> The conceptualization of security is an integral part of the project of insertion of Brazil in the world which, in turn, is a relevant part of the national project. Thus, the first step for the conceptualization of security is 'what is the national policy? What can we do to emphasize Brazil in the world? The answer is obvious – we need to move Brazil from the periphery to a central position.
>
> (Kumasaka and Barros 1988: 65)

Conceptualizing security to fit the project of international insertion reflects the same need to constantly reify and reproduce the discourse of Brazilian identity examined throughout the thesis. That is, facts as well as conceptualizations are only made intelligible through what they can say about a particular interpretation of identity and development. Bringing Brazil from the periphery to the centre is central to thinking not only about security, but also about international politics in general. In addition, the idea of countering US influence is the key discursive element in this strategy of international insertion and development. On this point, another panellist of the 2004 conference argued:

> The security of Brazil in the international realm is primarily threatened by those actions that strike the sovereignty of our national-state. Where may these actions come from? They can only come from the core [the West/the USA].

The geographic position, the level of power, and Brazil's national objectives preclude any perspective that the source of external insecurity may come from the periphery.

(Velasco e Cruz *et al.* 2004: 41)

The relationship with the USA not only permeates the majority of analysis in Brazilian IR, it is also used to justify any behaviour in Brazilian foreign policy. By making the USA the source of otherness, Brazilian IR works within the paradigm of the TEA but instead of using the USA as the example of rationality (as espoused in other forms of social theorizing) it strategically places the USA as the counterpoint to Brazilian international identity. If, on the one hand, Brazil is portrayed as peaceful, law-abiding, champion of multilateral organizations, of the right to sovereignty and as a representative of the developing world; on the other, the USA is depicted as being naturally inclined to wage wars, to disrespect treaties and other countries' right to sovereignty, and to be one of the main obstacles to development. This chapter analysed thinking about security in Brazil between 1985 and 2010 in the light of the TEA. It did so by applying the three tenets of the TEA in three steps. First, the section 'Being' looked at the conceptualization of security developed in Brazilian IR after redemocratization. For the second step, becoming, the chapter looked at how underlying claims of resistance to the USA and assertions of Brazilian international identity dictated the agenda of security in the discipline. Third, in 'The Method', it explored how members of the community developed practices of resistance against the neo-liberal policies of the Cardoso government. Lastly, and linked to 'worlding', the chapter looked at how the themes explored were presented in the 2003 and 2010 conferences on security and defence sponsored by the federal government. The arguments proposed in this chapter may be summarized in five points. First, Brazilian IR has been more concerned with establishing the place and role of Brazil in the world than with thinking about the international. Thinking about security follows the same pattern of the discipline and is highly concerned with Brazilian foreign policy in the area of security. Second, in the section 'Being', the contingencies of thinking about and conceptualizing security in Brazilian IR have not been determined by intellectual debates on security elsewhere. My analysis briefly explored the politics of talking security in post-redemocratization Brazil and the politically charged meanings that the two dictatorships rendered for the concept. Despite political differences concerning the redemocratization process, military and civilian thinking about security were not strange bedfellows. By comparing conceptualizations of security provided by contemporary members of the community of Brazilian IR with those provided by the ESG during the regime, this chapter argued that the depoliticization of the concept of security in post-redemocratization Brazil served not only to bring civilians and military together but also to submit security to the idea of Brazilian international insertion. Third, through 'Becoming' this chapter argued that the teleological aim of development, central to the TEA, was inscribed in Brazilian IR as *inserção internacional*. Brazil's international insertion has been pervaded by two ideas. The first is the need to counter US influence on the continent and the second is the claim that Brazil has an international identity. By exploring how these two ideas both determine and underpin the security agenda in IR, this chapter argued that the discipline is embedded in the same ontological assumptions as other forms of social theorizing in Brazil. Fourth, in 'Method', by exploring how Brazilian IR organized forms of resistance to those governments that pursued neo-liberal policies, this chapter investigated how the defining disciplinary claim of opposition to the USA was internalized within the national realm and justified in the community of Brazilian IR. Furthermore, it argued that members of the Brazilian IR community act as intellectuals and defenders of the state in much the same way that intellectuals of the 1920s and 1930s behaved as guardians of the centralized state. Fifth, the section entitled 'Worlding' explored two arguments previously presented in this chapter. These two arguments relate to how the Brazilian IR community worked with essentialized views on identity. Instead of 'Brazilian national identity', Brazilian IR intellectuals refer to 'Brazilian international identity' in order to put forward their own positions of the development of the state and the political platform they favoured.

Part III

Worlding Brazil, reworlding the self

6   Conclusion

The introduction to this volume set out a discussion about the place of knowledge production in IR outside the global core. As argued there, IR in the periphery has often been the concern of academic enquiry only in relation to what it can offer to the discipline at the core. One strand of academic enquiry has attempted to search for critical understandings in the discipline that are not available in the West. Another has sought to ask why there is no IR theory in other geocultural settings. This way, Western IR engaged with scholars in the periphery either as first-hand accounts of the state of the art of the discipline outside the core or as subaltern voices that may offer critical understandings to the discipline in the West.

The argument raised then was that the engagement proposed by both strands was yet to attempt (a) analysing the core–periphery axis of the discipline, (b) investigating power relations in the non-core of the discipline, and (c) pushing forward critical self-reflection in the periphery. Thus, this volume proposes investigating knowledge production on security in Brazil in ways that address the processes that connect the formulation of claims embedded in the deep structure of thought to the policy outcomes that are enabled by them.

The first part of my engagement with the question proposed by Tickner and Wæver in relation to Brazilian IR – Why is this the case? – was to rework Souza's critique of Brazilian sociology and include an analytical framework that accounted for intellectual agency and interests in knowledge production. This allowed chapters to highlight the linearity of intellectual heterodoxy in Brazil. By furthering Souza's work to include the role of Brazilian intellectuals in reifying and reproducing the TEA, this volume provides a narrative on knowledge production in Brazil that takes into account the 'interplay of interests and ideas' (Wyn Jones 1999: 112).

This analytical framework (*being, becoming* and *the method*) resonates with the one proposed by Booth (2008: chap. 4) when analysing the process by which practising security emerges from deep political assumptions to policy outputs. Booth argues that one can look at this process as a movement that begins in the deep structure of politics, namely the main political theories and philosophies that inform different worldviews. From this stems the 'interplay of underlying ideas', the violent and non-violent political struggles that ultimately define 'who gets what, when, and how' (an old definition of 'politics' – Lasswell 1950). The final step of the process is the policy outcomes that derive from the deep structure and the interplay of ideas. Being, becoming and the method are tied to this rationale. These three levels of analysis were especially helpful in that they allowed the argument that political and academic discussions in Brazil only take place at the level of the fracture zone and of policy outputs.

The deep structure of thought entailed by the claims of Brazilian identity remained largely unchallenged in the eight decades preceding 2014 in Brazil. What has changed, however, is the way that different intellectual groups have strategized those claims to fit their own political purposes in each of the contexts analysed in this book. Thus, although being (claims about identity), becoming (the teleological aim of development) and the method (the political choices that enable development) are identifiable constants in intellectual practice in Brazil, they also have had specific characteristics and meanings in each of the contexts.

Being, as the deeply ingrained assumptions about Brazilian identity, is the main structure of Brazilian theorizing. Becoming is the teleological aim of state development. The method is the enactment of being and becoming in political and academic practice. It corresponds to the fracture zone in which political gains are struggled for and decided on: who profits from development, when and how. Booth calls attention to the policy outcomes that are embedded in the deep structure of thought. These policy outcomes, which are a reflection of the deep structure and the fracture zones of politics, refer to the way I have conceived *worlding*. That is, worlding is the political output produced by the political and social theorizing that has been hegemonic in Brazil in the last eight decades. Before turning to worlding, let us look at the main findings provided by each of the three tenets explored in Part II.

Being

Being relates to the essentialization of Brazilian identity and culture. In all three historic contexts, the division of society between those who are adapted to lead development efforts and those who are not also served to justify and legitimize the place of intellectuals who were able to 'speak security'. Implied in each of these claims about Brazilian identity is an elitist vision of society falling into two groups: one composed of pre-modern irrational beings driven by passion, and another of rational leaders who are in charge of the development process. What gave the TEA momentum and allowed it to become both an academic and political common sense was the work of intellectuals who were able to claim authority for structuring authoritative knowledge and political ideas already espoused, to different extents, by certain segments of society (Pécaut 1989: 59).

In Chapter 3, the analysis of the journal *A Defeza Nacional*, published since 1913 by army officers, provided an illustration for the contextualization of Freyre's and Buarque de Holanda's work within the general crisis of the republican system. It explored how some of the ideas put forward by these two authors had been discussed, at least partially, by other sectors of society. Chapter 3 argued that, in the first decades of the twentieth century, the army assigned itself the true

Brazilian identity, for they were 'the only truly organized force' (*ADN* 1913: 1) that could not only lead the effort of modernization but also cleanse the country of civilian politics. Here the armed forces were the only rational and morally correct sector, while civilians, despite their status or role in politics, were perceived as being incapable of representing the *pátria*.

In Chapter 4, claims about the nature of Brazilian identity were present in the most fundamental concepts of the DSN. The doctrine made an explicit differentiation between society and nation. The former was taken to be the collective of *personalista* beings that inhabited the country and whom were deemed not rational enough to serve the modernization effort. The latter was understood as the advanced stage of society, one populated by rational individuals who could both lead the country to development and represent the values that were to be made secure. Thus, according to the DSN, the nation – not society – provided the country with national power. Moreover, the state was perceived as a direct reflection of the nation, hence the need to rationalize society in order to acquire more national power and to become a part of the international status quo. At the ESG, the lines between civilians and armed forces were blurred to include other like-minded conservative sectors. In that case, irrationality and, thus, a lack of modernity was assigned to those who, either through dissent or unrealized potential, could not take part in the development effort.

In Chapter 5, claims about Brazilian identity were discussed not in relation to Brazilian citizens but to the Brazilian state. As portrayed by the Brazilian IR community, the Brazilian state is endowed with a peaceful, law-abiding, treaty-respecting, cooperative nature that propels it to be a natural regional leader and representative of the developing world. For the Brazilian IR community, the divide between pre-modern and rational citizens is implied rather than explicit as it had been in the two previous contexts. As argued earlier, Brazilian intellectuals have often claimed to speak in the name of disadvantaged peoples. However, as was the case with the other two contexts, these take the form of moral exhortations rather than a meaningful attempt to include ordinary people in political processes.

Becoming

This relates to the underlying teleological aim of social theorizing in Brazil: the development of the state. Although *becoming developed* was a general trend in social theorizing in Brazil, Part II explored what development meant in each of these contexts. That is, it investigated how the teleological aim of development had different meanings for different intellectual sectors. These different strategies of becoming are reflective of the political choices of each group and their own vision of what rationality means for Brazil. As such, they do not presuppose a specific path to development – a specific method – rather they focus on the endpoint of thinking about security.

For the authoritarian actors in Chapter 3, development meant the establishment of heavy industries, the development of roads and ports, the supply of staff and armaments to the armed forces and, above all, the militarization of the state. During the *Estado Novo*, that endpoint was the complete militarization of society. For the conservative and authoritarian forces that reconvened at the ESG after the end of the *Estado Novo* (Chapter 4), the goal of development was related to becoming a Western Christian Democracy. Chapters 5 argued that, for the Brazilian IR community, development has been understood in terms of the possibility of political and economic autonomy from the USA. At the ESG, development aimed to raise Brazil to the sphere of the West, while the Brazilian IR community perceives development to be also secured through the attainment of specific security goals such as a seat in the United Nation's SC, leadership in South America, and representing developing countries in international forums.

The method

As the political platform of each group that spoke security, *the method* (strategy of development) also differed significantly. Political and academic debates have never required intellectuals to think about the deep structure of their thought and to move away from the usual claims about Brazilian identity. As such, political and academic discussions have confined themselves to discussing different methods of development.

In the first context, the most authoritarian sector of the armed forces developed a legal and security apparatus to implement their specific method of modernization. They argued that national security was devised to justify that method – the scrutiny of civilian life by the armed forces. Thus, any thinking or institutional arrangement of security was pre-emptively marked not only as an area of the military but also as authoritarian and conservative. As argued in Chapters 3 and 4, this early politicization of the word 'security' had long-term political consequences, especially the lack of willingness by more progressive sectors to discuss security, either during the democratic interregnum (1945–64) or in the post-1985 redemocratization period. Chapter 4 argued that the doctrine itself was the method of development proposed by the ESG. The DSN worked using a circular logic that started from the concepts of society, nation, state and national power and, from there, derived its rationale from the power of the ruling elite to lead the country to national security.

In the post-authoritarian context, the method was derived from opposition to the neo-liberal project of the government. That is, the strategy devised by the Brazilian IR community was to stand in opposition to the government (because it espoused neo-liberal policies) and to defend the centralization of the state and of the economy.

Chapter 3 used the critique of the *Princípios Fundamentais* (PF) proposed by Montarroyos (1979) to argue that, since political and academic debates on security are circumscribed to the TEA, they remain attached to politics – who gets what, when and how. That is, they focus on the legitimacy of different sectors in talking security and their proposed method of development. As the critique offered by Montarroyos exemplified, she did not disagree with the ideas of rationalization of society, with the need for a method of development or even that an elite was necessary to lead that project of development. Her criticism focused on the legitimacy of the ESG to lead that project and the possibility of authoritarian measures to justify it. Whilst these concerns revealed the very pragmatic (and necessary) aim of questioning the regime, it also revealed how deeper philosophical questions that informed the TEA were not challenged.

In Chapter 5, the discussion of the method also highlighted how political and academic discussions in Brazil have remained at the policy output level and have seldom sought to transcend it. In the case of the Brazilian IR community, its intellectuals offered political resistance to government policies through the organization of seminars, conferences and publications (Cervo and Bueno 2002), but that political opposition was in terms of policy outputs. It did not question the basic assumptions about identity and development. In fact, if anything, it further strengthened their own claims of being intellectuals and defenders of the centralized state. In this sense, as argued, intellectuals of the Brazilian IR community in the 2000s behaved much like intellectuals of the 1920s and 1930s –as intellectuals of the centralized state. Once that was threatened by the liberal republican system – in the first three decades of the last century, and by post-1985 civilian governments that pursued neo-liberal policies – intellectuals organized resistance to defend the state.

The narrative that emerged was one of continuity and similarity. Continuity in relation to the claims about Brazilian identity, the teleological aim of economic development, and the fierce elitism that divides the country between the rational elite that is to lead the modernization effort and the pre-modern irrational people on whose name they speak. Another constant underlying theme was the way that the TEA allowed me to question the divides between military and civilian thought and right and left wing. I do not mean to argue that there are no differences between right and left or between those who profess the free-market as a solution to Brazilian problems and those who argue that a centralized state with economy-intervening powers. There are serious political and economic consequences at stake that define these different approaches. Rather, the argument is that they have been historically similar in the way they are informed by the same elitist exclusionary ideas based on claims about Brazilian identity. That is to say, while they differ in their policy outputs, they are much alike in the deep structure of thought that sustains their discussions. Consequently, they both contribute to the exclusion of other actors' agency, to the status quo of intellectuals as agents of modernization and to the invisibility of other forms of identity that strive to be recognized outside the limitations imposed by the all-encompassing and essentialized Brazilian identity.

Worlding

As mentioned before, worlding constituted the second part of my engagement with the GEP. Worlding connects the basic informing views about the world in here (academic and political circles of those who get to speak security) to the world out there (where the deep structure of thought is materialized). Thus, worlding has been understood as the process through which reality is made intelligible in the global context and by which we determine who we are in relation to others (Tickner and Wæver 2009b: 9). That means to say that worlding is the representation of Brazil offered by Brazilian intellectuals to themselves and to the world. Exploring the relationship between worlding and the deep structure of thought that informs it constitutes a fundamental step of critical engagement in Brazil. It concerns how local interpretations of security promote different forms of exclusion and which are obscured if their formative processes are not put under scrutiny.

Examining worlding entails not only exploring the deep structure of thought that informs political views, but also establishing links between those perspectives and policy outcomes, discursive representations and assumptions used in everyday life. This means that the process of worlding, making reality intelligible, relates to and is a reflection of all three tenets of the TEA. 'Worlding Brazil' meant examining the way in which representations of Brazil were inscribed in policy outcomes (Chapter 4) and in intellectual thinking (Chapter 5). Upon representing Brazil to themselves and to the world, Brazilian intellectuals have promoted a specific series of images about Brazil outwards, as well as inwards, that reflect their exclusionary and essentializing ideas about both identity and politics.

In Chapter 4, worlding Brazil through security was explored in relation to the two characteristics of the DSN. The first one related to the idea of making secure specific traits of Brazilian identity whilst the second concerned securing the project of *Brasil Potência* (Brazil World Power). In the schoolbooks analysed in Chapter 4, the representation of Brazil and its people was infused in essentialized ideas of rationality, gender, race, religion, and belonging (to the West). By offering a representation of Brazil as a Catholic, rational country devoted to the principles of national security, those schoolbooks also excluded difference whilst setting out what character traits should be made secure.

In Chapter 5, representations of Brazil were analysed in two instances. First, it explored representations of Brazil as a natural leader and peaceful country that had all necessary requirements to be a representative of the developing world. Second, it investigated the relationship between *inserção internacional* as a counterweight to US influence in the world. In Chapters 4 and 5, 'worlding Brazil' meant portraying the country as a benevolent leader of the developing world. As such, it fed back into the claims about identity and the rationality of those who led the development effort. For the most part of the past eight decades, worlding Brazil has meant silently excluding difference and denying agency to those outside policy-making and policy-advising circles.

Currently, the uncritical acceptance of terms used in Brazilian IR abounds in the recent Western scholarship on Brazil. Brazil's rapid economic growth in the past 10 years has caught the attention of the West and it has inspired the literature on Brazil as an emerging power. Slowly making their way to the discipline's core are terms such as 'international insertion' (Tickner 2003: 340), statements about Brazilian identity in IR and/or foreign politics (Hurrell 2006: 19;

Alden and Vieira 2006), comments on Brazil's natural disposition to become a regional power (Klom 2003; Burges 2006, 2008; Brainard and Martinez-Diaz 2009) and the assumption that Brazil is a representative of the developing world (Huelsz 2009). All these developments serve to reify the claims of Brazilian IR by embedding this story of Brazil within the core of the discipline. This move represents a significant consequence of the way that mainstream IR scholarship has engaged with knowledge production by Brazilian academia. What is necessary then is to engage with heterodoxy in its local meanings and forms in Brazil. Such engagement entails not only critically assessing the terms of the Brazilian IR debate, but also offering ways to re-world Brazil. Before moving on to the ways Brazil might be re-worlded in IR academia, there is a third level of analysis – introduced in Chapter 1 – that needs to be considered, namely, the personal.

Re-worlding the self

In his *Ralé Brasileira: Quem é e como vive,* Jessé Souza wrote: 'becoming uncomfortable is always a risk, we end up discovering things about those people we love and about ourselves that are by no means a comfortable truth'. As an academic and personal exercise, the research that led to this volume was not only uncomfortable but also deeply emotional. It required distancing myself – both geographically and academically – from what and whom I loved and from the deepest assumptions I held about my discipline in Brazil and my political praxis.

My encounter with critical scholarship allowed me to rethink the historical role of academia and theoretical underpinnings. For me, this rethinking occurred in two ways. First, as a personal encounter with the history of my family, which, generation after generation, was subjected to different politics of security deriving from particular deep structures of political ideas. My own political situatedness led me to look for ways to appraise the different historical contexts in which thinking about security took place.

To recall the history of the family members mentioned in the Introduction, my great-grand uncle was tried by the Tribunal of National Security – one of the string of security institutions established to support the project of militarization of the state analysed in Chapter 3. My grandmother was accompanied more than once by members of the political police in her preaching of Liberation Theology. My father had to send me, his first born, to live my first 2 years 3,000 km away from him for fear of what could happen to those who engaged in the establishment in left-wing politics in the late 1970s and early 1980s. Lastly, me, who came to Aberystwyth University to think about security in Brazil in non-militarized ways.

As a child of the last years of the Brazilian dictatorship, I had learned to dichotomize politics between military and civilian thought, in which the former was understood as authoritarian and top-down and the latter simply was not. This deep political divide in national politics hindered self-criticism towards the democratic basis of civilian thought. Through reassessing the deep structure of thought of Brazilian academic and political debates of each generation of my family, I was able to understand that the 'people' – on whose name so many have spoken – were seldom given any agency or place. On a very personal basis, my non-white, immigrant, uneducated, historically hungry and thirsty family had no place in any of this. Even though we had been subjected to the politics of security, we were largely absent from Brazilian intellectual thought beyond rhetoric. By drilling down Brazilian knowledge production on security I was able to challenge my place as part of the intellectual elite of my country; as an interlocutor of IR from outside the core; as a Brazilian IR student who left her native country sponsored by a government that had historically denied public education to the majority of its population, as a political activist who had justified her praxis with an exclusionary and elitist discourse and, lastly, as somebody who had defined politics through civilian/military and neo-liberal/nationalist lenses. Researching the political place of my family in twentieth-century Brazil led me to enquire into my own political situatedness in relation to Brazilian IR. As a student, IR had attracted me for what it could say about the place of Brazil in the world. However, as I followed critical debates on IR at the core, I started to question my own place in the world of Brazilian IR. Criticism of Anglo-European academic culture and the Western views it imposes on the non-core was not a novelty. Back then, and for some time already, critical voices had started to denounce the white male-dominated, upper class environment of Western IR (see discussion in Sjoberg 2013).

Those arguments gave me an opportunity to look back at the Brazilian academic environment and see that gender, class and racial divides remained largely unquestioned, lurking behind the idea of a homogenous, zealous Brazilian IR. I had myself denied those questions for a long time. In informal conversations with peers, the subject of power relations inside the discipline in Brazil would often come up but only to be quickly tucked away under an 'accept and conform' mantra.

I often spoke of Brazilian identity and the national goal of development, but seldom thought of who was represented by that identity. I wished to distance myself from exclusively military forms of thinking about security, but never considered whether there were great differences in the way the armed forces and civilians thought about security nor what I meant by 'civilian and military thinking'. Due to my family history and personal activism, it was extremely emotional and challenging to look back and realize I was myself conforming to the academic discourse that spoke in the name of the people but saw no place for their agency. In doing so, I was not only denying my background, I was working hard to maintain that status quo.

Ultimately, what had started as sociological observations became the research project that paved the way for this volume. Questioning the fabric of political assumptions that defined my work allowed me to reposition myself in relation to the assumptions I once held so dear. Through *Worlding Brazil* I have 'reworlded' myself. The national identity discourse that was once central to my political activism was replaced with a more critical engagement with politics through being, becoming and the method through which Brazil might re-world itself. The question then is What might it mean to re-world Brazil?

Re-worlding Brazil

While space does not allow more than a brief indication future directions, such an ending to this book is appropriate given its personal origins, the Critical Security Studies (CSS) approach adopted and the endorsement at the start of this Conclusion that the personal is political and global. I would like to propose re-worlding Brazil by addressing ways in which being, becoming and the method may contribute to bringing about the politics of inclusion, diversity and emancipatory ideals rather than nationalistic, elitist, exclusionary practices that have for so long characterized thinking about security in Brazil. In other words, being becomes a different identity, becoming is conceived with a different aim and the method (of enacting) a new being and becoming is reconceived.

The essentialization of identity has been the most basic informing idea of social theorizing in Brazil since the 1930s. Therefore, being has been marked by perspectives that not only silence and exclude diversity, it also renders Brazilian inequality invisible by reducing issues such as race, gender and class to a matter of national identity. Furthermore, being, as currently practised and theorized in Brazilian academia is not only myopic, it also serves to maintain the status quo of the limited sector of Brazilian society that is not perceived as irrational, premodern and passion-driven. In a brief interview I conducted with J. Souza, he argued that making national identity the most basic assumption of social theorizing has engendered:

> Superficial knowledge that cannot account for the pragmatic dimension of everyday life. It is there [everyday life] that we find silenced conflict, pain, and suffering – including those silenced by science. It is in everyday life that we find subtle and non-transparent domination mechanisms – of class, gender, race and groups of all sorts – that are not intelligible to those who imagine a world divided into nation-states, for example.
>
> (J. Souza 13/08/2011)

The world of Brazilian national identity is mandatorily a world of nation-states, a world in which political borders, and not any other form of association, have most prominently defined identity. In order to think of re-worlding Brazil, other forms of community, both internally and externally, must be brought to the forefront of political theorizing. Internally, that means politicizing other forms of identity that are not based on nationality. It requires thinking about those groups that have been silenced and made insecure by the practices of national identity, such as native peoples, women, sexual minorities and people in the many social categories of blackness. Externally, thinking about security in ways that are not tied to national identity means placing the individual and different forms of community as the main referent object of security. In other words, it means re-conceptualizing the subject of security as the security of the subjected.

Becoming in Brazil has focused on the teleology of social theorizing in relation to the development of the state. Re-worlding then means that the guiding principle of development needs to be replaced by forms of theorizing and practices that seek to change the insecurity of those subjected to oppressive relations and threatening life conditions. This requires that the limit of security theorizing in Brazil (or anywhere) be defined not through geopolitical and identity essentializations but through human suffering and exclusion. That means having emancipation as a process of inclusion and egalitarianism instead of development as a teleological aim.

Method in Brazilian social theorizing has concerned the establishment of political platforms of development pursued by different sectors of Brazilian intellectuals. A political platform that places the security of the subjected at the forefront of politics and emancipation as the guiding principle of inclusion and security must work with a more ambitious idea of what problem-solving theory might mean. In relation to this issue, Booth (2008: 48) highlights that 'the task of students of world politics is to construct a security studies that goes beyond problem-solving within the status quo, and instead seeks to help engage through critical theory with the problem of the status quo'. As Booth suggests, critical theory has an important role to play in actively engaging with the problems engendered by the status quo and in promoting critique as a way of theorizing 'reflexively beyond current orthodoxies' to oppose those 'structures that produce, perpetuate, and naturalize human wrongs' (Booth 2008: 44). Again, from a personal perspective, these guiding principles of critical theory allowed me to look at the positions I had previously defended about Brazil and its place in the world and reflect on the structures that I myself was reproducing and naturalizing.

In other words, re-worlding Brazil requires a basic rethinking of being, becoming and method from the deep structures of political thought upwards. It requires moving beyond its traditional worlding, embedded in its colonial and postcolonial legacies, beyond embedded assumptions about its geopolitical situation and beyond traditional theorizing about society and politics. Instead, Brazil has the opportunity to begin to re-construct itself – guided by social inclusivity, emancipatory politics and critical theorizing – into a condition of being what Hedley Bull, in a well-known phrase, called a 'local agent of the world common good' (Bull 1983: 11–12).

Bibliography

Acharaya A and Buzan B (2007) Why is there no Non-Western International Relations Theory? An Introduction. *International Relations of the Asia-Pacific* 7(3): 287–312.

ADESG (1955) O Problema da Recuperação Moral do País. Escola Superior de Guerra.

___ (2013) *Diplomados da ADESG por Estado.* Associacao dos Diplomados da Escola Superior de Guerra. Available at: www.adesg.net.br/diplomados-por-estado (accessed 15/05/13).

ADN (1913) Editorial. A Defeza Nacional.

ADN (1915) Editorial. A Defeza Nacional. 'Adeus Brasil Potência' (2000) *Folha de São Paulo.* São Paulo, 1 August.

Albuquerque J (1998) *ALCA: Relações Internacionais e Sua Construção Jurídica.* Sao Paulo: FTD.

Alden C and Vieira A (2006) The new diplomacy of the South: South Africa, Brazil, India and trilateralism, *Third World Quaterly* 26(7): 1077–95.

Alexander R (1956) Tenentismo. *The Hispanic American Historical Review* 36(2): 229–42.

Alker H and Biersteker T (1984) The Dialectics of World Order: Notes for a Future Archeologist of International Savoir Faire. *International Studies Quarterly* 28(2): 121–48.

Almeida P (1998) Revista Brasileira de Política Internacional: Quatro Décadas ao Serviço da Inserção Internacional do Brasil. *Revista Brasileira de Política Internacional* 41: 42–55.

___ (2004) Uma Política Externa Engajada: A Diplomacia do Governo Lula. *Revista Brasileira De Política Internacional* 47(1): 162–84.

___ (2006) *O Estudo das Relações Internacionais do Brasil.* Brasilia: LGE Editora.

Almino J (2002) Inserção Internacional de Segurança do Brasil: A Perspectiva Diplomática. In: Brigadão C and Proença J (eds) *Brasil e o Mundo: Novas Visões.* Rio de Janeiro: Francisco Alves.

Alves MH (1984) *Estado e Oposição no Brasil (1964–1984).* Petrópolis: Editora Vozes.

Amorim C (1996) *A Reforma da ONU.* Instituto de Estudos Avançados da Universidade de São Paulo. Texto apresentado no seminário *O Brasil e as Novas Dimensões da Segurança Internacional,* set 1–10.

___ (1999) Entre o Desequilíbrio Unipolar e a Multipolaridade: O Conselho de Segurança da ONU no Período pós-Guerra Fria. In: Dupas G and Vigevani T (eds) *O Brasil e as Novas Dimensões de Segurança Internacional.* Sao Paulo: Alfa-Omega.

___ (2004). O Brasil e o Novos Conceitos Globais e Hemisféricos do Conceito de Segurança. In: Rocha A, Silva R and Pinto J (eds) *Reflexões Sobre Defesa e Segurança: Uma Estratégia para o Brasil.* Brasília: Ministério da Defesa.

Andrade M (1972) *Os Contos de Belazarte*. ãSao Paulo: Martins.

Anselmo R and Bray S (2002) Geografia e Geopolítica na Formação Nacional Brasileira: Everardo Backheuser. In: Gerardi L and Mendes I (eds) *Do Natural, Do Social e de Suas Interações: Visões Geográficas*, pp. 109–19.

Armitage D (2004) The Fifty Years' Rift: Intellectual History and International Relations. *Modern Intellectual History* 1: 97–109.

Arraes V (2005) O Brasil e o Conselho de Segurança da Organização das Nações Unidas: Dos anos 90 a 2002. *Revista Brasileira De Política Internacional* 48(2): 152–68.

Arruda A (1967) *O Poder Nacional: Fundamentos e Fatores Psicossociais*, C1-06–67. Rio de Janeiro: Escola Superior de Guerra.

___ (1980) *ESG: História de Sua Doutrina*. Rio de Janeiro: GRD/INL-MEC.

___ (1983) A Escola Superior de Guerra: Origens (I), Revista da Escola Superior de Guerra. *Revista da Escola Superior de Guerra* 1(I): 113–24.

Avelino Filho G (1990) Cordialidade e civilidade em Raízes do Brasil. *Revista Brasileira de Ciências Sociais* 5(12): 5–14.

Aydinli E and Mathews J (2009) Turkey – Towards Homegrown Theorizing and Building a Disciplinary Community. In: Tickner A and Wæver O (eds) *International Relations Scholarship Around the World*. Abingdon, Oxon: Routledge, pp. 208–22.

Azevedo CMM de (1987) *Onda Negra, Medo Branco: O Negro no Imaginário das Elites– Século XIX*. São Paulo: Annablume.

Azevedo T (1975) *Democracia Racial*. Petrópolis: Vozes.

Backheuser E (1948) *Curso de Geopolítica Geral do Brasil*. Rio de Janeiro: Laemmert.

Baran P (1984) *A Economia Política do Desenvolvimento*. São Paulo: Abril Cultural.

Barbosa R (2002) Os Estados Unidos pós 11 de Setembro de 2001: Implicações para o Brasil. *Revista Brasileira De Política Internacional* 45(1): 72–91.

Batista P (2003) A Alca e o Brasil. *Estudos Avançados* 17(48): 267–93.

Beattie P (2001) *The Tribute of Blood: Army, Honor, Race, and Nation in Brazil, 1864–1945*. Durham: Duke University Press.

Behera N (2007) Re-Imagining IR in India. *International Relations of the Asia-Pacific* 7(3): 341–68.

___ (2009) South Asia: A 'Realist' Past and Alternative Futures. In: Tickner A and Wæver O (eds) *International Relations Scholarship Around the World*. Abingdon, Oxon: Routledge, 134–57.

Bell D (2009) Writing the World: Disciplinary History and Beyond. *International Affairs* 85(1): 3–22.

Bellintani A (2009) *O Exército Brasileiro e a Missão Militar Francesa: Instrução, Doutrina, Organização, Modernidade e Profissionalismo (1920–1940)*. Brasília: Universidade de Brasília.

Berghahnh V (1981) *Militarism: The History of an International Debate, 1861–1979*. London: Berg Publishers.

Bernal-Meza R (2000) *Sistema Mundial y Mercosur: Globalización, Regionalism y Políticas Exteriores Comparadas*. Buenos Aires: Grupo Editor Latinoamericano.

___ (2005) Multilateralismo e Unilateralismo na Política Mundial: América Latina Frente À Ordem Mundial em Transição. *Revista Brasileira de Política Internacional* 48(1): 5–23.

Bielschowski R (1988) *O pensamento econômico brasileiro*. Rio de Janeiro: IPEA-INPES.

Bilac O (1917) Instrução e Patriotismo. *Conferências Literárias*. Rio de Janeiro: Editora Nacional.

Bilgin P (2008) Thinking past 'Western' IR? *Third World Quarterly* 29: 5–23.

Birkner W (2002) *O Realismo de Golbery: Segurança Nacional e Desenvolvimento Global no Pensamento de Golbery do Couto e Silva*. Itajaí: Univale.

Bocco H and Hirst M (1989) Cooperação Nuclear e Integração Brasil–Argentina. *Contexto Internacional* 9: 63–78.

Bonemy H (1999) Três Decretos e um Ministério: A Propósito da Educação no Estado Novo. In: Pandolfi D (ed) *Repensando o Estado Novo*. Rio de Janeiro: FGV.

Booth K (1997) Security and Self: Reflections of a Fallen Realist. In: Krause K and Williams N (eds) *Critical Self Studies – Concepts and Cases*. Minneapolis: University of Minnesota Press, 83–120.

____ (2008) *Theory of World Security*. Cambridge: Cambridge University Press.

____ and Vale P (1995) Security in Southern Africa: After Apartheid, beyond Realism. *International Affairs* 71(2): 285–304.

Braga P (2002) Os Interesses Econômicos dos Estados Unidos e a Segurança Interna no Brasil entre 1946 e 1964: Uma Análise sobre os Limites Entre Diplomacia Coercitiva e Operações Encobertas. *Revista Brasileira de Política Internacional* 45(2): 46–65.

Brainard L and Martinez-Diaz L (2009) *Brazil as an Economic Superpower? Understanding Brazil's Changing Role in the Global Economy*. Washington DC: The Brookings Institute.

Braz M (1979) *Moral e Civismo*. São Paulo: FTD.

Brazil (1927) *Mensagem Apresentada ao Congresso Nacional na Abertura da Primeira Sessão da Décima Terceira Legislatura*. Presidência da República. Available at: http:// brazil.crl.edu/bsd/bsd/u1319/000002.html (accessed 12/07/11).

____ (1934) *Constituição da República Federativa dos Estados Unidos do Brasil*. Presidência da República. Available at: www.planalto.gov.br/ccivil_03/constituicao/constitu-i%C3%A7ao34.htm (accessed 11/05/13).

____ (1935) *Plano de Reorganização do Ministério da Educação e Saúde Pública*. Rio de Janeiro: Imprensa Nacional.

____ (1943) Conferências Marcha para o Oeste (1939–1943). Rio de Janeiro: Companhia Editora Nacional.

____ (1967) Address of the President of the Republic of Brazil on Foreign Policy. Embassy of Brazil in Washington, DC.

Brazil-DOU (1902) Decreto 4.464, de 12 de Julho de 1902. Diário Oficial da União.

____ (1903) Decreto 979 de 6 de Janeiro de 1903. Diário Oficial da União, Seção 1: 138.

____ (1904) Decreto 5.389, de 10 de Dezembro de 1904. Diário Oficial da União.

____ (1905) Decreto 5.478, de 13 de Marco de 1905. Diário Oficial da União.

____ (1906) Decreto 5.919, de 7 de Marco de 1906. Diário Oficial da União.

____ (1912) Decreto 9.521, de 21 de Abril de 1912. Diário Oficial da União.

____ (1915) Decreto 11.498, de 23 de Fevereiro de 1915. Diário Oficial da União.

____ (1916) Decreto 12.310, de 13 de Fevereiro de 1916. Diário Oficial da União.

____ (1921a) Decreto 14.989, de 10 de Setembro de 1921. Diário Oficial da União.

____ (1921b) Decreto 4.354 de 25 de Outubro de 1921. Diário Oficial da União.

____ (1922a) Decreto 7.267, de 12 de Maio de 1922. Diário Oficial da União.

____ (1922b) Decreto 14.447, de 19 de Abril de 1922. Diário Oficial da União.

____ (1923) Decreto 4.629, de 5 de Janeiro de 1923. Diário Oficial da União.

____ (1927) Decreto 17.999, de 3 de Dezembro de 1927. Diário Oficial da União.

____ (1931a) Decreto 176.654, de 11 de Setembro de 1931. Diário Oficial da União.

___ (1931b) Decreto 20.246, de 31 de Julho de 1931. Diário Oficial da União, Seção 1: 138.

___ (1932a) Decreto 23.454, de 9 de Fevereiro de 1932. Diário Oficial da União.

___ (1932b) Decreto 21.985, de 25 de Outubro de 1932. Diário Oficial da União.

___ (1934) Decreto 23.873, de 15 de Fevereiro de 1934. Diário Oficial da União.

___ (1935) Lei 38, de 4 de Abril de 1935. Diário Oficial da União, Seção 1: 138.

___ (1939a) Decreto 1.058, de 19 de Janeiro de 1939. Diário Oficial da União, Seção 1: 138.

___ (1939b) Decreto 869, de 12 de Setembro de 1969. Diário Oficial da União, Seção 1: 138.

Bresser-Pereira L (1999) Do Estado Patrimonial ao Gerencial. In: Pinheiro W (ed) *Brasil: Um Século de Transformações*. São Paulo: Companhia das Letras.

Brigagão C (2004) O Brasil Diante dos Desafios Internacionais em Material de Segurança e Defesa. In: Pinto AR and Silva R (eds) *Pensamento Brasileiro Sobre Defesa e Segurança*, vol. 2, *O Brasil no Cenário Internacional de Defesa e Segurança*. Brasília: Ministério da Defesa.

___ and Proença J (1988) A Projeção Externa do Brasil: A Questão da Segurança. *Contexto Internacional* 7: 85–110.

___ and Seabra R (2009) Panorama Estratégico da Política Externa Brasileira: Os Caminhos da Inserção Internacional. *Relações Internacionais* 24: 75–91.

Brincat S, Lima L and Nunes J (2011) For Someone and for Some Purpose: An Interview with Robert W. Cox. In: Brincat S, Lima L and Nunes J (eds) *Critical Theory in International Relations and Security Studies: Interviews and Reflections*. London: Routledge.

Buarque de Holanda S (1936) *Raízes do Brasil*. (Reprint 1999). São Paulo: Companhia das Letras.

___ (2004) Corpo e Alma do Brasil: Entrevista de Sérgio Buarque de Holanda. *Novos Estudos* 69: 3–14.

Buger C and Gadinger F (2007) Reassembling and Dissecting: International Relations Practice from a Science Studies Perspective. *International Studies Perspective* 8(1): 90–110.

Bull H (1983) The Emergence of a Universal International Society. In Bull and Watson (eds) *The Expansion of International Society*. Oxford: Clarendon Press.

Burges, S (2006) Without Sticks or Carrots: Brazilian Leadership in South America During the Cardoso Era, 1992–2003. *Bulletin of Latin American Research* 25(1): 23–42.

___ (2008) Consensual Hegemony: Theorizing Brazilian Foreign Policy after the Cold War. *International Relations* 22(1): 65–84.

Cabral F and Cunha P (2006) *Nelson Werneck Sodré: Entre o Sabre e a Pena*. São Paulo: UNESP.

Camargo A and Goés W (1981) *Meio Século de Combate: Diálogo com Cordeiro de Farias*. Rio de Janeiro: Nova Fronteira.

Campos F (1940) *Educação e Cultura*. Rio de Janeiro: José Olympio.

Campos J (1964) *Os Interesses e as Aspirações do Povo Brasileiro: Os Objetivos Nacionais Permanentes*. Rio de Janeiro: Escola Superior de Guerra.

Campos R (1982) *O Tribunal de Segurança Nacional, 1935–1945*. Rio de Janeiro: Achiame.

Capanema G (1982) *Discursos e Outros Escritos*. Rio de Janeiro: Pallas.

Carneiro J (1966) *Elementos Básicos da Nacionalidade*. Rio de Janeiro: Escola Superior de Guerra.

Carneiro M (1988) *O Anti-Semitismo na Era Vargas: Fantasmas de Uma Geração (1930–1945)*. São Paulo: Brasiliense.

Carone E (1965) *Revoluções do Brasil Contemporâneo*. São Paulo: Buriti.

Carranza M (1993) Segurança Regional e Integração Econômica na América Latina e no Sudeste Asiático: Um Estudo Comparado. *Contexto Internacional* 15(1): 57–95.

Carvalho J (1980) *A Construção da Ordem: A Elite Política Imperial.* Rio de Janeiro: Campus.

___ (1982) Armed Forces and Politics in Brazil (1930–1945). *Hispanic American Historical Review* 62(2): 193–223.

___ (1987) *Os bestializados: O Rio de Janeiro e A República que Não Foi.* São Paulo: Companhia das Letras.

___ (2005) *Forças Armadas e Política no Brasil.* Rio de Janeiro: Zahar.

Castelo Branco H (1966) *Discursos.* Brasília: Editora Nacional.

Castro C and D'Áraújo MC (2001) *Militares e Política na Nova República.* Rio de Janeiro: FGV.

Castro J (1972) O Congelamento do Poder Mundial. *Revista Brasileira de Estudos Políticos* 33: 7–30.

Cavagnari Filho G (2000) Estratégia e Defesa (1960–1990). In: Albuquerque J (ed) *Sessenta Anos De Política Externa Brasileira (1930–1990): Prioridades, Atores e Políticas.* São Paulo: Annablume.

Cepik M (2001) Segurança Nacional e Segurança Humana: Problemas Conceituais e Consequências Políticas. *Security and Defence Studies Review* 1: 1–19.

Cervo A (2000) Sob o Signo Neoliberal: as Relações Internacionais da América Latina. *Revista Brasileira De Política Internacional* 43(2): 5–27.

___ (2001) *Relações Internacionais da América Latina: Velhos e Novos Paradigmas.* Brasília: Funag.

___ (2003) Política Exterior e Relações Internacionais do Brasil: Enfoque Paradigmático. *Revista Brasileira De Política Internacional* 46(2): 5–25.

___ (2008) *Inserção Internacional – Formação dos Conceitos Brasileiros.* São Paulo: Saraiva.

___ and Bueno C (2002) *História da Política Exterior do Brasil.* Brasília: UnB.

Chaui M (1983) *Seminários.* São Paulo: Brasiliense.

___ (2000) *Brasil: Mito Fundador.* São Paulo: Perseu Abramo.

___ and Franco M (1978) *Ideologia e Mobilização Popular.* Rio de Janeiro: Paz e Terra.

Cheeseman G and Kettle S (1990) Introduction. *The New Australian Militarism: Undermining Our Future Secutiy.* Melbourne: Pluto Press Australia.

Chiavenato J (1981) *Geopolítica: Arma do Fascismo.* São Paulo: Global.

Child J (1979) Geopolitical Thinking in Latin America. *Latin American Research Review* 14(2): 89–111.

Chong A and Hamilton-Hart N (2009) Teaching International Relations In Southeast-Asia: Historical Memory, Academic Context, and Politics – An Introduction. *International Relations of the Asia-Pacific* 9: 1–18.

Codato A and Oliveira A (2004) A Marcha, o Terço e o Livro: Catolicismo Conservador e a Ação Política na Conjuntura do Golpe de 1964. *Revista Brasileira de História* 24(47): 201–302.

Coelho EC (2000) *Em Busca Da Identidade: O Exército e a Política na Sociedade Brasileira.* Rio de Janeiro: Record.

Comblin J (1978) *A Ideologia da Segurança Nacional: O Poder Militar na América Latina.* Rio de Janeiro: Civilização Brasileira.

Cordeiro JM (2009) Femininas e Formidáveis: O Público e o Privado na Militância Política da Campanha da Mulher pela Democracia (CAMDE). *Revista Gênero* 8: 175–208.

Correia A (1976) *Estudos Dirigidos de Educação Moral e Cívica*. São Paulo: Ática.
Costa D (1999) Segurança e Defesa: Uma Única Visão Abaixo do Equador. *Revista Brasileira De Política Internacional* 42(1): 127–43.
Costa e Silva A (1968) *Mensagem ao Congresso Nacional*. Brasília: Imprensa Nacional.
Costa T éíé (1989) Bases da Postura Estratégica dos Países Sul-Americanos para a Década de 90. *Contexto Internacional* 10: 55–66.
___ (1994) Política de Defesa: Uma Discussão Conceitual e o Caso do Brasil. *Revista Brasileira de Política Internacional* 37(1): 106–20.
Coutinho L (1956) O General Góes Depõe. *Rio de Janeiro: Livraria Editora Coelho Branco.*
___ (2009) O Conceito de Vontade Coletiva em Gramsci. *Katálysis* 12(1): 32–40.
Couto e Silva G (1957) *Aspectos Geopolíticos do Brasil*. Rio de Janeiro: Biblioteca do Exército.
___ (1958) *Geoplítica do Brasil*. Rio de Janeiro: José Olympio.
___ (1959) *Aspectos Geopolíticos do Brasil* II. Rio de Janeiro: José Olympio.
Cowan B (2007) Sex and the Security State: Gender, Sexuality and 'Subversion' at Brazil's Escola Superior de Guerra. *Journal of History of Sexuality* 16(3): 459–81.
Cox R (1981) Social Forces, States and World Orders: Beyond International Relations Theory. *Millennium-Journal of International Studies* 10(2): 126–55.
___ (1983) Gramsci, Hegemony and International Relations. *Millennium-Journal of International Studies* 10(2): 162–75.
Crawford A and Jarvis D (2001) *International Relations–Still an American Social Science? Toward Diversity in International Thought*. Albany: State University of New York Press.
Cunha L (2006) Sintonia Oscilante: Religião. Moral e Civismo no Brasil 1931–1997. *Cadernos de Pesquisa* 37(131): 285–302.
Cunha PR (2008) *A Esquerda Militar no Brasil: Uma Leitura e Várias Agendas*. Available at www.abed-defesa.org/page4/page7/page23/files/PauloCunha.pdf (accessed 20/08/14).
D'Araújo MS, Soares GAD and Castro C (1994) *Os Anos De Chumbo: A Memória Militar Sobre A Repressão*. Rio de Janeiro: Relume Dumará.
D'Ávila J (2003) *Diploma of Whiteness: Race and Social Policy in Brazil, 1917–1945*. London: Duke University Press.
Davidoff C (1982) A Ideologia da Modernização em Gilberto Freyre e Oliveira Vianna. *Perspectivas* 5: 29–38.
Debert G (1986) *A política do significado no início dos anos 60: O nacionalismo no Instituto Superior de Estudos Brasileiros (ISEB) e na Escola Superior de Guerra (ESG)*. São Paulo, Universidade de São Paulo.
De Kock L (1992) Interview with Gayatri Chakravorty Spivak: New Nation Writers Conference in South Africa. *ARIEL: A Review of International English Literature* 23(3): 29–47.
De La Reza G (2002) Ilusão de acesso: O modelo ALCA. *Contexto Internacional* 24(2): 363–95.
De Souza A (2008) *O Brasil na Região e no Mundo: Percepções da Comunidade Brasileira de Política Externa*. Rio de Janeiro: Centro Brasileiro de Relações Internacionais. Available at: www.iadb.org/intal/intalcdi/PE/2009/02620.pdf (accessed 15/09/11).
Diniz E (1985) A Transição Política no Brasil: Uma Reavaliação da Dinâmica da Abertura. *Dados* 3: 329–46.
___ and Boschi R (1989) A Consolidação Democrática no Brasil: Atores Políticos, Processos Sociais e Intermediação de Interesses. In: Diniz E, Boschi R and Lessa R (eds) *Modernização e Consolidação Democrática no Brasil: Dilemas da Nova República*. São Paulo: Vertice.

Dodds K (2000) Geopolitics and the Geographical Imagination of Argentina. In: Dodds K and Atkinson D (eds) *Geopolitical Traditions: A Century of Geopolitical Thought.* London: Routledge, pp. 150–84.

Dreifuss R (2008) *1964: A Conquista do Estado – Ação Política, Poder e Golpe de Classe.* São Paulo: Editora Vozes.

Drulak P, Karlas J and Konigova L (2009) Central and Eastern Europe–Between Continuity and Change. In: Tickner A and Wæver O (eds) *International Relations Scholarship Around the World.* Abingdon, Oxon: Routledge, pp. 242–60.

Duarte S (2006) A Sétima Conferência de Exame do TNP – Uma Avaliação. *Revista Política Externa* 14(4): 119–26.

Elman C and Elman M, eds. (1993) *Progress in International Relations Theory: Appraising the Field.* Chicago: MIT Press.

Enloe C (2000) *Bananas, Beaches and Bases: Making Feminist Sense of International Politics.* Berkeley: University of California Press.

Enloe C and Rejai M (1969) Nation-States and State-Nations. *International Studies Quarterly* 13(2): 140–58.

Escola Superior de Guerra (1978) *Manual Básico da Escola Superior de Guerra.*

Evans R (1958) Review of *Planejamento Estratégico* by Golbery do Couto e Silva. *International Affairs* 34(2): 2000.

Faoro R (1975) *Os Donos do Poder.* São Paulo: Companhia das Letras.

___ (2000) *Os Donos do Poder.* São Paulo: Companhia das Letras.

Faria M (1979) A Guarda Nacional em Minas Gerais, 1831–1873. *Revista Brasileira de Estudos Políticos* 49: 145–99.

Fausto B (1988) *Revolução de 1930: História e Historiografia.* São Paulo: Brasiliense.

___ (1995) O Estado Novo no Contexto Internacional. In: Pandolfi D (ed) *Repensando o Estado Novo.* Rio de Janeiro: FGV.

___ (2001) *História concisa do Brasil.* São Paulo: Imprensa Ofical : EDUSP.

Fávero M de L de A (2007) A Universidade no Brasil: Das Origens à Reforma Universitária de 1968. *Educar em Revista* 28. Available at: http://ojs.c3sl.ufpr.br/ojs-2.2.4/index.php/educar/article/view/7609 (accessed 24/05/13).

Ferreira E (1996) *Mulheres.* MilitÃ¢ncia e Memória, Rio de Janeiro: Fundação Getúlio Vargas.

Ferreira J (2006) A democratização de 1945 e o Movimento Queremista. In: Ferreira J (ed) *O Brasil Republicano: O Tempo da Experiência Democratica.* Rio de Janeiro: Civilização Brasileira.

Fico C (2004) Versões e Controvérsias sobre 1964 e a ditadura military. *Revista Brasileira de História* 24(47): 29–60.

Figueiredo L (2005) *Ministério do Silêncio.* Rio de Janeiro: Record.

Figueiredo M (1971) Civilismo e Segurança Nacional. *Revista Brasileira De Política Internacional* 53/54: 55–68.

Filho E (2005) A Sociologia no Brasil: História, Teorias e Desafios. *Sociologias*, Porto Alegre 7(14): 376–437.

Flauzina A (2006) *Corpo Negro Caído no Chão: O Sistema Penal e o Projeto Genocida do Estado Brasileiro.* Brasília, Universidade de Brasília.

Flemes D (2006) *Brazil's Nuclear Policy: From Technological Dependence to Civil Nuclear Power.* Working paper. Available at www.isn.ethz.ch/isn/Digital-Library/Publications/Detail/?id=47033&lng=en (accessed 10/09/11).

Fonseca Jr C (1989) Studies on International Relations in Brazil: Recent Times (1950–1980). In: Dyer H and Mangasarian L (eds) *Study of International Relations: The State of the Art*. London: Macmillan.

___ and Lafer C (1994) Questões para a Diplomacia no Context Internacional das Polaridades Indefinidas (Notas Analíticas e Algumas Sugestões). In: Fonseca Jr C and Lafer C (eds) *Temas de Política Externa Brasileiras* II. São Paulo: Paz e Terra.

Forjaz M (1979) De como a Autonomia do Político Aprisionou os Cientistas Sociais Brasileiros. *Cadernos de Opinião* 14: 11–6.

___ (1989) Cientistas e Militares no Desenvolvimento do CNPq (1950–1985). *Boletim Informativo e Bibliográfico de Ciências Sociais* 28: 75–89.

___ (1997) A Emergência da Ciência Política no Brasil: Aspectos Institucionais. *Revista Brasileira de Ciências Sociais* 12(35). Available at www.scielo.br/scielo. php?pid=S0102-69091997000300007&script=sci_arttext#back (accessed 02/09/11).

Fragoso A (1975) *Legislação de Segurança Nacional*. Rio de Janeiro: Escola Superior de Guerra.

Freyre G (1933). Casa Grande & Senzala. (Reprint 2003). São Paulo: Global.

___ (1938) *Conferências na Europa*. Rio de Janeiro: Ministério da Educação e Saúde.

Friedrichs J (2004) *European Approaches to International Relations Theory: A House with Many Mansions*. London: Routledge.

Galache G, Pimentel M and Zanuy F (1971) *Construindo o Brasil – Educação Moral, Cívica e Política*. São Paulo: Edições Loyola.

Galvão T (2009) América do Sul: Construção pela Reinvenção (2000–2008). *Revista Brasileira de Política Internacional* 52(2): 63–80.

Garcia E (1972) *Educação Moral e Cívica na Escola de Primeiro Grau*. São Paulo: LISA.

Garcia M (2010) *Recursos Naturais e conflito no Subcontinente Sul-Americano*. Paper presented at the Seguranca Internacional: Perspectivas Brasileiras. FIESP–Federação das Indústrias do Estado de São Paulo. São Paulo/SP. Available at: www.segurancainternacional.com.br/Programacao-3.html (accessed 10/04/13).

Gaspari E (2002) *A Ditadura Escancarada: As Ilusões Armadas*. São Paulo: Companhia das Letras.

Goés Monteiro P (1934) *A Revolução de 30 e a Finalidade Política do Exército*. Rio de Janeiro: Andersen.

Goldenberg J (1987) A Questão Nuclear no Brasil. *Lua Nova* 3(3): 6–20.

Gonçalves JF (2000) *Rui Barbosa: Pondo as idéias no lugar* (1st edn). Rio de Janeiro, Brasil: FGV Editora.

Gramsci A (1971a) *Prison Notebooks*. New York: International Publishers.

___ (1971b) *Selections from the Prison Notebooks*. London: Lawrence & Wishart.

___ (1978) *Selections from Political Writings, 1910–1920*. London: Lawrence & Wishart.

___ (1985) *Selections from Cultural Writings*, ed. D Forgacs and G Nowell-Smith, trans. W Boelhower. London: Lawrence and Wishart.

___ (1996) *Prison Notebooks*, vol.2, ed. and trans. J A Buttigieg. New York: Columbia University Press.

Guerreiro Ramos A (1960) *O Problema Nacional do Brasil*. Rio de Janeiro: Saga.

Guimarães S (1999) *ALCA e MERCOSUL: Riscos e Oportunidades para o Brasil*. Brasília: Funag.

Gurgel J (1978) *Segurança e Democracia*. Rio de Janeiro: José Olympio.

Haeckel E (1908) *O Monismo: Laço entre Religião e a Sciencia*. Porto: Imprensa Moderna Manoel Lello.

Harris M (1964) *Patterns of Race in the Americas*. New York: Walker.

Harvey D (2010) *Organizing for the Anti-Capitalist Transition.* [online]. Available at: http://davidharvey.org/2009/12/organizing-for-the-anti-capitalist-transition/.

Hentschke J (ed) (2006) *Vargas and Brazil: New Perspectives.* New York: Palgrave Macmillan.

Hepple L (1992) Metaphor, Geopolitical Discourse and the Military in South America. In: Barnes T and Duncan J (eds) *Writing Worlds: Discourse, Text and Metaphor in the Representation of Landscape.* Abingdon, Oxon: Routledge.

___ (2004) South American Heartland: The Charcos, Latin American Geopolitics and Global Strategies. *The Geographical Journal* 170(4): 359–67.

Hermógenes J (1977) *Educação Moral e Cívica: Faixa F.* Rio de Janeiro: Record.

Herz M (2002a) O Crescimento da Área de Relacões Internacionais no Brasil. *Contexto Internacional* 24(1): 7–40.

___ (2002b) Política de Segurança dos EUA para a América Latina após o Final da Guerra Fria. *Estudos Avançados* 16(46): 85–104.

___ and Wrobel P (2002) A Política Brasilsiera de Segurança no Pós-Guerra Fria. In: Brigadão C and Proença J (eds) *Brasil e o Mundo: Novas Visões.* Rio de Janeiro: Francisco Alves.

Hilton S (1982) The Armed Forces and Industrialists in Modern Brazil: The Drive for Military Autonomy (1889–1954). *The Hispanic American Historic Review* 62(4): 629–73.

Hirst M (2001) Atributos e Dilemas Políticos do Mercosul. *Cadernos do Forum Euro-Latino-Americano.* Available at: http://ieei.pt/files/WP8_MHirst.pdf.

___ (2006) Os Cinco a das Relações Brasil-Estados Unidos: Aliança, Alinhamento, Autonomia, Ajustamento e Afirmação. In: Altemani H and Lessa A (eds) *Relações Internacionais do Brasil: Temas e Agendas.* São Paulo: Saraiva.

___ and Pinheiro L (1995) A Politica Externa do Brasil em Dois Tempos. *Revista Brasileira de Política Internacional* 38(1): 5–23.

Hochman G (1998) *A Era do Saneamento: As Bases da Política de Saúde Pública no Brasil.* São Paulo: Hucitec.

Hoffmann S (1977) An American Social Science: International Relations. *Daedalus* 106(3): 41–60.

Holanda F (2001) Idiossincrasias do Liberalismo Brasileiro. In: Holanda F (ed) *Do Liberalismo ao Neoliberalismo: O Itinerário de Uma Cosmovisão Impertinente.* Porto Alegre: EDIPUCRS.

Holden G (2001) The Politer Kingdoms of the Globe: Context and Comparison in the Intellectual History of IR. *Global Society* 15(1): 27–51.

Holloway T (1980) *Immigrants on the Land: Coffee and Society in São Paulo.* Chapel Hill: University of North Carolina Press.

Holsti K (1985) *The Dividing Discipline: Hegemony and Diversity in International Theory.* Boston: Allen & Unwin.

Huelsz C (2009) Middle Power Theories and Emerging Powers in International Political Economy: A Case Study of Brazil. PhD, Manchester, University of Manchester.

Hunter W (1997) *Eroding Military Influence in Brazil: Politicians Against Soldiers.* Chapell Hill: University of North Carolina Press.

Hurrell A (2006) Hegemony, liberalism and global order: what space for would-be great powers? *International Relations* 82(1): 1–19.

Ianni O (1986) *Classe e Nação.* Petrópolis: Vozes.

___ (1998) Neoliberalismo. *Contexto Internacional* 20(1): 91–106.

INEP (2010) Censo da Educacao Superior no Brasil. Ministério da Educação. Available at: http://download.inep.gov.br/educacao_superior/censo_superior/resumo_tecnico/resumo_tecnico_censo_educacao_superior_2010.pdf (accessed 20/08/14).

Inoguchi T (2007) Are There any Theories of International Relations in Japan? *International Relations of the Asia-Pacific* 7(3): 369–90.

Jobim N (2010) *O Cenario Global.* Paper presented at the Segurança Internacional: Perspectivas Brasileiras. Available at: www.segurancainternacional.com.br/ (accessed 24/05/13).

Katzman J (1974) Social Relations of Production in the Brazilian Frontier. In: Steffan J (ed) *The Frontier: Comparative Studies.* Norman: University of Oklahoma Press.

Kehl R (1913) *A Cura da Fealdade: Eugenia e Medicina Social.* São Paulo: Brasiliana.

___ (1923) *Aparas Eugênicas: Sexo e Civilização (Novas Diretrizes).* Rio de Janeiro: Francisco Alves.

Kelly P (1984) Geopolitical Themes in the Writings of General Carlos Meira Mattos of Brazil. *Journal of Latin American Studies* 16(2): 439–61.

Klom A (2003) Mercosur and Brazil: A European Perspective. *International Affairs* 79(2): 351–68.

Korany B and Makdisi K (2009) Arab Countries–The Object Worlds Back. In: Tickner A and Wæver O (eds) *International Relations Scholarship Around the World.* Abingdon, Oxon: Routledge, pp. 172–90.

Kossoy B and Carneiro M (2004) *A Imprensa Confiscada Pelo Deops, 1924–1954.* São Paulo: Ateliê Editorial.

Kramer P, Wrobel P and Moura G (1985) Os Caminhos (Difíceis da Autonomia): As Relações Brasil-Estados Unidos. *Contexto Internacional* 1(2): 35–52.

Kumasaka H and Barros L (1988) Entrevista com o Professor Hélio Jaguaribe de Mattos. *História da Ciência.* Available at: www.cle.unicamp.br/arquivoshistoricos/ehelio.pdf (accessed 15/09/11).

Lacerda J (1911) *Sur Les Metis au Brésil.* Paris: Imprimerie Devougue.

Lafer C (2000) Brazilian International Identity and Foreign Policy: Past, Present, and Future. *Daedalus* 192(2): 207–38.

Lamounier B (1982) A Ciência Política no Brasil: Roteiro para um Balanço Crítico. In: Lamounier B (ed) *A Ciência Política nos Anos 80.* Brasília: UnB, pp. 407–33.

___ (1989) Brazil: Inequality Against Democracy. *Democracy in Developing Countries and Latin America.* Boulder: Lynne Reinner.

Lapid Y (1989) The Third Debate: On the Prospects of International Theory in a Post-Positivist Era. *International Studies Quarterly* 33(3): 235–54.

Lessa A (2005a) O Ensino das Relações Internacionais do Brasil. In: Saraiva J and Cervo A (eds) *O Crescimento das Relações Internacionais do Brasil.* Brasília: UnB.

___ (2005b) Trinta Anos de Ensino de Relações Internacionais em Nível de Graduação no Brasil. *Meridiano 47* 54(Jan): 7–9.

___ (2005c) Instituições, Atores e Dinâmicas no Ensino e da Pesquisa em Relações Internacionais no Brasil: O Diálogo Entre a História, a Ciência Política e os Novos Paradigmas de Interpretação (Dos Anos 90 aos Nossos Dias). *Revista Brasileira de Política Internacional* 48(2): 169–84.

___ and Almeida P (2004) O IBRI e a Revista Brasileira de Política Internacional: Tradição, Continuidade e Renovação. *Revista Brasileira de Política Internacional* 47(1): 7–30.

___ and Meira F (2001) Brasil e os Atentados de 11 de Setembro de 2001. *Revista Brasileira de Política Internacional* 44(2): 46–61.

___, Couto L and Farias, R. (2009) Política Externa Planejada: Os Planos Plurianuais e a Ação Internacional do Brasil, de Cardoso a Lula (1995–2008). *Revista Brasileira de Política Internacional* 52(1): 89–109.

Lasswell H (1950) *Politics, Who Gets What When and How*. New York: Peter Smith.

Levine R (1968) Brazil's Jews during the Era Vargas and After. *Luso-Brazilian Review* 5(1): 45–58.

Levy J (1997) Too Important to Leave to the Other: History and Political Science in the Study of International Relations. *International Security* 22(1): 22–33.

Lima A (1953) *Aspirações e Interesses Nacionais Permanentes do Brasil*, C-31–53. Rio de Janeiro: Escola Superior de Guerra.

Lima N and Hochman G (2000) Pouca Saúde, Muita Saúva, os Males do Brasil são... Discurso Médico-Sanitário e Interpretação do País. *Ciência e Saúde Coletiva* 5(2): 313–32.

Lipkin S (1985) Impondo o Livre Comércio? A Política Comercial do Governo Reagan. *Contexto Internacional* 2: 53–62.

Loureiro M (2009) Economists in the Brazilian Government: From Developmentalist State to Neoliberal Policies. In: Markoff J and Montecinos V (eds) *Economists in the Americas*. Northampton: Edward Elgar.

Luz M (1982) *Medicina e Ordem Política Brasileira: Políticas e Instituições de Saúde (1850–1930)*. Rio de Janeiro: Graal.

Lyra Tavares A (1958) Razões que Levaram Criação da ESG. *ESG: Doutrina e Pensamento*. Rio de Janeiro: Escola Superior de Guerra.

Macedo Soares L (2004) O Brasil no Cenário Regional de Defesa e Segurança. In: Pinto A, Rocha A and Silva L (eds) *Pensamento Brasileiro Sobre Defesa e Segurança*. Brasília: Ministério da Defesa.

Madeira A (1955) *Características Psicológicas do Povo Brasileiro*, C-51–55. Rio de Janeiro: Escola Superior de Guerra.

Mainwaring S (1986) The Transition to Democracy in Brazil. *Journal of Interamerican Studies and World Affairs* 28(1): 149–79.

Markoff J and Baretta R (1985) Professional Ideology and Military Activism in Brazil: Critique of a Thesis by Alfred Stepan. *Comparative Politics* 17(2): 175–91.

Marson A (1979) *A Ideologia Nacionalista em Alberto Torres*. São Paulo: Duas Cidades.

Martins C (1975) A Evolução da Política Externa Brasileira na Década 64–74. *Cadernos Cebrap* 9: 55–98.

Martins L (1986) The liberalization of the authoritarian rule in Brazil. In: O'Donnell P, Schmitter P and Whitehead L (eds) *Transitions from Authoritarian Rule in Latin America*. Baltimore: John Hopkins University.

___ (1997) ALCA: Uma Pauta para Discussão. *Política Externa* 5(4): 39–54.

Martins Filho J (2006) As Forças Armadas e o Plano Colômbia. In: Castro C (ed) *Amazônia e defesa nacional*. Rio de Janeiro: FGV.

Mathias K, Guzzi A and Giannini R (2008) Aspectos da Integração Regional em Defesa no Cone Sul. *Revista Brasileira de Política Internacional* 51(1): 70–86.

Matos J (2005) *Sérgio Buarque de Holanda: Raízes do Brasil, Diálogos com a Política e a História do Brasil*. Pontifícia Universidade Católica do Rio Grande do Sul.

Mattos I (1989) Do Império à República. *Revista Estudos Históricos* 2(4): 163–71.

McCann F (1980) The Brazilian Army and the Problem of a Mission. *Journal of Latin American Studies* 12: 107–26.

___ (1983) The Brazilian General Staff and Brazil's Military Situation, 1900–1945. *Journal of Interamerican Studies and World Affairs* 25(3): 299–324.

___ (1984) The Formative Period of Twentieth-Century Brazilian Army Thought, 1900–1922. *The Hispanic American Historic Review* 64(4): 737–65.

___ (2004) *Soldiers of the Pátria: A History of the Brazilian Army (1889–1937)*. Stanford: Stanford University Press.

McLain W (1967) Alberto Torres, Ad Hoc Nationalist. *Luso-Brazilian Review* 4(2): 17–34.

Medeiros M (1995) Relações Exteriores do Mercosul: Uma Abordagem Brasileira. *Revista Brasileira de Política Internacional* 38(2): 35–60.

Meira Mattos C (1973) Poder Militar e Política Internacional. *Revista Brasileira de Política Internacional* 63–4: 63–80.

___ (1975) *Brasil: Geopolítica e Destino*. Rio de Janeiro: José Olympio.

___ (1977) *A Geopolítica e as Projeções do Poder*. Rio de Janeiro: José Olympio.

___ (1980) *Uma Geopolítica Pan-Amazônica*. Rio de Janeiro: Biblioteca do Exército.

___ (1984) *Geopolítica e Trópicos*. Rio de Janeiro: Biblioteca do Exército.

___ (1990) *Geopolítica e Teoria de Fronteiras*. Rio de Janeiro: Biblioteca do Exército.

___ (2000) Geopolítica Brasileira: Predecessores e Geopolíticos. *Revista da Escola Superior de Guerra* XVII (39): 58–82.

Mello V (2002) Paz e Segurança na ONU: A Visão do Brasil. In: Brigadão C and Proença J (eds) *Brasil e o Mundo: Novas Visões*. Rio de Janeiro: Francisco Alves.

Melo M and Costa N (1995) A Difusão das Reformas Neoliberais: Análise Estratégica, Atores e Agendas Internacionais. *Contexto Internacional* 17(1): 89–113.

Menezes L (1987) Para Entender a Questão Nuclear. *Lua Nova* 3(3): 9–12.

Mercadante P (1980) *Militares & Civis: A Ética e o Compromisso*. Rio de Janeiro: Zahar.

Meyer A (1999) A Europa Atual: Questões de Segurança Coletiva e Integração Econômica. *Revista Brasileira de Política Internacional* 42(1): 183–92.

Miceli S (1990) *A Desilusão Americana: Relações Acadêmicas Entre Brasil e Estados Unidos*. São Paulo: Sumaré/Idesp.

Miranda J (2004) A Comissão Nacional de Moral e Civismo, 1969–1986. Sao Paulo: Pontificia Universidade Catolica de Sao Paulo (PUC-SP).

Miyamoto S (1987) Escola Superior de Guerra: Mito e Realidade. *Política e Estratégia* V (1): 76–97.

___ (1999) O Estudo das Relações Internacionais no Brasil: O Estado da Arte. *Revista de Sociologia e Política* 12: 83–98.

___ (2000) A Política de Defesa Brasileira e Segurança Regional. *Contexto Internacional* 22(2): 431–72.

___ (2002) O Mercosul e a Segurança Regional – Uma Agenda Comum? *São Paulo Perspectiva* 16(1): 54–62.

___ and Gonçalves W (1995) A Política Externa Brasileira e o Regime Militar. *Premissas* 10: 5–62.

Moniz Bandeira L (2002) As Políticas Neoliberais e a Crise na América do Sul. *Revista Brasileira de Política Internacional* 45(2): 135–46.

Montarroyos J (1979) Educação de Adultos como Doutrinação: Fundamentos e Métdoso da Divulgação da Doutrina de 'Segurança e Desenvolvimento' do Brasil. MSc, Joao Pessoa, Universidade Federal da Paraíba.

Monteiro M and Coelho M (2004) As Políticas Federais e Reconfigurações Espaciais na Amazônia. *Novos Cadernos NAEA* 7(2): 91–122.

Morel R (1979) A Política Científica no Brasil. In: Morel R (ed) *Ciência e Estado: A Política Científica no Brasil*. São Paulo: Queiroz.

Morton AD (2007) *Unravelling Gramsci: Hegemony and Passive Revolution in the Global Political Economy*. London, Ann Arbor, MI: Pluto Press.

Mota A (2003) *Quem é Bom Já Nasce Feito: Sanitarismo e Eugenia no Brasil*. Rio de Janeiro: DP&A.

Mota Filho (1958) *Elementos Básicos da Nacionalidade – O Homem*, C-43–68. Rio de Janeiro: Escola Superior de Guerra.

Moura G (1982) Brazilian Foreign Relations, 1939–1950. PhD, London, University College London.

___ (1986) *Tio Sam Chega ao Brasil: A Penetração Cultural Americana*. São Paulo: Brasiliense.

Muñoz H (1980) Los Estudios Internacionales en América Latina: Problemas Fundamentales. *Estudios Internacionales* 51: 328–44.

Muricy A (1993) *Antônio Carlos Murici* I (depoimento, 1981). FGV/CPDOC. Available at: www.fgv.br/cpdoc/historiaoral/arq/Entrevista35_2.pdf (accessed 31/12/2012).

Nabuco J (2003) *O Abolicionismo [1883]*. Brasília: Edições do Senado Federal.

Nunn F (1972) Military Professionalism and Professional Militarism in Brazil, 1870–1970: Historical Perspectives and Political Implications. *Journal of Latin American Studies* 4(1): 29–54.

___ (1983) *Yesterday's Soldiers: European Military Professionalism in South America 1890–1940*. Lincoln: University of Nebraska Press.

Ofuho C (2009) Africa: Teaching IR where It's Not Supposed To Be. In: Tickner A and Wæver O (eds) *International Relations Scholarship Around the World*. Abingdon, Oxon: Routledge, pp. 71–85.

Oliveira E (1976) Os Tempos da ADESG – Passado, Present e Futuro. *Segurança e Desenvolvimento* 25(166): 13–20.

Oliveira L (1995) As Ciências Sociais no Rio de Janeiro In: Miceli S (ed) *História das Ciências Sociais no Brasil*, vol. 2. São Paulo: Sumaré.

Oliveira A and Onuki J (2000) Brasil, Mercosul e a Segurança Regional. *Revista Brasileira de Política Internacional* 43(2): 108–29.

Pagliai G (2006) Segurança Hemisférica: Uma Discussão Sobre a Validade E Atualidade de seus Mecanismos Institucionais. *Revista Brasileira de Política Internacional* 49(1): 26–42.

Pandolfi D (1999) Apresentação. In: Pandolfi D (ed) *Repensando o Estado Novo*. Rio de Janeiro: FGV.

Parola A (2007) *A Ordem Injusta*. Brasília: Funag.

Pasha M (2013) Return to the Source: Gramsci, Culture, and International Relations. In: Ayers AJ (ed) *Gramsci, Political Economy, and International Relations Theory: Modern Princes and Naked Emperors*. Basingstoke: Palgrave Macmillan.

Patriota A (2010) *O Cenário Global*. Paper presented at the Segurança Internacional: Perspectivas Brasileiras. Conference Lecture. Rio de Janeiro. Available at: http://itv.netpoint.com.br/segurancainternacional/principal.asp?id=2 (accessed 15/09/11).

Paulino L (2002) O Brasil, Seus Sócios e Seus Negócios. *São Paulo Perspectiva* 16(2): 82–93.

Pécaut D (1989) *Intelectuais e a Política no Brasil: Entre o Povo e a Nação*. São Paulo: Atica.

Pedro, J and Wolff, C (2010) *Gênero, feminismos e ditaduras no Cone Sul*. Porto Alegre: Editora Mulheres.

Penna Filho P (2004) Segurança Seletiva no Pós-Guerra Fria: Uma Análise da Política e dos Instrumentos de Segurança das Nações Unidas para os Países Periféricos – O Caso Africano. *Revista Brasileira de Política Internacional* 47(1): 35–50.

Pereira M (1922) O Brasil é Ainda um Imenso Hospital: Discurso Pronunciado pelo Professor Miguel Pereira por Ocasião do Regresso do Professor Alo Aloysio de Castro, da República Argentina, em Outubro de 1916. *Revista de Medicina* 7(21): 3–7.

Pereira M and Medeiros O (1965) *O Comunismo e os Movimentos da Juventude*, C4-39–65. Rio de Janeiro: Escola Superior de Guerra.

Petras J (2005) Imperialismo e resistência na América Latina. *Tensões Mundiais* 1(1): 193–228.

Pimenta J (1919) Somos um Povo Engermo. *Revista Acadêmica da Faculdade de Direito do Recife* 1: 50–60.

Pinto J (1967) Fundamentos da Politica Exterior do Brasil. *Revista Brasileira de Política Internacional* 37–8(March to June): 10–25.

Pontes H (2001) Entrevista com Antonio Cândido. *Revista Brasileira de Ciências Sociais* 16(47): 5–30.

Prado A (2001) Os Conceitos de Homem e de Educação no Brasil no Period do Estado Novo (1937–1945). *Educação e Filosofia* 15(30): 9–22.

Prado P (1928) *Retrato do Brasil*. São Paulo: Duprat-Mayença.

Prado L and Earp F (1984) O 'Milagre' Brasileiro: Crescimento Acelerado, Integração Internacional e Concentração De Renda (1967–1973). *Revista de Economia Política* 12(4): 209–40.

Procopio Filho A and Vaz A (1997) Brasil no Contexto do Narcotráfico Internacional. *Revista Brasileira de Política Internacional* 40(1): 75–122.

Proença Jr D and Diniz E (2007) The Brazilian Conceptualization of Security: Philosophical, Ethical and Cultural Contexts and Issues. In: Brauch H and Brauch H (eds) *Globalisation and Environmental Challenges: Reconceptualising Security in the 21st Century*. Berlin: Springer-Verlag.

____ and Duarte E (2003) Projeção de Poder e Intervenção Militar Pelos Estados Unidos da América. *Revista Brasileira de Política Internacional* 46(1): 135–52.

Queiroga M (2011) O Governo dos Corpos Infantis: A Produção do Discurso da Eugenia no Campo da Educação. *Vivência* 37: 123–40.

Rebelo A (2004) O Brasil no Cenário Regional de Defesa e Segurança. In: Pinto J, Rocha A and Silva A (eds) *Pensamento Brasileiro Sobre Defesa e Segurança*. Brasília: Ministério da Defesa.

Reis A (1978) Porque a Amazônia Deve ser Brasileira? *Revista Brasileira de Política Internacional* 11(41/42): 7–17.

Reis DA (2000) *Ditadura Militar*. Esquerdas e Sociedades, Rio de Janeiro: Jorge Zahar.

Ricupero R (2002) Os Estados Unidos e o Comércio Mundial: Protecionistas ou Campeões do Livre-Comércio? *Estudos Avançados* 16(46): 7–18.

Rocha A (2005) O Lugar Do Brasil Na Geopolítica Global. In: Saraiva J and Cervo A (eds) *O Crescimento das Relações Internacionais no Brasil*. Brasília: UnB.

____ (2010) *O Futuro das Operações de Paz da ONU*. Paper presented at the Segurança Internacional: Perspectivas Brasileiras. Rio de Janeiro. Available at: http://itv.netpoint.com.br/segurancainternacional/principal.asp?id=2 (accessed 01/09/11).

Rocha H (2003) Educação Escolar e Higienização da Infância. *Cadernos CERES* 23(59): 39–56.

Rocha J (2006) O Brasil e os Regimes Internacionais. In: Oliveira H and Lessa A (eds) *Relações Internacionais do Brasil – Temas e Agenda*. São Paulo: Saraiva.

Rodrigues L (1947) *Geopolítica do Brasil*. Rio de Janeiro: Editora Nacional.

Rodrigues N (1899) *Métissage, Dégénérescence et Crime*. Lyon: Archives d'Anthropologie Criminelle.

____ (1915) *O Animismo Fetichista dos Negros Baianos*. Rio de Janeiro: Civilização Brasileira.

Rogers E (1968) Brazilian Success Story: The Volta Redonda Iron and Steel Project. *Journal of Inter-American Studies* 10(4): 637–52.

Rogers T (2006) 'I choose this means to be with you always': Getúlio Vargas's Carta Testamento (1st edn). *Vargas and Brazil: New Perspectives.* New York, NY: Palgrave Macmillan, pp. 227–55.

Romero S (1868) *O Naturalismo em Literatura.* São Paulo: Lucta.

___ (1882) *O Brasil Social.* Rio de Janeiro: Typographica Jornal do Commercio.

Rosa L (1985) Da gênese da bomba à política nuclear brasileira. In: Arnt R (ed) *O Armamentismo no Brasil: A Guerra Deles.* São Paulo: Brasiliense.

Rosenbaum J and Cooper G (1970) Brazil and the Nuclear Non-Proliferation Treaty. *International Affairs* 46(1): 74–90.

Rouquié A (1984) *O Estado Militar na América Latina.* São Paulo: Alfa-Omega.

Saes D (1984) *Classe Média e Sistema Político no Brasil.* São Paulo: T. A. Queiroz.

Salgado P (1971) *Compêndio de Instrução Moral e Cívica.* Rio de Janeiro: FTD.

Salomao L (2010) *As Vulnerabilidades Estratégicas Nacionais.* Paper presented at the Segurança Internacional: Perspectivas Brasileiras. Lecture. Rio de Janeiro. Available at: http://itv.netpoint.com.br/segurancainternacional/principal.asp?id=2 (accessed 15/12/11).

Santana A (1999) A Globalização do Narcotráfico. *Revista Brasileira de Política Internacional* 42(2): 99–116.

Santos Filho J (2002) *Busca-se a Segurança, Planeja-se a Defesa: Uma Introdução à (Re) Discussão dos Conceitos de Segurança e Defesa Nacional na Realidade Brasileira Ontem e Hoje.* Paper presented at the REDES 2002. Centro de Estudios Hemisféricos de Defensa.

Santos L (1985) O Pensamento Sanitarista na Primeira República: Uma Ideologia de Construção da Nacionalidade. *Dados* 28(2): 193–210.

Santos M (2004) A Nova Missão das Forças Armadas Latino-Americanas no Mundo Pós-Guerra Fria: O caso do Brasil. *Revista Brasileira de Ciências Sociais* 19(54): 115–28.

Santos N (2003) História das Relações Internacionais do Brasil: Esboço de Uma Avaliação Sobre a Área. *História* 24(1): 11–39.

___ and Fonseca F (2009) A pós-Graduação em Relações Internacionais no Brasil. *Contexto Internacional* 31(2): 353–80.

Santos W (1962) *Quem Dará O Golpe No Brasil?* Rio de Janeiro: Civilização Brasileira.

Saraiva J (1994) Do Silêncio à Afirmação: Relações do Brasil com a África. In: Cervo A (ed) *O Desafio Intenacional: A Política Exterior do Brasil de 1930 a Nossos Dias.* Brasília: UnB.

Saraiva M (2004) A União Européia como Ator Internacional e os Países do Mercosul. *Revista Brasileira de Política Internacional* 47(1): 84–111.

___ (2007) As Estratégias de Cooperação Sul-Sul nos Marcos da Política Externa Brasileira de 1993 a 2007. *Revista Brasileira de Política Internacional* 50(2): 42–59.

Sardenberg R (2005) Brasil, Política Multilateral e Nações Unidas. *Estudos Avançados* 19(53): 347–67.

Sariolghalam M (2009) Iran: Accomplishments and limitations in IR. In: Tickner A and Wæver O (eds) *International Relations Scholarship Around the World.* Abingdon, Oxon: Routledge, pp. 158–71.

Schilling P (1981) *O Expansionismo Brasileiro.* São Paulo: Global.

Schmidt B (1998) *The Political Discourse of Anarchy: A Disciplinary History of International Relations.* Albany: State University of New York Press.

Schoeman M (2009) South Africa: Between History and a Hard Place. In: Tickner A and Wæver O (eds) *International Relations Scholarship Around the World*. Abingdon, Oxon: Routledge, pp. 53–70.

Schoultz L (2000) *Estados Unidos: Poder e Submissão, Uma História da Política Norte-Americana em Relação à América Latina*. Bauru: Edusc.

Schwarcz L (1993) *O Espetáculo das Raças: Cientistas, Instituicões e Questão Racial no Brasil*. São Paulo: Companhia das Letras.

___ (2002) *As Barbas do Imperador*. São Paulo: Companhia das Letras.

Schwartzman S (1977) *Avaliação e Perspectivas da Área de Ciência Política*. Brasília: CNPq. Available at: www.schwartzman.org.br/simon/cpolitica.htm (accessed 02/09/11).

___ (1983) *Estado Novo: Um Auto-Retrato*. Rio de Janeiro: Campus.

___ (1988) *Bases do Autoritarismo Brasileiro*. Rio de Janeiro: Campus.

Secco V (1957) A Seguranca Nacional e a Escola Superior de Guerra. Escola Superior de Guerra.

Seitenfus R (2000) *A Entrada Do Brasil Na Segunda Guerra Mundial*. Porto Alegre: EDIPUCRS.

Sevcenko N (1983) *Literatura como Missão*. São Paulo: Brasiliense.

Sharp J (2008) *Geographies of Postcolonialism*. London: Sage.

Ship S (1994) and what about Gender? Feminism and International Relations Theory's Third Debate. In: Sjolander CT and Cox WS (eds) *Beyond Positivism: Critical Reflections on International Relations*. Boulder: Lynne Rienner, pp. 129–52.

Silva C (1987) Proliferação Nuclear e o Tratado de Não-Proliferação. *Revista Brasileira de Política Internacional* 117/118: 5–8.

___ (1992) Tratado de Não-Proliferação de Armas Nucleares: contexto político e jurídico. *Revista Brasileira de Política Internacional* 137/138: 79–88.

Silva L (2006) Desenvolvimentismo e Intervencionismo Militar. *e-Premissas: Revista de Estudos Estratégicos* 1(June-December): 92–119.

Silva M (2003) Aquém e Além da Modernidade: Aproximações e Distanciamentos Entre Sérgio Buarque de Holanda e Gilberto Freyre. *Trabalhos de Antropologia e Etnologia* 43(3/4): 83–96.

Simoes S (1985) *Deus, Patria e Familia*. Petrópolis: Vozes.

Simmons F and Emeny B (1935) *The Great Powers in World Politics: International Relations and Economic Nationalism*. New York: American Book Co.

Simon R (1982) *Gramsci's Political Thought*. London: Lawrence and Wishart.

Singer P (1972) O Milagre Brasileiro: Causas e consequências. *Cadernos Cebrap* 6. Available at: www.cebrap.org.br/v1/template.php?lang=pt&area=7&pagina=31&item_biblio=201 (accessed 02/09/11).

Sjoberg L (ed) (2013) *Gender and International Security: Feminist Perspectives*. London: Routledge.

Skidmore T (1988) *Brasil: De Castelo e Tancredo*. Rio de Janeiro: Paz e Terra.

___ (1989) Brazil's Slow Road to Democratization: 1974–1985. In: Stepan A (ed) *Democratizing Brazil: Problems of Transition and Consolidation*. New York: Oxford University Press.

Skjelsbæk K (1980) Militarism, Its Dimensions and Corollaries: An Attempt at Conceptual Clarification. In: Eide A and Thee M (eds) *Problems of Contemporary Militarism*. London: St. Martin's Press.

Smallman SC (2002) *Fear & Memory in the Brazilian Army and Society, 1889–1954*. Chapel Hill, NC: University of North Carolina Press.

Smith S (1995) The Self-Images of a Discipline: A Genealogy of International Relations Theory. In: Booth K and Smith S (eds) *International Relations Theory Today*. University Park: Pennsylvania State University Press.

___ (2000) The Discipline of International Relations: Still an American Social Science? *British Journal of Politics and International Relations* 3(3): 216–55.

___ (2005) The Contested Concept of Security. In: Booth K (ed) *Critical Security Studies and World Politics*. London: Rienner.

Soares de Lima M (2005a) Aspiração Internacional e Política Externa'. *Revista Brasileira de Comércio Exterior* 82: 4–19.

___ (2005b) A Política Externa Brasileira e os Desafios da Cooperação Sul-Sul. *Revista Brasileira de Política Internacional* 48(1): 24–59.

___ and Cheibub Z (1983) *Relações Internacionais e Política Externa Brasileira: Debate Intellectual e Produção Acadêmica*. Rio de Janeiro: Instituto de Pesquisas do Estado do Rio de Janeiro.

Sodré N (1962) Quem é O Povo No Brasil? In *Introdução À Revolução Brasileira*. São Paulo: Ciências Humanas.

___ (1968) *História Militar do Brasil*. Rio de Janeiro: Civilização Brasileira.

Sorj B (2005) Segurança Humana: Conceito e Agenda. *Revista Internacional de Direitos Humanos* 3(2): 41–59.

___ (2008) *A Construção Intelectual do Brasil ContemporÂ¢neo*. São Paulo: Centro Edelstein de Pesquisas Sociais.

Souto Maior L (2001) Brasil-Estados Unidos: Desafios de um Relacionamento Assimétrico. *Revista Brasileira de Política Internacional* 44(1): 55–68.

___ (2003) *O Brasil Em Um Mundo Em Transição*. Brasília: UnB.

___ (2011) The Politics of Personality in Brazil. *Journal of Democracy* 22(2): 75–88.

Souza J (1998) A Ética Protestante e a Ideologia do Atraso Brasileiro. *Revista Brasileira de Ciências Sociais* 13(38). Available at: www.scielo.br/scielo.php?pid=S0102-69091998000300006&script=sci_arttext (accessed 06/06/13).

___ (2006a) A Gramática Social da Desigualdade Brasileira. In: Souza J (ed) *A Invisibilidade da Desigualdade Brasileira*. Belo Horizonte: UFMG.

___ (2006b) É Preciso Teoria para Compreender o Brasil Conteporâneo?–Uma Crítica a Luis Eduardo Soares. In: Souza J (ed) *A Invisibilidade da Desigualdade Brasileira*. Belo Horizonte: UFMG, pp. 117–52.

___ (2006c) Apresentação. In: Souza J (ed) *A Invisibilidade da Desigualdade Brasileira*. Belo Horizonte: UFMG.

___ (2006d) O Casamento Secreto entre Identidade Nacional e 'Teoria Emocional da Razao' ou Por Que é tao Dificil o Debate Critico e Aberto entre nos. In: Souza J (ed) *A Invisibilidade da Desigualdade Brasileira, Belo Horizonte:* Editora UFMG, pp. 97–116.

Stepan A (1971) *The Military in Politics: Changing Patterns in Brazil*. Princeton: Princeton University Press.

___ (1975) *Os Militares na Política: As Mudanças de Padrões na vida Brasileira*. Rio de Janeiro: Arte Nova.

___ (1988) *Rethinking Military Politics: Brazil and the Southern Cone*. Princeton: Princeton University Press.

Svartman S (2006) Guardiões da Nação: Formação Profissional, Experiências Compartilhadas e Engajamento Político dos Generais de 1964. PhD, Porto Alegre, Universidade Federal do Rio Grande do Sul.

Tan S (2009) Southeast Asia–Theory and Praxis in International Relations. In: Tickner A and Wæver O (eds) *International Relations Scholarship Around the World*. Abingdon, Oxon: Routledge, pp. 120–33.

Tavares M (1994) O Consenso e o Dissenso de Washington. *Revista de Economia Política* 14(2): 140–65.

Távora J (1959) *A Segurança Nacional. Sua Conceituação e seu Estudo na ESG*, C-01–59. Rio de Janeiro: Escola Superior de Guerra.

___ (1983) A Segurança Nacional, a Política e a Estratégia – Conceituação e Inter-Relações [23 March 1953]. *Revista da Escola Superior de Guerra* 1(1): 9–20.

Teti A (2007) Bridging the Gap: IR, Middle East Studies and the Disciplinary Politics of the Area Studies Controversy. *European Journal of International Relations* 13(1): 117–45.

Thomas C (1999) Introduction. In: Thomas C and Wilkin P (eds) *Globalization, Human Security, and the African Experience*. London: Lynne Reinner.

Thorstensen V (1998) A OMC – Organização Mundial do Comércio e as Negociações Sobre Comércio, Meio Ambiente e Padrões Sociais. *Revista Brasileira de Política Internacional* 41(2): 29–58.

Tickner A (2003) Hearing Latin American Voices in International Relations Studies. *International Studies Perspective* 4(4): 325–50.

___ (2009) Latin America: Still Policy Dependent after All These Years? In: Tickner A and Wæver O (eds) *International Relations Scholarship Around the World*. Abingdon, Oxon: Routledge.

___ and Wæver O (2009a) (eds) *International Relations Scholarship Around the World*. Abingdon, Oxon: Routledge.

___ and Wæver O (2009b) Introduction: Geocultural Epistemologies. In: Tickner A and Wæver O (eds) *International Relations Scholarship Around the World*. Abingdon, Oxon: Routledge.

___ and Wæver O (2009c) Conclusion: Worlding Where the West Once Was. In: Tickner A and Wæver O (eds) *International Relations Scholarship Around the World*. Abingdon, Oxon: Routledge, pp. 328–41.

Toledo C (2009) Crônica Política Sobr um Documento Contra a 'Ditabranda'. *Revista de Sociologia Política* 17(34): 208–17.

Topik S (1980) State Interventionsim in a Liberal Regime: Brazil, 1889–1930. *The Hispanic American Historical Review* 60(4): 593–616.

Travassos M (1930) *Projeção Continental do Brasil*. Rio de Janeiro: Editora Nacional.

___ (1941) *Introdução à Geografia de Comunicações Brasileiras*. Rio de Janeiro: Editora Nacional.

Trindade H (2005) Social Sciences in Brazil in Perspective: Foundation, Consolidation and Diversification. *Social Sciences Information* 44(2/3): 283–357.

___ (2007) Ciências Sociais no Brasil em Perspectiva: Fundação, Consolidação e Expansão. In: Trindade H (ed) *As Ciências Sociais na América Latina em Perspectiva Comparada*. Porto Alegre: UFRGS.

Triner G (1999) Banks, Regions, and Nation in Brazil, 1889–1930. *Latin American Perspectives* 26(1): 129–50.

United Nations Development Programme (1994) Human Development Programme: New Dimensions on Human Security. New York: United Nations. Available at: http://hdr.undp.org/en/reports/global/hdr1994/chapters/ (accessed 11/05/13).

Vargas E (1997) Átomos na Integração: A Aproximação Brasil-Argentina no Campo Nuclear e a Construção do Mercosul. *Revista Brasileira de Política Internacional* 40(1): 41–74.

Vaz A (1993) Neoliberalismo na América Latina: Impacto e Perspectivas para o Regionalismo Econômico. *Revista Brasileira de Política Internacional* 2: 67–79.

Velasco e Cruz S, Brigadão C, Herz M, Rizzo M and Costa D (2004) Relato da Primeira Rodada de Discussao. In: Pinto A, Ramalho A and Silva R (eds) *O Brasil no Cenário Internacional de Defesa e Segurança.* Brasília: Ministério da Defesa.

Ventura R (1991) *Estilo Tropical: História Cultural e PolêMicas Literárias no Brasil, 1870–1914.* São Paulo, Brazil: Companhia das Letras.

Vidigal A (1987) Dissuasão Convencional nos Países em Desenvolvimento. *Dissuasão Convencional nos Países em Desenvolvimento* V(3): 324–41.

Vidigal C, Herz D, Rizzo M and Brigagão E (2004) Relato da Terceira Rodada de Debates Elaborado pelos organizadores. In: Pinto AR and Silva R (eds) *O Brazil no Cenário Internacional de Defesa e Segurança.* Brasília: Ministério da Defesa.

___ (2010) Brazil: A Cordial Power? Brazilian Diplomacy in the Early 21st Century. *Revista Eletrônica de Comunicação, Informação & Inovação em Saúde* 4(1): 33–41.

Vigevani T (1999) Ciclos Longos e Cenários Contemporâneos da Sociedade Internacional. *Revista Lua Nova* 46(2): 5–53.

___ and Capaluni G (2007) A Política Externa de Lula da Silva: Estratégia da Autonomia Pela Diversificação. *Contexto Internacional* 29(2): 273–335.

Villa R (2002) Estados Unidos – a Difícil Escolha. *Revista de Sociologia e Política* 18: 157–63.

Viola E and Leis H (2004) Unipolaridade, Governabilidade e Intervenção Unilateral Anglo-Americana no Iraque. *Revista Brasileira de Política Internacional* 47(2): 29–58.

Viotti da Costa E (1997) *Da Monarquia à República: Momentos Decisivos.* São Paulo: UNESP.

Vizentini P (2001) Dez Anos do Mercosul: A Crise da Integração e o Desafio da ALCA. *Indicadores Econômicos* 29(1): 9–29.

___ (2007) O Brasil, o Mercosul e a Integração da América do Sul. *de Estudos e Pesquisas sobre as Américas* 1(1): 82–94.

Wæver O (1994) *Insecurity and Identity Unlimited.* Working Paper 14. Copenhagen: Copenhagen Centre for Peace and Conflict Research.

___ (1995) Securitization and Desecuritization. In: Lipschutz R (ed) *On Security.* New York: Columbia University Press.

___ (1998) The Sociology of a Not So International Discipline: American and European Developments in International Relations. *International Organization* 52(4): 687–727.

Walker RBJ (1993) *Inside/Outside: International Relations as Political Theory.* Cambridge: Cambridge University Press.

Waltz K (1990) Realist Thought and Neorealist Theory. *Journal of International Affairs* 44: 21–37.

Wang Y (2009) China–Between Copying and Constructing. In: Tickner A and Wæver O (eds) *International Relations Scholarship Around the World.* Abingdon, Oxon: Routledge, pp. 103–19.

Weffort F (1972) *Origens Do Sindicalismo Populista No Brasil: A Conjuntura Do Após-Guerra.* São Paulo: Universidade de São Paulo.

Wrobel P (1993) A Diplomacia Nuclear Brasileira: A Não-Proliferação Nuclear e o Tratado de Tlatelolco. *Contexto Internacional* 15(1): 27–56.

___ (1996) O Brasil e o TNP: Resistência à Mudança? *Contexto Internacional* 18(1): 143–56.

Wyn Jones R (1999) *Security, Strategy, and Critical Theory*. Boulder: Lynne Reinner.

Yaqing Q (2007) Why is there no Chinese International Relations theory? *International Relations of the Asia-Pacific* 7(3): 313–40.

Zaverucha J (1992) As Prerrogativas Militares nas Transições Brasileiras, Argetina e Espanhola. *Revista Brasileira de Ciências Sociais* 7(19): 56–65.

___ (2000) *Frágil Democracia*. São Paulo: Civilização Brasileira.

___ and Pereira A (1998) *Democracia e Instituições Políticas Brasileiras no Século* XX. Recife: Edições Bagaço.

Index

For Product Safety Concerns and Information please contact our EU
representative GPSR@taylorandfrancis.com
Taylor & Francis Verlag GmbH, Kaufingerstraße 24, 80331 München, Germany

www.ingramcontent.com/pod-product-compliance
Lightning Source LLC
Chambersburg PA
CBHW050446280326
41932CB00013BA/2265